Table of Contents

Introduction

Do you want to become a healthier and happier person but at the same time you need to lose some of the extra weight that's bothering you so much? Are you looking for a healthy lifestyle that will change your life forever? If that's the case, then you are definitely in the right place. We want to present you the most popular diet these days. It the Whole food diet.

Each day, millions of people all over the world decide to give up their unhealthy dietary habits and to follow this incredible diet. Why? Well, the answer is pretty simple.

The reason why this lifestyle is loved by so many people is because it can help you in so many ways. The Whole food diet increases your energy levels, improves your immune system and the balance of your hormone levels. It also prevents the appearance of many other illnesses and of course, it helps you lose weight in a healthy manner.

The main thing you need to remember when you decide to follow this diet is that you need to give up consuming some unhealthy products. You will no longer be allowed to consume dairy products, grains, alcohol, legumes, any kind of sweeteners, or junk food.

On the other hand, you are allowed to eat fresh vegetables, fruits, meat, poultry, seafood, eggs, seeds, nuts and healthy oils.

As you can see, this is not a restrictive diet. You can make many delicious meals using Whole food diet approved ingredients. In order to help you with your Whole food meals, we gathered the best Whole food recipes just for you. Try these rich dishes and enjoy your new life! We can assure you it will be the best experience of your life!

Whole Food Breakfast Recipes

Veggie and Fried Egg Bowls

Preparation time: *10 minutes* | ***Cooking time:*** *10 minutes* | ***Servings:*** *2*

Ingredients:

- 2 zucchinis, cubed
- ½ avocado
- 2 tablespoons water
- Salt and ground black pepper, to taste
- ¼ cup extra virgin olive oil
- 2 eggs
- 1 sweet potato, peeled and cubed
- 1 red onion, chopped
- 2 garlic cloves, peeled and chopped
- 2 sweet potatoes, peeled and chopped

Directions:

Heat a pan with half of the olive oil over medium-high heat, add the potatoes, stir, and cook for 8 minutes. Heat the pan again over medium heat, crack the eggs, cook until done and take off heat. In a food processor, mix the avocado with the rest of the oil, garlic, water, salt, and pepper and blend well. Divide the zucchinis, avocado and garlic mix and sweet potatoes in 2 bowls and toss. Divide the fried eggs on top of this mix, season with salt and pepper, sprinkle the red onion all over and serve.

Nutrition: Calories - 93, Fat - 3, Fiber - 3, Carbs - 11, Protein – 4

Coconut, Almond and Cashew Porridge

Preparation time: *7 hours* | ***Cooking time:*** *7 minutes* | ***Servings:*** *4*

Ingredients:

-
- 1 cup raw almonds
- ½ cup raw cashews
- ⅓ cup coconut flakes
- 1 egg yolk
- 1 banana, peeled and chopped
- 1 tablespoon clarified butter
- A pinch of nutmeg
- 1 apple, peeled and chopped
- 14 ounces canned pure coconut milk
- 2 teaspoons vanilla extract
- ½ cup raisins
- A pinch of salt
- 2 teaspoons ground cinnamon

Directions:

Put the almonds, cashews and coconut flakes in a bowl, add filtered water to cover and a pinch of salt and set aside for 7 hours. Drain this mix, put them in your food processor, add the egg yolk and banana and pulse well. Heat up a pan with the clarified butter over medium heat, add the apples and nutmeg, stir, and cook for 2 minutes. Add the vanilla, raisins, coconut milk, cinnamon, and nut mix, stir well, bring to a simmer, cook for 5 minutes, divide into bowls, and serve for breakfast

Nutrition: Calories - 100, Fat - 2, Fiber - 1, Carbs - 2, Protein - 2

Egg and Meatball Breakfast Salad

Preparation time: 10 minutes | Cooking time: 15 minutes | Servings: 4

Ingredients:

- 8 eggs, hard boiled, peeled and each cut into 8 pieces
- 1 pound breakfast pork sausage, casings removed
- 3 cups cherry tomatoes, halved
- 2 avocados, pitted, peeled, and chopped
- ¼ cup onion, chopped
- ½ cup fresh cilantro, chopped
- Juice of 2 lemons
- Salt and ground black pepper, to taste

Directions:

Shape the sausage meat into small meatballs. Heat a pan over medium-high heat, add the meatballs, brown them on all sides and transfer to a plate. In a salad bowl, mix the meatballs with the eggs, onion, tomatoes, lemon juice, cilantro, avocado, salt and pepper and serve.

Nutrition: Calories - 120, Fat - 4, Fiber - 0.5, Carbs - 4, Protein – 10

Banana Omelette

Preparation time: 10 minutes | Cooking time: 7 minutes | Servings: 2

Ingredients:

-
- 4 eggs, whisked
- 1 teaspoon vanilla extract
- 2 banana
- 1 big green apple, sliced
- 2 tablespoons dried coconut flakes
- 2 tablespoons almond butter
- 1 teaspoon coconut oil, melted
- 1 teaspoon cinnamon powder

Directions:

In a bowl, mix the eggs with the banana and the vanilla and whisk everything. Heat a pan brushed with the coconut oil over medium heat, add the eggs mixture and cook until eggs are done, stirring often. Divide between 2 plates, also divide the apple, top with the almond butter, cinnamon, and coconut flakes, and serve for breakfast.

Nutrition: Calories - 120, Fat - 3, Fiber - 1, Carbs - 4, Protein - 6

Coconut Banana Pudding

Preparation time: 30 minutes | Cooking time: 0 minutes | Servings: 2

Ingredients:
- 2½ tablespoons chia seeds
- 2 bananas, peeled and chopped
- 1 cup water
- 1 cup coconut milk
- A pinch of salt
- ½ teaspoon ground cinnamon

Directions:

In a jar, mix the chia seeds with the water, cover, stir and set aside for 30 minutes. In a food processor, mix the coconut milk with the bananas and pulse very well. Transfer this mixture to a bowl, add the chia seeds, cinnamon and a pinch of salt, stir and serve cold for breakfast.

Nutrition: Calories - 132, Fat - 9, Fiber - 3 Carbs 12, Protein - 2.2

Zucchini Scramble

Preparation time: 10 minutes | Cooking time: 10 minutes | Servings: 1

Ingredients:
- ¾ cup vanilla almond milk
- 1 zucchini, grated
- ¾ cup egg whites
- 1½ tablespoons flaxseed, ground
- 1 small banana, peeled and mashed
- ½ teaspoon ground cinnamon

Directions:

In a bowl, mix the zucchini with the mashed banana and stir. Heat a pan over medium heat, add the milk and egg whites, and stir well. Add the flaxseed and the zucchini mixture, stir, and cook for 5 minutes. Add the cinnamon, stir, reduce heat to low, and cook for 3 minutes. Transfer to a bowl and serve.

Nutrition: Calories - 100, Fat - 1, Fiber - 2, Carbs - 0.6, Protein - 4

Blueberry Salad

Preparation time: 5 minutes | Cooking time: 0 minutes | Servings: 1

Ingredients:

- ¼ cup raw cashews
- ¼ cup blueberries
- A pinch of cinnamon powder
- 1 banana, peeled and sliced
- 1 tablespoon almond butter

Directions:

In a bowl, mix the banana with the cashews, blueberries, cinnamon and almond butter, stir gently and serve.

Nutrition: Calories - 90, Fat - 0.3, Fiber - 1, Carbs - 0, Protein - 5

Apple and Sweet Potato Mash

Preparation time: 10 minutes | Cooking time: 1 hour and 15 minutes | Servings: 1

Ingredients:

-
- 2 pounds sweet potatoes
- 2 tablespoons water
- A pinch of salt
- ½ pound apples, cored and chopped
- 1 tablespoon ghee, melted

Directions:

Put the potatoes on a lined baking sheet, bake in the oven at 400 degrees Fahrenheit for 1 hour, let them cool down, peel them, and mash them in a food processor. Put the apples in a pot, add the water, bring to a boil over medium heat, reduce the temperature, and cook until they are soft. Add this to mashed sweet potatoes, blend again, transfer to a bowl, and serve for breakfast.

Nutrition: Calories - 80, Fat - 1, Fiber - 0, Carbs - 0, Protein - 6

Salmon and Chives Frittata

Preparation time: 10 minutes | Cooking time: 30 minutes | Servings: 6

Ingredients:

-
- 10 eggs
- 1 tablespoon chives, chopped
- 1½ pounds salmon fillets
- 2 tablespoons clarified butter
- Salt and ground black pepper, to taste
- 1 tablespoon fresh dill, chopped
- 1 tablespoon capers, drained

Directions:

Heat a pan with the butter over medium-high heat, add the salmon, salt and pepper, and cook for 5 minutes on one side and for 3 minutes on the other. Take off the heat, flake the salmon and put in a greased baking dish. In a bowl, mix the eggs with the salt, pepper, capers, chives and dill, whisk well, pour over the salmon, spread and bake in the oven at 375°F for 30 minutes. Leave the frittata to cool down before serving.

Nutrition: Calories - 100, Fat - 2, Fiber - 1, Carbs - 0.3, Protein - 3

Zucchini, Spinach and Eggs Breakfast

Preparation time: 10 minutes | Cooking time: 30 minutes | Servings: 4

Ingredients:

- 2 cups Brussels sprouts, chopped
- 4 eggs
- 1 teaspoon cumin, ground
- 1 small onion, peeled and chopped
- 2 tablespoons extra virgin olive oil
- 1 zucchini, grated
- Salt and ground black pepper, to taste
- 4 garlic cloves, peeled and minced
- 2 cups baby spinach
- ¼ cup fresh cilantro, chopped

Directions:

Heat a pan with the oil over medium heat, add the onion, stir, and cook for 5 minutes. Add the garlic and the Brussels sprouts, stir, and cook for another 5 minutes. Add the salt, pepper, cumin, cilantro and zucchini, stir, and cook for 1 minute. Add the spinach, stir, crack the eggs on top, cook in the oven at 375°F for 8 minutes, divide between plates and serve hot.

Nutrition: Calories - 160, Fat - 6, Fiber - 2, Carbs - 9, Protein - 2

Marinara Eggs

Preparation time: *10 minutes* | ***Cooking time:*** *25 minutes* | ***Servings:*** *4*

Ingredients:

- 1 cup hot water
- 4 eggs
- 1 cup homemade marinara sauce
- Salt and ground black pepper, to taste

Directions:

Divide the marinara sauce into 4 ramekins, crack 1 egg into each, season with salt and pepper, place the ramekins in a baking dish, add the water to the baking dish, place in the oven, and cook at 350°F for 25 minutes. Serve hot.

Nutrition: Calories - 126, Fat - 1, Fiber - 0.7, Carbs - 4, Protein - 6

Kale and Broccoli Breakfast Pie

Preparation time: *10 minutes* | ***Cooking time:*** *50 minutes* | ***Servings:*** *4*

Ingredients:

- 6 kale stalks, chopped
- 2 sweet potatoes, peeled and sliced
- 2 eggs
- 2 egg whites
- 1 teaspoon olive oil
- 1 onion, peeled and chopped
- 1 broccoli head, separated into florets
- 2 garlic cloves, peeled and minced
- Salt and ground black pepper, to taste

Directions:

In a bowl, mix the eggs with the egg whites, salt and pepper and whisk. Heat a pan with the oil over medium high heat, add the onion, stir and cook for 3 minutes. Add kale, broccoli and garlic, stir, cook for 4 minutes more, take off heat, cool the mixture down, add over the eggs and stir everything. Arrange the sweet potatoes slices on the bottom of a pie dish in a circular way, bake in the oven at 400°F for 15 minutes and leave aside. Pour the kale and broccoli mix over the sweet potatoes, place in the oven, cook at 375°F for 30 minutes and serve hot.

Nutrition: Calories - 200, Fat - 12, Fiber - 2, Carbs - 12, Protein - 10

Eggs and Creamy Sauce

*Preparation time: 10 minutes | **Cooking time:** 15 minutes | **Servings:** 4*

Ingredients:

- 4 eggs
- 2 teaspoons apple cider vinegar
- 8 asparagus stalks, trimmed and sliced lengthwise

For the hollandaise sauce:

- 2 egg yolks
- ¼ cup clarified and melted butter
- 2 teaspoons lemon juice

- 1 tablespoon fresh chives, minced

- Salt, to taste
- ¼ teaspoon sweet paprika

Directions:

Heat a pot with some water over medium-high heat, add the asparagus, cook for 5 minutes, transfer to a bowl filled with the ice water, cool down, and drain. Add the vinegar to asparagus water, bring to a simmer, slide the eggs in the pot, cover, poach for 9 minutes, drain the eggs, and set aside. In a blender, mix the egg yolks with the salt, paprika, lemon juice, and the butter, and pulse well. Arrange the asparagus on plates, add the eggs on top, sprinkle the chives all over and serve with the hollandaise sauce on top.

Nutrition: Calories - 200, Fat - 12, Fiber - 1, Carbs - 9, Protein - 10

Bacon Breakfast Hash

Preparation time: 10 minutes | Cooking time: 30 minutes | Servings: 4

Ingredients:

- 7 bacon slices, chopped
- 1 yam, peeled and cubed
- 1 onion, chopped
- 1 teaspoon smoked paprika
- 1 celery root, cut into small cubes
- 2 tablespoons clarified butter
- 4 garlic cloves, peeled and minced
- Salt and ground black pepper, to taste
- 2 tablespoons fresh parsley, minced

Directions:

Put some water and a pinch of salt in a pot, bring to a boil over medium-high heat. Add the yams, cook for 15 minutes, and drain them. Heat a pan over medium-high heat, add the bacon, brown for a few minutes, and transfer to a plate. Heat the same pan over medium heat, add the onion, stir, and cook for 5 minutes. Add the celery, the yams, garlic, salt, pepper, paprika and bacon, stir, and cook for 8 minutes. Divide between plates and serve with the parsley sprinkled on top for breakfast.

Nutrition: Calories - 240, Fat - 2, Fiber - 5, Carbs - 8, Protein - 10

Sweet Potato and Avocado Breakfast

Preparation time: 10 minutes | Cooking time: 20 minutes | Servings: 3

Ingredients:

-
- 1 sweet potato, sliced thick
- Salt and ground black pepper, to taste
- 1 avocado, pitted and sliced
- 1 teaspoon sesame seeds
- Juice of 1 lime
- 2 tablespoons extra virgin olive oil
- A pinch of garlic powder
- A pinch of red pepper flakes
- 1 tablespoon green onions, chopped

Directions:

Heat a pan with the oil over medium-high heat, add the potato slices, season with salt, pepper, garlic powder, and cook for 10 minutes on each side. Add the avocado, red pepper, lime juice, sesame seeds, and green onions, stir, cook for 3 minutes, and serve for breakfast.

Nutrition: Calories - 100, Fat - 7, Fiber - 1, Carbs - 5, Protein - 10

Bacon Sandwich with Avocado Spread

Preparation time: 10 minutes | **Cooking time:** 4 minutes | **Servings:** 2

Ingredients:

-
- 4 bacon slices
- 1 avocado, pitted and
- Salt and ground black pepper, to taste

- 1 avocado, pitted and peeled
- Juice from 1 lime

Directions:

Put the avocado in a blender, add the salt, pepper and lime juice, and pulse well. Heat a pan over medium-high heat, add the bacon, brown on all sides, drain on paper towels and leave aside. Spread the avocado paste on 2 bacon slices, top with the other 2 bacon slices, and serve for breakfast.

Nutrition: Calories - 90, Fat - 1, Fiber - 3, Carbs - 6, Protein - 8

Zucchini Patties

Preparation time: 10 minutes | Cooking time: 10 minutes | Servings: 4

Ingredients:

- 1 cup zucchini, grated
- 1 egg, whisked
- 2 tablespoons olive oil
- 1 tablespoon coconut flour
- 1 cup sweet potato, peeled and shredded

- Salt and ground black pepper, to taste
- ¼ teaspoon cumin
- ½ teaspoon garlic powder
- ½ teaspoon dried parsley

Directions:

In a bowl, mix the flour with the salt, pepper, cumin, garlic powder, and parsley. Add the zucchini, egg and sweet potatoes, stir and shape medium patties out of this mix. Heat a pan with the oil and butter over medium-high heat, drop the patties into the pan, cook until they are gold on both sides, drain the excess grease, divide between plates, and serve hot for breakfast.

Nutrition: Calories - 122, Fat - 8, Fiber - 2, Carbs - 7, Protein - 3

Date and Walnut Granola

Preparation time: 2 hours | Cooking time: 0 minutes | Servings: 3

Ingredients:

- 2 cups walnuts, toasted
- 3 tablespoons water
- 2 cups coconut, desiccated
- 1 cup dates, pitted
- ¾ cup dried cranberries

Directions:

In a food processor, mix the dates with the coconut, cranberries, walnuts and the water gradually, blend, arrange mixture in a square baking dish, press well, keep in the refrigerator for 2 hours. Cut into bars, and serve for breakfast.

Nutrition: Calories - 100, Fat - 1, Fiber - 1, Carbs - 4, Protein – 2

Ham and Veggie Breakfast Wrap

Preparation time: 10 minutes | Cooking time: 5 minutes | Servings: 1

Ingredients:

- 3 ham slices
- 2 teaspoons olive oil
- 2 eggs, whisked
- 1 tablespoon cilantro, chopped
- 1 tablespoon spinach leaves, torn
- 1 tablespoon black olives, pitted and chopped
- 1 tablespoon red bell pepper, seeded and chopped
- 3 cherry tomatoes, cut in half
- Homemade salsa, for serving
- Guacamole, for serving

Directions:

Heat a pan with the oil over medium-high heat, add the bell pepper, olives, tomatoes, and spinach, stir, and cook for 3 minutes. Add the eggs, stir, spread, cook until done, transfer the eggs to a cutting board, roll the ham around them, and serve with the salsa, cilantro and guacamole on top.

Nutrition: Calories - 108, Fat - 2, Fiber - 1.4, Carbs - 10, Protein - 8

Pumpkin and Coconut Shake

Preparation time: 5 minutes | Cooking time: 0 minutes | Servings: 2

Ingredients:

- 1 cup coconut milk
- 1 cup ice
- 1 banana, sliced
- 2 teaspoons pumpkin pie spice
- ¼ cup pumpkin puree

Directions:

In a blender, mix the pumpkin with the banana, the coconut milk, pumpkin spice, and ice, blend, divide into 2 glasses and serve for breakfast.

Nutrition: Calories - 100, Fat - 1, Fiber - 1, Carbs - 0, Protein - 5

Almond Spinach Breakfast Smoothie

Preparation time: 10 minutes | Cooking time: 0 minutes | Servings: 2

Ingredients:

- 1 cup almond milk
- 2 cups spinach
- 1 apple, cored, peeled and cubed
- 1 small ginger piece, grated
- Juice of ½ lime
- 1 orange, peeled and chopped
- 1 cup ice cubes

Directions:

In a blender, mix the spinach with the apple, ginger, orange, lime juice, ice cubes, milk and pulse well. Divide into glasses, and serve for breakfast.

Nutrition: Calories - 100, Fat - 2, Fiber - 2, Carbs - 6, Protein - 8

Kale and Berries Smoothie

Preparation time: 10 minutes | Cooking time: 0 minutes | Servings: 2

Ingredients:

- 1 cup berries
- 1 cup kale, chopped
- 1 avocado, pitted, peeled, and chopped
- 1 cup water
- 1 tablespoon chia seeds
- 1 banana, peeled and chopped
- 1 tablespoon hemp seeds
- ½ cup coconut milk

Directions:

In a blender, mix the berries with the kale, avocado, water and banana and pulse. Add chia seeds, hemp seeds and the coconut milk, pulse well again, divide into glasses and serve for breakfast.

Nutrition: Calories - 120, Fat - 3, Fiber - 4, Carbs - 6, Protein - 3

Pear and Plum Smoothie

Preparation time: 10 minutes | Cooking time: 0 minutes | Servings: 3

Ingredients:

- 1 small avocado, peeled and pitted
- 1 cup water
- 2 big bananas, peeled and chopped
- 1 bunch parsley
- 2 pears, peeled, cored and chopped
- 1 cup ice
- 2 plums, pitted
- 1 apple, cored and chopped

Directions:

In a blender, mix the avocado with the bananas, water, pears, plums, ice, apple and parsley, pulse well, divide into glasses and serve for breakfast.

Nutrition: Calories - 120, Fat - 3, Fiber - 4, Carbs - 6, Protein - 9

Papaya Smoothie

Preparation time: 10 minutes | Cooking time: 0 minutes | Servings: 3

Ingredients:

-
- 2 cups papaya, peeled
- 1 parsley spring
- 1 teaspoon lemon juice
- ½ teaspoon fresh ginger, grated
- 4 ice cubes

Directions:

In a blender, mix the papaya with the parsley, lemon juice, ginger and ice, pulse well, divide into glasses and serve for breakfast.

Nutrition: Calories - 90, Fat - 1, Fiber - 2, Carbs - 5, Protein - 4

Cauliflower Rice and Sausage Bowls

Preparation time: 10 minutes | Cooking time: 8 minutes | Servings: 1

Ingredients:

- 1 teaspoon olive oil
- 1 egg
- ½ cup cauliflower rice
- 2 breakfast sausages, chopped
- ½ cup Brussels sprouts, roasted and chopped
- ½ cup sweet potato wedges, roasted

Directions:

Heat a pan with the oil over medium heat, crack the egg, fry it for 4 minutes and transfer it to a bowl. Heat the pan again over medium heat, add the sausages, potato wedges, cauliflower rice and Brussels sprouts, stir gently, cook for 1 minute, add next to the fried egg and serve for breakfast

Nutrition: Calories - 129, Fat - 3, Fiber - 4, Carbs - 7, Protein - 8

Mexican Scramble
Preparation time: 10 minutes | Cooking time: 5 minutes | Servings: 6

Ingredients:
- 3 cups tomatoes, chopped
- 8 eggs, whisked
- Juice of 1 lime
- A pinch of sea salt
- 1 bunch green onions, chopped
- 1 bunch fresh cilantro, chopped
- 1 cup onion, chopped
- 2 habanero chilies, chopped
- 2 garlic cloves, peeled and minced
- 1 teaspoon olive oil

Directions:
In a bowl, mix the tomatoes with the green onions, onion, cilantro, garlic, habaneros, a pinch of salt and lime juice, toss well and keep in the fridge. Heat a pan with the oil over medium heat, add the eggs, scramble them for 4-5 minutes, divide between plates, top with the salsa and serve for breakfast.

Nutrition: Calories - 187, Fat - 4, Fiber - 2, Carbs - 5, Protein - 16

Sausage, Mushroom and Egg Mix
Preparation time: 10 minutes | Cooking time: 32 minutes | Servings: 4

Ingredients:
- 2 tablespoons olive oil
- 2 tomatoes, cored, and flesh removed
- ¼ teaspoon dried thyme
- 4 eggs
- A pinch of salt and ground black pepper
- 12 mushrooms, halved
- 8 ounces small sausages, halved

Directions:
In a bowl, mix the tomatoes with the thyme, half of the oil, salt and black pepper, toss to coat, arrange on a lined baking sheet, and roast in the oven at 425°F for 15 minutes. Meanwhile, in a bowl, mix the mushrooms with salt, black pepper and remaining oil, toss to coat, arrange on the same baking sheet as the tomatoes. Add the sausages and roast in the oven at 425°F for 12 minutes. Make 4 holes in mix, crack an egg into each, roast for 5 minutes more, divide everything between plates, and serve for breakfast.

Nutrition: Calories - 302, Fat - 4, Fiber - 2, Carbs - 8, Protein - 17

Paprika Poached Egg

Preparation time: 5 minutes | Cooking time: 4 minutes | Servings: 1

Ingredients:

-
  - 1 tablespoon rice vinegar
  - 2 cups water
  - 2 teaspoons sweet paprika
  - 1 egg
- A pinch of salt and black pepper
- Ground black pepper, to taste

Directions:

Put the water into a pot, heat over medium, add the vinegar and whisk. Crack the egg into the water, and cook for 4 minutes, transfer the egg to a plate and serve seasoned with salt and black pepper and with paprika sprinkled on top.

Nutrition: Calories - 65, Fat - 2, Fiber - 0, Carbs - 1, Protein - 5

Rosemary Breakfast Hash

Preparation time: 10 minutes | Cooking time: 1 hour and 10 minutes | Servings: 8

Ingredients:

- 2 onions, peeled and chopped
- 1 tablespoon rosemary, chopped
- 8 eggs
- 3 sweet potatoes, peeled and cubed
- 1 pound Italian sausage, sliced
- 6 garlic cloves, peeled and minced
- A pinch of sea salt and black pepper, ground
- 4 tablespoons olive oil

Directions:

Heat a pan with 1 tablespoon oil over medium-high heat, add the onions, a pinch of salt and black pepper, stir, and cook over low heat for 20 minutes. Add the sausages, stir, cook everything for 10 minutes more and take off heat. In a bowl, mix the sweet potatoes with the garlic, rosemary, the remaining olive oil, a pinch of salt and black pepper, toss to coat well, arrange this on a lined baking sheet, also add the sausages and onions, toss to coat, and roast in the oven at 450°F for 40 minutes. Spread mix onto a baking dish, make 8 holes in the mixture, crack an egg into each, bake in the oven at 425°F for 10 minutes. Divide between plates and serve for breakfast

Nutrition: Calories - 430, Fat - 7, Fiber - 5, Carbs - 30, Protein – 16

Herbed Eggs

Preparation time: 10 minutes | Cooking time: 15 minutes | Servings: 2

Ingredients:

-
- 4 eggs
- 1 tablespoon olive oil
- A pinch of salt and black pepper
- 1 tablespoon fresh parsley, chopped
- 1 tablespoon chives, chopped
- 1 tablespoon fresh cilantro, chopped

Directions:

In a bowl, mix the eggs with salt, black pepper, parsley, chives and cilantro and whisk well. Heat a pan with the oil over low heat, add the eggs. Cook for 15 minutes, stirring often, divide between plates, and serve for breakfast.

Nutrition: Calories - 189, Fat - 6, Fiber - 1, Carbs - 2, Protein - 12

Spinach Frittata

Preparation time: 10 minutes | Cooking time: 33 minutes | Servings: 8

Ingredients:

- 1 tablespoon olive oil
- 1 pound pork sausage, chopped and casing removed
- 8 eggs, whisked
- A pinch of red pepper flakes
- 1 bunch spinach, chopped
- 2 tablespoons fresh basil, chopped
- ½ teaspoon onion powder
- 2 tomatoes, sliced
- A pinch of salt and black pepper

Directions:

Heat a pan with the oil over medium-high heat; add the sausage, stir, and brown for 5 minutes. Add the red pepper, basil and spinach, stir for 1-2 minutes, take off heat and transfer to a baking dish. In a bowl, mix the eggs with the salt, pepper, and onion powder, whisk well, and add to the sausage mix. Arrange tomato slices on top, bake in the oven at 375°F for 25 minutes, slice, and serve for breakfast.

Nutrition: Calories - 140, Fat - 3, Fiber - 1, Carbs - 6, Protein - 8

Mango Chicken Breakfast Balls

Preparation time: 10 minutes | Cooking time: 11 minutes | Servings: 6

Ingredients:

-
- 13 ounces ground chicken meat
- 1 tablespoon parsley, chopped
- 3 tablespoons olive oil
- 1 small yellow onion, chopped
- ½ cup mango, peeled and chopped
- 1 tablespoon red chili pepper, chopped
- 2 tablespoons potato flakes
- A pinch of salt and black pepper

Directions:

Heat a pan with 1 tablespoon oil over medium heat, add the onion, stir, sauté for 5 minutes, and transfer to a bowl. Add the meat, mango, chili pepper, parsley, potato flakes, salt, and pepper, stir and shape medium balls out of this mix. Heat a pan with remaining olive oil over medium heat, add the chicken meatballs, cook them for 3 minutes on each side, divide them between plates and serve for breakfast.

Nutrition: Calories - 234, Fat - 3, Fiber - 1, Carbs - 6, Protein - 16

Beef Hash and Fried Eggs

Preparation time: 10 minutes | Cooking time: 32 minutes | Servings: 4

Ingredients:

- 1 pound potatoes, chopped
- 1 red bell pepper, seeded and chopped
- 12 ounces beef, minced and browned
- 2 tablespoons olive oil
- 1 yellow onion, peeled and chopped
- A pinch of salt and black pepper
- 2 tablespoons fresh parsley, chopped
- 4 eggs, fried

Directions:

Put the potatoes into a pot, add water to cover, bring to a boil over medium heat, simmer for 3 minutes, and drain. Heat a pan with the oil over medium heat, add the bell pepper and onion, stir, and cook for 4 minutes. Add salt, black pepper, beef and potatoes, stir, and cook for 25 minutes. Divide the beef hash between plates and serve with the fried eggs.

Nutrition: Calories - 345, Fat - 6, Fiber - 2, Carbs - 20, Protein - 18

Paprika Hash Browns

Preparation time: 10 minutes | *Cooking time:* 45 minutes | *Servings:* 4

Ingredients:

- 2 teaspoons smoked paprika
- 1 egg, whisked
- 15 ounces hash browns
- 4 scallions, chopped
- ¼ cup olive oil+ 2 tablespoons
- A pinch of salt and black pepper

Directions:

In a bowl, mix the hash browns with the scallions, salt, pepper, ¼ cup oil, paprika, and egg and whisk. Heat a pan with 2 tablespoons oil over medium heat, add the hash browns mix, arrange well into the pan, place in the oven at 425°F, bake for 45 minutes, and serve for breakfast.

Nutrition: Calories - 198, Fat - 5, Fiber - 1, Carbs - 2, Protein - 2

Potato and Salmon Hash

Preparation time: 10 minutes | *Cooking time:* 35 minutes | *Servings:* 4

Ingredients:

- 4 tablespoons olive oil
- 2 pounds red potatoes, peeled and cubed
- 3 cups salmon, cooked and flaked
- 2 celery stalks, chopped
- 1 onion, peeled and chopped
- 1 tablespoon fresh dill, chopped
- A pinch of salt and black pepper
- ½ cup fresh parsley, chopped

Directions:

Heat a pan with the oil over medium heat, add the onion and potatoes, stir, and cook for 10 minutes. Add the celery, dill, salt, and pepper, stir, reduce heat to medium low, cover the pan, and cook for 25 minutes. Add the parsley and the salmon, stir gently, divide between plates and serve for breakfast.

Nutrition: Calories - 300, Fat - 3, Fiber - 7, Carbs - 15, Protein - 14

Breakfast Potato and Chard Mix

Preparation time: 10 minutes | Cooking time: 4 minutes | Servings: 2

Ingredients:

- 1 sweet potato, baked and halved
- 1 teaspoon lemon juice
- 1 garlic clove, minced
- A pinch of salt and black pepper
- 1 tablespoon olive oil
- 2 cups rainbow chard, chopped
- 1 teaspoon coconut chips, toasted

Directions:

Heat a pan with half of the oil over medium heat, add the garlic, stir, and cook for 1 minute. Add the lemon juice and chard, stir, cook for 3 minutes, and take off the heat. Stuff each potato half with the chard mixture, drizzle remaining oil over them, season with salt and pepper, divide between plates, sprinkle the coconut chips on top and serve for breakfast.

Nutrition: Calories - 150, Fat - 4, Fiber - 4, Carbs - 6, Protein - 7

Fennel and Arugula Breakfast Salad

Preparation time: 10 minutes | Cooking time: 0 minutes | Servings: 4

Ingredients:

- 5 cups arugula
- 1 fennel bulb, shaved
- 1 teaspoon lemon zest, grated
- 2 tablespoons olive oil
- 2 tablespoons lemon juice
- A pinch of salt and black pepper

Directions:

In a salad bowl, mix the fennel with the arugula, lemon zest, salt, pepper, the olive oil and lemon juice, toss and serve for breakfast.

Nutrition: Calories - 100, Fat - 2, Fiber - 3, Carbs - 4, Protein - 2

Salmon and Green Beans Breakfast Mix

Preparation time: 10 minutes | *Cooking time:* 10 minutes | *Servings:* 2

Ingredients:

-
- 1 pound small red potatoes, cut into wedges
- 7 ounces canned salmon, drained and flaked
- 1 onion, chopped
- 1 teaspoon mustard
- 1 pound green beans, trimmed and blanched
- 2 tablespoons fresh parsley, chopped
- 2 tablespoons vinegar
- ¼ cup olive oil
- A pinch of salt and black pepper

Directions:

Put the potatoes in a pot, add water to cover, bring to a simmer over medium heat, cook for 10 minutes, transfer to a bowl, add the green beans and toss a bit. Add the parsley, onion, and salmon and toss everything. Add the vinegar, salt, pepper, oil, and mustard, toss well, divide between plates, and serve for breakfast.

Nutrition: Calories - 225, Fat - 5, Fiber - 8, Carbs - 20, Protein - 22

Strawberry and Chia Smoothie

Preparation time: 10 minutes | *Cooking time:* 0 minutes | *Servings:* 1

Ingredients:

-
- 1 banana, peeled and sliced
- 1 cup coconut milk
- 1 teaspoon ginger, grated
- 1 cup strawberries, cored and halved
- 2 tablespoons chia seeds
- 1 tablespoon coconut oil, melted

Directions:

In a blender, mix the strawberries with the banana and the milk and pulse. Add the oil, ginger, and chia seeds, pulse well again, transfer to a glass and serve for breakfast.

Nutrition: Calories - 200, Fat - 12, Fiber - 5, Carbs - 16, Protein - 5

Kale and Spinach Smoothie

Preparation time: 10 minutes | Cooking time: 0 minutes | Servings: 1

Ingredients:

- 1 cup kale, chopped
- 1 cup spinach, chopped
- 2 tablespoons almond butter
- 1 cup coconut water, unsweetened
- 1 banana, peeled and chopped
- 1 tablespoon coconut oil, melted
- ½ teaspoon ground cinnamon

Directions:

In a blender, mix the kale with the spinach, banana and coconut water and pulse well. Add the oil, cinnamon, and almond butter, pulse again, pour into a glass and serve for breakfast.

Nutrition: Calories - 254, Fat - 4, Fiber - 10, Carbs - 30, Protein - 10

Pineapple, Mango and Coconut Smoothie

Preparation time: 10 minutes | Cooking time: 0 minutes | Servings: 2

Ingredients:

- 1 cup coconut milk
- ¾ cup pineapple, peeled and chopped
- 1 banana, peeled and sliced
- 1 tablespoon chia seeds
- ½ cup mango, peeled and chopped
- A pinch of ginger, grated
- 2 tablespoons coconut, toasted, shredded, and unsweetened
- 4 ice cubes

Directions:

In a blender, mix the pineapple with the banana, chia seeds, mango, ginger and the milk and pulse well. Add the coconut and the ice cubes, pulse well again, divide into 2 glasses and serve for breakfast.

Nutrition: Calories - 300, Fat - 3, Fiber - 3, Carbs - 15, Protein - 4

Fried Eggs and Roasted Veggies

Preparation time: 10 minutes | Cooking time: 1 hour and 7 minutes | Servings: 4

Ingredients:

- 2 tablespoons olive oil
- A pinch of salt and ground black pepper
- 2 pints cherry tomatoes, cut in half
- 7 ounces mushrooms, sliced
- 4 eggs, fried
- 2 avocados, pitted, peeled, and sliced

Directions:

Place tomatoes on a lined baking sheet, season with salt and black pepper, add the half of the oil, toss and bake in the oven at 300ºF for 1 hour. Add the mushrooms, remaining oil, season with more salt and pepper, toss and bake everything for 10 minutes more. Divide the mushrooms, the tomatoes and the avocado slices between plates, and serve with the fried eggs on the side.

Nutrition: Calories - 130, Fat - 3, Fiber - 1, Carbs - 4, Protein - 8

Beet and Cherry Smoothie Bowl

Preparation time: 10 minutes | Cooking time: 0 minutes | Servings: 1

Ingredients:

- ¾ cup coconut milk
- ½ cup cherries, pitted and cut in half
- ½ banana, peeled and chopped
- 1 small beet, peeled and chopped
- ½ cup raspberries
- 1 teaspoon vanilla extract
- 1 tablespoon coconut oil, melted

Directions:

In a blender, mix the cherries with the milk, beet, banana, vanilla and the oil, pulse well, transfer to a bowl, spread the raspberries all over and serve for breakfast.

Nutrition: Calories - 100, Fat - 3, Fiber - 4, Carbs - 6, Protein - 7

Zucchini Noodles and Veggies Mix

Preparation time: 10 minutes | Cooking time: 15 minutes | Servings: 2

Ingredients:

- 4 tablespoons olive oil
- 2 zucchinis, spiralized
- 2 garlic cloves, minced
- 1 small avocado, pitted and peeled
- 2 sweet potatoes, peeled and cubed
- 2 tablespoons green onions, chopped
- A pinch of salt and black pepper

Directions:

Heat a pan with half of the oil over medium-high heat, add the potatoes, stir, cook them for 5-6 minutes and set aside. In a food processor, mix the garlic with rest of the oil and the avocado and pulse well. In a bowl, mix the zucchini noodles with the avocado cream, toss, also add the sweet potatoes, sprinkle green onions at the end, season with salt and black pepper and serve for breakfast

Nutrition: Calories - 170, Fat - 4, Fiber - 3, Carbs - 7, Protein - 13

Pumpkin and Almond Bowls

Preparation time: 10 minutes | Cooking time: 5 minutes | Servings: 2

Ingredients:

-
- 1 cup pumpkin puree, unsweetened
- 1 tablespoon chia seeds
- 2 teaspoons stevia
- ⅓ cup almond milk
- ⅓ cup almond pulp
- ½ teaspoon ground cinnamon
- 2 teaspoons stevia

Directions:

Put the pumpkin puree in a small pot, heat over medium, add the chia sees, stevia, milk, almond pulp, cinnamon and stevia, toss, cook for 5 minutes, divide into bowls and serve for breakfast.

Nutrition: Calories - 111, Fat - 3, Fiber - 3, Carbs - 10, Protein - 4

Mixed Nut Porridge

Preparation time: 10 minutes | Cooking time: 6 minutes | Servings: 4

Ingredients:

-
- ⅓ cup coconut flakes, unsweetened, soaked overnight and drained
- ¼ cup walnuts, soaked overnight and drained
- 1 banana, chopped
- 2 teaspoons vanilla extract
- ½ cup almonds, soaked overnight and drained
- ½ cup cashews, soaked overnight and drained
- 1 tablespoon coconut oil, melted
- 1 apple, peeled, cored, and chopped
- ¼ teaspoon nutmeg, ground
- 1 teaspoon cinnamon, ground
- 14 ounces coconut milk
- ½ cup raisins

Directions:

In a food processor, mix the coconut flakes with the cashews, almonds, walnuts, and banana, pulse, and transfer to a bowl. Heat a pan with the oil over medium heat, add the apple, the nutmeg, cinnamon, raisins, coconut milk, vanilla extract and the nut mixture, stir well, bring to a simmer, cook for 10 minutes, divide into bowls and serve for breakfast.

Nutrition: Calories - 143, Fat - 2, Fiber - 3, Carbs - 20, Protein - 3

Easy Berry and Greens Smoother
Preparation time: 10 minutes | Cooking time: 0 minutes | Servings: 2

Ingredients:
- 1 cup spinach
- ½ cup strawberries
- ½ cup blueberries
- 1 tablespoon hemp hearts
- 1 tablespoon chia seeds
- 1 banana, peeled and chopped
- 1 teaspoon flaxseed, ground
- 1 cup coconut milk
- 6 mint leaves

Directions:
In a blender, mix the spinach with the strawberries, blueberries, hemp hearts, chia seeds, banana, flaxseed, mint and milk, pulse well, pour into 2 glasses and serve for breakfast.

Nutrition: Calories - 178, Fat - 4, Fiber - 2, Carbs - 7, Protein - 7

Veggie Muffins
Preparation time: 10 minutes | Cooking time: 20 minutes | Servings: 6

Ingredients:
-
- 1 red bell pepper, chopped
- 4 cherry tomatoes, chopped
- 3 green onions, chopped
- 6 eggs
- ½ cup spinach, chopped
- 2 teaspoons olive oil
- A pinch of salt
- ½ teaspoon curry powder

Directions:
In a bowl, mix the eggs with the salt and curry powder and whisk. Add the bell pepper, cherry tomatoes, onions, spinach, and stir. Grease a muffin tin with the olive oil, divide the muffin mixture into the tin, bake in the oven at 380°F for 20 minutes, divide them between plates and serve for breakfast.

Nutrition: Calories - 265, Fat - 4, Fiber - 5, Carbs - 15, Protein - 18

Egg Salad

Preparation time: 10 minutes | Cooking time: 0 minutes | Servings: 4

Ingredients:

-
  - 8 eggs, hard boiled, peeled and cut into wedges
  - ¼ cup onion, chopped
  - 3 cups cherry tomatoes, cut in half
  - 2 avocados, peeled, pitted and chopped
  - Juice of 2 lemons
  - ½ cup fresh parsley, chopped
  - A pinch of salt and black pepper

Directions:

In a salad bowl, mix the avocados with the eggs, onion, tomatoes, salt, pepper, parsley, and lemon juice, toss well, and serve for breakfast

Nutrition: Calories - 250, Fat - 5, Fiber - 3, Carbs - 8, Protein - 12

Banana Pudding

Preparation time: 30 minutes | Cooking time: 0 minutes | Servings: 6

Ingredients:

-
  - 1 cup coconut milk
  - ½ teaspoon ground cinnamon
  - 2 bananas, peeled
  - 2 tablespoons chia seeds
  - 1 cup water

Directions:

Put the chia seeds in a bowl, add the water, cover, and set aside for 30 minutes. In a food processor, mix the banana with the coconut milk and cinnamon. Pulse well, transfer to a bowl, add the chia mix, toss and serve for breakfast.

Nutrition: Calories - 140, Fat - 3, Fiber - 3, Carbs - 7, Protein - 6

Brussels Sprout, Potato and Sausage Mix
Preparation time: 10 minutes | Cooking time: 30 minutes | Servings: 6

Ingredients:

-
- 1 pound Italian sausage, chopped
- 1 tablespoon olive oil
- 2 garlic cloves, peeled and min
- 2 cups sweet potatoes, cubed
- 2 cups Brussels sprouts, cut into wedges
- 1 onion, peeled and chopped
- 1 red bell pepper, seeded and chopped

Directions:

Heat a pan over medium-high heat; add the sausage, stir, brown for 10 minutes, and transfer to a plate. Heat the same pan with the oil over medium heat, add the Brussels sprouts, the sweet potatoes, garlic, bell pepper, and onion, stir, cook for 15 minutes, return the sausage to the pan, stir again, divide between plates, and serve for breakfast.

Nutrition: Calories - 245, Fat - 6, Fiber - 3, Carbs - 16, Protein - 15

Yam Hash
Preparation time: 10 minutes | Cooking time: 25 minutes | Servings: 4

Ingredients:

-
- 7 bacon slices, cooked and crumbled
- 2 yams, peeled and cubed
- 1 teaspoons sweet paprika
- 2 tablespoons coconut oil, melted
- 4 garlic cloves, peeled and minced
- 1 onion, peeled and chopped
- 2 tablespoons fresh parsley, chopped
- A pinch of salt and black pepper

Directions:

Put some water in a pot, bring to a boil over medium heat, add the yams and some salt, cook for 15 minutes, drain and put them into a bowl. Heat a pan with the oil over medium heat, add the onions, stir, and cook for 5 minutes. Add the yams, garlic, bacon, paprika, and parsley, salt and ground black pepper, stir, cook for 5 minutes, divide between plates, and serve for breakfast.

Nutrition: Calories - 200, Fat - 3, Fiber - 3, Carbs - 6, Protein – 12

Pork and Chard Bowls

Preparation time: 10 minutes | Cooking time: 20 minutes | Servings: 4

Ingredients:

-
- 2 tablespoons olive oil
- 1 bunch chard, torn
- 1 pound ground pork
- ½ cup raisins
- 2 cups sweet potato, chopped
- 3 garlic cloves, peeled and minced
- 1 teaspoon turmeric, ground
- ½ teaspoon ground cinnamon
- 1 teaspoon apple cider vinegar

Directions:

Heat a pan over medium-high heat, add the pork, brown for 4 minutes and transfer to a bowl. Heat the same pan with the oil over medium heat, add the sweet potatoes, stir, and cook for 5 minutes. Add the chard, cinnamon, garlic, and turmeric, stir, and cook 5 minutes. Add the raisins, vinegar, and return the meat to the pan as well, stir, cook for 5 more minutes, divide between plates and serve for breakfast.

Nutrition: Calories - 300, Fat - 4, Fiber - 4, Carbs - 12, Protein - 17

Turkey Breakfast Pan

Preparation time: 10 minutes | Cooking time: 22 minutes | Servings: 4

Ingredients:

- 3 teaspoons olive oil
- 3 tablespoons water
- 3 cups kale, torn
- 1 butternut squash, peeled and cubed
- 12 ounces ground turkey meat
- 1 yellow onion, chopped
- 1 apple, cored, peeled, and chopped
- ¼ teaspoon dried thyme
- ½ teaspoon dried sage
- A pinch of ground nutmeg
- ¼-teaspoon garlic powder

Directions:

In a bowl, mix the turkey with the nutmeg, thyme, and sage and garlic powder and stir well. Heat a pan with half of the oil over medium heat, add the squash and onion, stir, and cook for 10 minutes. Add the apple, water, turkey mixture and the rest of the oil, stir, and cook for 10 minutes. Add the kale, stir, cook for 2 minutes, divide between plates, and serve for breakfast.

Nutrition: Calories - 300, Fat - 12, Fiber - 4, Carbs - 20, Protein - 23

Chicken, Squash and Apple Mix

Preparation time: *10 minutes* | **Cooking time:** *40 minutes* | **Servings:** *3*

Ingredients:

-
  - 1 summer squash, peeled and cubed
  - 1 bunch kale, torn
  - 2 tablespoons olive oil
  - 1 apple, cored and cubed
  - 2 chicken breasts, skinless and boneless

  - 1 tablespoon fresh thyme, chopped
  - A pinch of salt and black pepper

Directions:

In a bowl, mix the apple with salt, pepper, thyme, squash and half of the oil and toss. Heat a pan with the rest of the oil over medium heat, add the chicken, season with salt and black pepper, and cook for 5 minutes on each side. Add the squash mixture, stir, bake in the oven at 425°F for 20 minutes, add the kale, bake for 10 minutes, shred the meat, divide everything between plates and serve for breakfast.

Nutrition: Calories - 200, Fat - 4, Fiber - 3, Carbs - 10, Protein - 15

Chicken Bowls

Preparation time: *10 minutes* | **Cooking time:** *35 minutes* | **Servings:** *4*

Ingredients:

-
  - 2 chicken breasts, skinless and boneless
  - 2 cups butternut squash, cubed
  - 2 tablespoons olive oil
  - 6 cups mixed greens
  - 1 tablespoon lemon juice
  - ¼ cup tahini paste

  - 1 avocado, peeled, pitted, and cubed
  - 3 tablespoons water
  - 1 tablespoon apple cider vinegar
  - A pinch of salt and black pepper

Directions:

Arrange the squash pieces on a lined baking sheet, season with salt and pepper, drizzle half of the oil and roast in the oven at 425°F for 25 minutes. Heat a pan with the rest of the oil over medium-high heat, add the chicken, season with salt and black pepper, and cook for 5 minutes on each side and shred with a fork. In a bowl, mix the lemon juice with the tahini, vinegar, salt, pepper and water, and whisk well. Put the mixed greens in a bowl, add roasted squash, shredded chicken and avocado, drizzle the lemon and tahini dressing you've made, toss and serve for breakfast.

Nutrition: Calories - 245, Fat - 4, Fiber - 3, Carbs - 6, Protein - 12

Sprout Salad and Vinaigrette

Preparation time: 10 minutes | Cooking time: 0 minutes | Servings: 10

Ingredients:

- 24 ounces Brussels sprouts, shredded
- 1 cup onion, chopped
- 6 bacon slices, cooked and chopped

For the vinaigrette:

- 1 teaspoon orange zest, grated
- 1 teaspoon mustard
- Juice of 1 orange
- Juice of 1 lemon
- 2 tablespoons shallots, chopped

- ⅔ cup almonds, toasted and sliced
- ⅔ cup cherries, pitted and sliced

- ¾ cup olive oil
- 2 teaspoons fresh cilantro, chopped
- A pinch of salt and black pepper

Directions:

In a salad bowl, mix the Brussels sprouts with the onion, almonds, cherries, and bacon and toss. In another bowl, mix the orange zest with the mustard, lemon juice, orange juice, shallots, oil, salt, pepper and cilantro and whisk well. Add 1 cup of this mix over the salad, toss, divide between plates and serve for breakfast.

Nutrition: Calories - 150, Fat - 4, Fiber - 4, Carbs - 7, Protein - 8

Sweet Potato and Tomato Sauce Mix

Preparation time: 10 minutes | Cooking time: 45 minutes | Servings: 3

Ingredients:

-
- 2 tablespoons olive oil
- 3 tablespoons tomato sauce, no-salt added
- 3 tablespoons green onions, chopped
- 1 pound pork sausage, chopped
- 2 sweet potatoes, cubed
- 4 cups kale, chopped
- A pinch of salt and black pepper

Directions:

In a bowl, mix the sweet potatoes with the salt, pepper, and oil, toss, arrange on a lined baking sheet and bake in the oven at 400°F for 30 minutes. Heat a pan over medium heat, add the sausage, tomato sauce, green onions and kale, toss and cook for 15 minutes. Divide this mix into bowls, add toasted potatoes, toss and serve for breakfast.

Nutrition: Calories - 220, Fat - 4, Fiber - 2, Carbs - 6, Protein - 7

Turkey and Apple Breakfast Cakes

Preparation time: 10 minutes | Cooking time: 10 minutes | Servings: 12

Ingredients:

- ½ teaspoon garlic powder
- ¼ teaspoon fennel seeds, crushed
- 1 pound ground turkey meat
- ½ cup apples, peeled, cored and minced
- ½ teaspoon sweet paprika
- A pinch of salt and black pepper
- 2 tablespoons olive oil

Directions:

In a bowl, mix the turkey meat with garlic powder, fennel, apple, and paprika, salt and pepper, stir and shape 12 cakes out of this mix. Heat a pan with the oil over medium heat, add the turkey cakes to the pan, cook for 5 minutes on each side, divide between plates and serve.

Nutrition: Calories - 104, Fat - 4, Fiber - 0, Carbs - 3, Protein - 12

Pork Cakes with Blackberries

Preparation time: 10 minutes | Cooking time: 10 minutes | Servings: 8

Ingredients:

- 1 pound ground pork meat
- ½ cup blackberries, chopped
- ½ teaspoon garlic powder
- A pinch of salt and black pepper
- ½ teaspoon dried thyme
- ½ teaspoon dried sage
- 2 tablespoons olive oil

Directions:

In a bowl, combine the pork meat with the blackberries, garlic powder, salt, pepper, thyme and sage, stir well and shape 8 cakes out of this mix. Heat a pan with the oil over medium-high heat, add the cakes into the pan, and cook for 5 minutes on each side, divide between plates and serve for breakfast.

Nutrition: Calories - 233, Fat - 5, Fiber - 2, Carbs - 8, Protein – 12

Blueberry Smoothie

Preparation time: 10 minutes | Cooking time: 10 minutes | Servings: 2

Ingredients:

-
- 12 ounces blueberries
- 2 teaspoons cinnamon powder
- 5 cups water

Directions:

Heat a pot with 4 cups water over medium-high heat, add the cinnamon, boil for 10 minutes and strain into a blender. Add the rest of the water and the blueberries, pulse well, strain this again into 2 bowls and serve.

Nutrition: Calories - 68, Fat - 0, Fiber - 1, Carbs - 0, Protein - 2

Pineapple and Cucumber Bowls

Preparation time: 5 minutes | Cooking time: 0 minutes | Servings: 1

Ingredients:

- 1 cup pineapple, cubed
- ½ cup cucumber, sliced
- 1 small banana, peeled and chopped
- 1 teaspoon lime zest
- 2 tablespoons lime juice
- ½ cup kale leaves

Directions:

In a salad bowl, mix the pineapple with the cucumber, banana, lime zest, lime juice and kale, toss and serve for breakfast.

Nutrition: Calories - 78, Fat - 1, Fiber - 1, Carbs - 2, Protein - 2

Minty Cucumber Smoothie

Preparation time: 5 minutes | Cooking time: 0 minutes | Servings: 2

Ingredients:

-
- 1 cup cucumber, peeled, and chopped
- ¼ cup water
- 6 ice cubes
- ⅓ cup natural apple juice
- ¼ cup mint leaves, chopped

Directions:

In a blender, mix the cucumber with the water, apple juice, mint and ice, pulse well, divide into 2 glasses and serve.

Nutrition: Calories - 76, Fat - 1, Fiber - 0, Carbs - 0, Protein – 3

Cucumber and Berry Smoothie

Preparation time: 5 minutes | Cooking time: 0 minutes | Servings: 3

Ingredients:

- 2 big cucumbers, peeled and chopped
- 1 cup blackberries
- 1 tablespoon lemon juice
- 1 cup almond milk

Directions:

In a blender, mix the cucumbers with the blackberries, milk and lemon juice, pulse well, pour into 3 glasses and serve.

Nutrition: Calories - 80, Fat - 0, Fiber - 1, Carbs - 2, Protein - 3

Apple and Spinach Smoothie

Preparation time: 6 minutes | Cooking time: 0 minutes | Servings: 2

Ingredients:

-
  - 1 cucumber, peeled and chopped
  - 1 cup baby spinach
  - 1 cup water
  - ½ green apple, peeled and chopped

Directions:

In a blender, mix the cucumber with the apple, water and spinach, pulse well, divide into 2 glasses and serve.

Nutrition: Calories - 60, Fat - 1, Fiber - 1, Carbs - 2, Protein – 4

Cucumber and Ginger Smoothie
Preparation time: 5 minutes | Cooking time: 0 minutes | Servings: 3

Ingredients:

-
  - 2 cucumbers, sliced
  - 1 tablespoon ginger, grated
  - 1 cup water
  - ½ cup kale, torn
  - 1 apple, peeled and chopped
  - Juice of 1 lime

Directions:

In a blender, mix the cucumbers with the ginger, water, apple, kale and lime juice, pulse well, divide into 3 glasses and serve.

Nutrition: Calories - 78, Fat - 1, Fiber - 1, Carbs - 2, Protein - 2

Strawberry Smoothie

Preparation time: 5 minutes | Cooking time: 0 minutes | Servings: 2

Ingredients:

-
- 2 cups strawberries
- 1 cup coconut milk
- ½ cucumber, seedless and chopped
- 1 tablespoon lemon juice

Directions:

In a blender, mix the strawberries with the coconut milk, lemon juice and cucumber, pulse well, divide into bowls and serve for breakfast.

Nutrition: Calories - 100, Fat - 0, Fiber - 1, Carbs - 1, Protein – 2

Squash Boats

Preparation time: 10 minutes | Cooking time: 45 minutes | Servings: 4

Ingredients:

-
- 1 onion, peeled and chopped
- 1 pound Italian sausage, casings removed and chopped
- 2 acorn squash, cut in half and deseeded
- 3 tablespoons olive oil
- 2 cups spinach, chopped
- 2 garlic cloves, peeled and minced
- 1 apple, cored and chopped
- 1 tablespoon fresh rosemary, chopped
- A pinch of salt and black pepper

Directions:

Arrange the acorn squash halves on a lined baking sheet, place in the oven at 400°F, and roast for 20 minutes. Heat a pan with the oil over medium heat, add the onion, stir, reduce heat to low, cook them for 15 minutes, add the garlic, apples, salt, pepper, spinach, rosemary and sausage, stir, cook for 7 minutes more and take off heat. Stuff the roasted acorn halves with this mix, broil for 10 minutes over medium heat, divide between plates, and serve.

Nutrition: Calories - 300, Fat - 4, Fiber - 4, Carbs - 7, Protein - 12

Almond Milk and Berries Smoothie Bowls
Preparation time: 10 minutes | Cooking time: 3 minutes | Servings: 3

Ingredients:

- ½ cup coconut flakes
- 2 and ½ cups almond milk
- 1 tablespoon ground cinnamon
- 1 teaspoon allspice
- 2 teaspoons ground ginger
- 1 teaspoon cardamom powder
- 2 tablespoons pumpkin seeds
- 1½ cups berries
- 1 tablespoon chia seeds

Directions:

In a blender, mix the almond milk with the coconut flakes, cinnamon, allspice, ginger, cardamom and berries, pulse well, divide into 3 bowls, top with pumpkin seeds and chia seeds and serve.

Nutrition: Calories - 150, Fat - 4, Fiber - 2, Carbs - 6, Protein - 3

Grapes Smoothie
Preparation time: 10 minutes | Cooking time: 0 minutes | Servings: 3

Ingredients:

-
- 1 cup apple juice
- 1 small avocado, pitted and peeled
- ¼ cup mint leaves
- 3 cups grapes
- 2 cups baby spinach
- 1 teaspoon green tea powder
- ½ tablespoon chia seeds

Directions:

In a blender, mix the apple juice with the avocado, mint, grapes, spinach, tea powder and pulse well. Add the chia seeds, stir, divide into glasses and serve.

Nutrition: Calories - 90, Fat - 1, Fiber - 2, Carbs - 5, Protein - 2

Blueberry Pudding

Preparation time: 3 hours and 10 minutes | Cooking time: 0 minutes | Servings: 2

Ingredients:

-
  - 2 cups almond milk
  - 1 cup matcha green tea powder
  - 4 tablespoons chia seeds
  - 2 cups blueberries
  - 1 banana, peeled and sliced

Directions:

In a bowl, mix the almond milk with the tea powder and chia seeds, stir and leave aside for 10 minutes. Add the blueberries and the banana, toss and serve.

Nutrition: Calories - 130, Fat - 1, Fiber - 1, Carbs - 4, Protein - 2

Spinach Omelette

Preparation time: 10 minutes | Cooking time: 6 minutes | Servings: 3

Ingredients:

-
  - 3 tablespoons coconut milk
  - 2 eggs
  - 1 teaspoon olive oil
  - 2 green onions, chopped
  - 1 red bell pepper, seeded and chopped
  - 1 cup spinach, torn

Directions:

In a bowl, mix the eggs with the milk, green onions, bell pepper and spinach, and whisk. Heat a pan with the oil over medium-high heat, add the eggs mix, stir, cook for about 3 minutes on each side, slice, divide between plates, and serve.

Nutrition: Calories - 160, Fat - 3, Fiber - 3, Carbs - 7, Protein - 3

Stuffed Mushroom Caps

Preparation time: 10 minutes | Cooking time: 32 minutes | Servings: 12

Ingredients:

-
- 1 pound chorizo, chopped
- 1 small onion, peeled and chopped
- 1 tablespoon olive oil
- 2 pounds button mushroom caps, half of the stems reserved and chopped
- 3 garlic cloves, peeled and minced
- 2 cups spinach, chopped
- ¼ cup fresh parsley, chopped

Directions:

Heat a pan with the oil over medium heat, add the mushroom stems, stir, and cook for 3 minutes. Add the onion and the garlic, stir, and cook for 5 minutes. Add the spinach and parsley, stir, take off the heat, mix with the chorizo, stuff the mushroom caps with mix, arrange them on a lined baking sheet, bake in the oven at 350°F for 25 minutes, divide between plates and serve.

Nutrition: Calories - 124, Fat - 4, Fiber - 1, Carbs - 3, Protein – 9

Chicken, Apple and Grape Salad

Preparation time: 10 minutes | Cooking time: 0 minutes | Servings: 4

Ingredients:

-
- 2 tablespoons lemon juice
- 1 avocado, peeled, pitted and cubed
- 3 tablespoons fresh basil, chopped
- 1 tablespoon olive oil
- A pinch of salt and black pepper
- 2 cups chicken, cooked and shredded
- 1 onion, peeled and chopped
- ⅓ cup celery, chopped
- ½ cup apple, cored and chopped
- ½ cup grapes, cut in half
- ¼ cup walnuts, chopped

Directions:

In a salad bowl, mix the onion with the chicken, apples, celery, walnuts, and grapes and toss. In a food processor, mix the avocado with the oil, basil, lemon juice, salt and pepper, pulse well, and add over the salad, toss and serve.

Nutrition: Calories - 243, Fat - 12, Fiber - 4, Carbs - 10, Protein – 22

Pear and Berry Sandwich

Preparation time: 10 minutes | Cooking time: 0 minutes | Servings: 6

Ingredients:

-
- 1 pear, cored and sliced
- 2 tablespoons almonds, chopped
- 6 tablespoons almond butter
- 6 tablespoons blueberries

Directions:

Spread the almond butter on the pear slices, arrange them on a platter, sprinkle the almonds all over, divide the blueberries and serve.

Nutrition: Calories - 154, Fat - 12, Fiber - 2, Carbs - 9, Protein - 4

Avocado Boats

Preparation time: 10 minutes | **Cooking time:** 0 minutes | **Servings:** 4

Ingredients:

- ½ cup red cabbage, shredded
- 2 cups chicken breasts, skinless, boneless, cooked, and chopped
- ½ cup mango, peeled and cubed
- 3 tablespoons fresh cilantro, chopped
- 3 green onions, chopped
- 2 tablespoons olive oil
- 2 tablespoon red vinegar
- A pinch of salt and black pepper
- 2 avocados, pitted and halved
- 2 tablespoons lemon juice

Directions:

In a bowl, mix the cabbage with the chopped chicken, mango, cilantro, onions, lemon juice, salt, pepper, vinegar and oil and toss well. Stuff the avocado boats with the mix and serve.

Nutrition: Calories - 265, Fat - 12, Fiber - 5, Carbs - 12, Protein - 27

Whole Food Lunch Recipes

Flavoured Chicken Mix
Preparation time: 10 minutes | Cooking time: 10 minutes | Servings: 4

Ingredients:

-
- 1 red bell pepper, seeded and chopped
- 2 cups chicken meat, cooked and shredded
- 1 avocado, pitted and chopped
- Salt and black pepper, to taste
- 2 scallions, diced
- Juice of 1 lime
- ¼ cup fresh cilantro, chopped
- ¼ teaspoon smoked paprika

Directions:

In a salad bowl, mix the bell pepper with the avocado, scallions, chicken, salt, pepper, lime juice, paprika and cilantro, toss and serve.

Nutrition: Calories - 120, Fat - 1, Fiber - 2, Carbs - 2, Protein - 7

Shrimp, Carrots and Cabbage Salad
Preparation time: 10 minutes | Cooking time: 0 minutes | Servings: 4

Ingredients:

- 1 cup carrots, grated
- 1 cup red cabbage, shredded
- A pinch of salt and black pepper
- A handful fresh parsley, chopped
- Juice of 1 lime
- 2 teaspoons red curry paste
- 12 shrimp, peeled, deveined, and cooked

Directions:

In a salad bowl, mix the carrots with the cabbage, shrimp, curry paste, lime juice, salt, pepper and parsley, toss and serve.

Nutrition: Calories - 120, Fat - 3, Fiber - 3, Carbs - 6, Protein - 8

Carrot and Coconut Cream

Preparation time: 10 minutes | *Cooking time: 40 minutes* | *Servings: 8*

Ingredients:

-
- 1 cup onion, chopped
- 2 tablespoons coconut oil, melted
- 1 sweet potato, cubed
- 4½ cups carrots, sliced
- 28 ounces vegetable stock
- 1 teaspoon fresh ginger, grated
- 2 cup coconut milk
- 1 teaspoon dried rosemary
- A pinch of salt and white pepper

Directions:

Heat a pot with the oil over medium heat, add the onion, stir, and cook for 5 minutes. Add the ginger, carrots, potato and stock, stir, bring to a simmer, cover, cook for 30 minutes, cool down, and puree using an immersion blender, return to heat. Add the coconut milk, rosemary, salt and pepper, stir, and cook for 5 minutes. Ladle into soup bowls and serve for lunch.

Nutrition: Calories - 187, Fat - 4, Fiber - 4, Carbs - 10, Protein - 6

Spiced Potato Cream

Preparation time: 10 minutes | *Cooking time: 1 hour and 40 minutes* | *Servings: 6*

Ingredients:

-
- 3 sweet potatoes, scrubbed
- ½ cup coconut cream
- 28 ounces vegetable stock
- A pinch of salt and black pepper
- ¼ teaspoon ground nutmeg

Directions:

Arrange the sweet potatoes on a lined baking sheet, bake in the oven at 350ºF for 1 hour and 30 minutes, peel the potatoes, and transfer them to a pot. Add the stock, nutmeg, cream, salt and pepper, pulse well using an immersion blender, heat the soup up for 10 minutes more, ladle into bowls and serve.

Nutrition: Calories - 245, Fat - 4, Fiber - 5, Carbs - 10, Protein - 6

Sweet Potato and Zucchini Cream

Preparation time: 10 minutes | Cooking time: 25 minutes | Servings: 8

Ingredients:

-
- 4 cups vegetable stock
- 2 tablespoons olive oil
- 2 sweet potatoes, peeled and cubed
- 8 zucchinis, chopped
- 2 onions, peeled and chopped
- 1 cup coconut milk
- A pinch of salt and black pepper
- 1 teaspoon dried rosemary
- 4 tablespoons fresh dill, chopped
- ½ teaspoon fresh basil, chopped

Directions:

Heat a pot with the oil over medium heat, add the onion, stir, and cook for 2 minutes. Add the zucchini, rosemary, basil, potato, stock, salt, and pepper, stir, and simmer for 20 minutes. Add the milk, puree the soup using an immersion blender, also add the dill, stir, ladle into soup bowls and serve.

Nutrition: Calories - 133, Fat - 3, Fiber - 4, Carbs - 10, Protein - 5

Chicken and Lemongrass Soup

Preparation time: 10 minutes | Cooking time: 20 minutes | Servings: 4

Ingredients:

- 4 cups vegetable stock
- 1 lemongrass stalk, chopped
- 1 small ginger piece, peeled and grated
- A pinch of salt and black pepper
- 12 ounces coconut milk
- 1 pound chicken breast, skinless, boneless, and cut into thin strips
- 8 ounces mushrooms, chopped
- 4 Serrano chilies, chopped
- 4 tablespoons coconut aminos
- ¼ cup lime juice
- ¼ cup fresh parsley, chopped

Directions:

Put the stock into a pot, add the lemongrass and ginger, stir, and cook over medium heat for 10 minutes. Strain this mix into another pot, heat over medium, add the mushrooms, chicken, milk, chilies, salt, pepper, lime juice and aminos, stir and simmer for 10 minutes. Add the parsley, stir, ladle into bowls, and serve.

Nutrition: Calories - 150, Fat - 4, Fiber - 4, Carbs - 6, Protein - 7

Turkey Patties

Preparation time: 10 minutes | **Cooking time:** 10 minutes | **Servings:** 4

Ingredients:

-
  - 1 pound ground turkey
  - Zest of 1 lime, grated
  - 2 teaspoons lime juice
  - 1 shallot, peeled and minced
  - 3 teaspoons olive oil
  - 1 jalapeño pepper, minced

  - Salt and ground black pepper, to taste
  - 1 teaspoon cumin
  - 1-teaspoon paprika

Directions:

In a bowl, mix the turkey meat lime zest, lime juice, shallot, jalapeno, salt, pepper, cumin and paprika, stir well and shape medium patties out of this mix. Heat a pan with the oil over medium-high heat, add the turkey burgers, cook them for 4-5 minutes on each side, divide between plates and serve.

Nutrition: Calories - 200, Fat - 12, Fiber - 0, Carbs - 0, Protein - 12

Turkey, Kale and Broccoli Soup

Preparation time: 10 minutes | Cooking time: 35 minutes | Servings: 4

Ingredients:

-
  - 4 shallots, peeled and chopped
  - 3 carrots, peeled and chopped
  - 1 pound turkey, ground
  - 6 cups chicken stock
  - Salt and ground black pepper, to taste

  - 1 red bell pepper, seeded and chopped
  - 2 cups broccoli florets, chopped
  - 4 cups kale, chopped
  - 2 tablespoons coconut oil
  - 15 ounces canned diced tomatoes

Directions:

Heat a pot with the oil over medium-high heat, add the shallots, broccoli, carrots and bell pepper, stir, and cook for 10 minutes. Add the turkey, tomatoes, stock, salt and pepper, stir, bring to a boil, add the kale, cover the pot, reduce heat, simmer soup for 25 minutes, ladle into bowls and serve.

Nutrition: Calories - 150, Fat - 1, Fiber - 0, Carbs - 5, Protein - 6

Smoked Salmon Lunch Mix

Preparation time: 10 minutes | Cooking time: 23 minutes | Servings: 4

Ingredients:

- 1 pound asparagus, trimmed
- 1 tablespoon olive oil
- 1 teaspoon sweet paprika
- Salt and ground black pepper, to taste
- A pinch of garlic powder
- 4 ounces smoked salmon

Directions:

Put the asparagus spears on a lined baking sheet, season with salt, pepper, paprika, garlic powder and rub. Add the oil, toss, and roast in the oven at 390 ° F for 15 minutes. Wrap 4 asparagus spears in 1 ounce smoked salmon and put the wrap on a lined baking sheet. Repeat this with the remaining asparagus and salmon, broil over medium high heat for 3 minutes, divide between plates and serve.

Nutrition: Calories - 90, Fat - 1, Fiber - 1, Carbs - 1.2, Protein - 4

Tuna Lunch Mix

Preparation time: 30 minutes | Cooking time: 0 minutes | Servings: 4

Ingredients:

- 10 ounces canned tuna in water, drained and flaked
- 2 avocados, pitted, peeled, and cubed
- Salt and ground black pepper, to taste
- 2 tablespoons onion, chopped
- ½ cup cilantro, diced
- Juice of ½ lime
- 1 shallot, chopped

Directions:

In a salad bowl, mix the tuna with the avocados, salt, pepper, onion, shallot, cilantro and lime juice. Toss well and serve.

Nutrition: Calories - 130, Fat - 1.5, Fiber - 2.4, Carbs - 6, Protein - 10

Lemony Salmon

Preparation time: 10 minutes | *Cooking time:* 20 minutes | *Servings:* 4

Ingredients:

-
- 4 salmon fillets, boneless
- 3 garlic cloves, peeled and minced
- 1 onion, peeled and chopped
- Salt and ground black pepper, to taste
- 2 tablespoons olive oil
- ¼ cup fresh parsley, chopped
- Juice of 1 lemon
- 1 lemon, sliced
- 1 tablespoon fresh thyme, chopped
- 4 cups water

Directions:

Heat a pan with the oil over medium-high heat, add the onion and garlic, salt and pepper stir, and cook for 5 minutes. Add the parsley, thyme, water, lemon juice, and lemon slices, stir, bring to a boil. Add the salmon pieces, cook for 15 minutes, drain, divide between plates and serve.

Nutrition: Calories - 133, Fat - 3, Fiber - 1, Carbs - 1, Protein - 12

Beef Lunch Bowls

Preparation time: 10 minutes | *Cooking time:* 15 minutes | *Servings:* 4

Ingredients:

-
- 2 tomatoes, cored and chopped
- 2 avocados, pitted and chopped
- 6 cups romaine lettuce leaves, chopped
- 1 onion, peeled and chopped
- Juice of 2 limes
- 1 pound ground beef
- 2 garlic cloves, peeled and minced
- 1 teaspoon cumin
- 2 teaspoons olive oil
- Salt and ground black pepper, to taste
- 1 bunch fresh cilantro, chopped
- 2 teaspoons chili powder

Directions:

Heat a pan with the oil over medium-high heat, add the onion, stir, and cook for 5 minutes. Add the garlic, salt, pepper, chili powder, cumin and the beef, stir, and cook for 10 minutes. In a salad bowl, mix the lettuce with the avocados, tomatoes, beef, salt, pepper, lime juice and cilantro, toss and serve.

Nutrition: Calories - 143, Fat - 6, Fiber - 4, Carbs - 12, Protein - 6

Sausage and Kale Lunch Mix
Preparation time: 10 minutes | Cooking time: 15 minutes | Servings: 2

Ingredients:
- 1 pound sausage, casings removed and chopped
- 1 tomato, cubed
- 1 onion, peeled and chopped
- 1 bunch kale, chopped
- Salt and ground black pepper, to taste

Directions:
Heat a pan over medium-high heat; add the sausage meat, stir, and brown for 5 minutes. Add the onions, kale, salt, pepper and the tomato stir, and cook for 10 minutes. Divide between plates and serve.

Nutrition: Calories - 170, Fat - 3, Fiber - 4, Carbs - 10, Protein - 12

Beef Burgers
Preparation time: 10 minutes | Cooking time: 10 minutes | Servings: 7

Ingredients:
- ½ pound bacon, minced
- 1½ pounds ground beef
- A drizzle of olive oil
- Salt and ground black pepper, to taste
- 6 garlic cloves, peeled and minced

Directions:
In a bowl, mix the beef with the bacon, garlic, salt, and pepper, stir well and shape medium patties from this mixture. Heat a pan with the oil over medium-high heat, add the patties, cook for 5 minutes on each side, transfer to plates and serve.

Nutrition: Calories - 200, Fat - 5, Fiber - 4, Carbs - 12, Protein - 14

Tomato and Sweet Potato Bake

Preparation time: 10 minutes | Cooking time: 1 hour | Servings: 4

Ingredients:

- 2½ tablespoons olive oil
- 2 cups sweet potatoes, grated
- 6 eggs
- A drizzle of olive oil
- 5 bacon slices, cooked and crumbled
- Salt and ground black pepper, to taste
- 8 cherry tomatoes, cut in quarters
- 1 small onion, peeled and chopped
- ½ cup arugula leaves
- 3 garlic cloves, peeled and minced

Directions:

Arrange the sweet potatoes in a baking dish and bake in the oven at 450°F for 20 minutes. Heat a pan oven to medium-high heat, add the bacon, stir, and cook until it browns. Heat a pan with the oil over medium heat, add the onions, stir, and cook for 5 minutes. Add the arugula, the garlic and tomatoes, stir, cook for 5 minutes and take off the heat. In a bowl, mix the eggs with the salt, pepper, bacon, and the veggie sauté, stir, pour this over the potatoes, bake in the oven at 350°F for 30 minutes and serve hot.

Nutrition: Calories - 200, Fat - 5, Fiber - 3, Carbs - 12, Protein - 9

Egg and Sausage Muffins

Preparation time: 10 minutes | Cooking time: 25 minutes | Servings: 12

Ingredients:

- 2 garlic cloves, peeled and minced
- ¾ pound sausage, casings removed
- Salt and ground black pepper, to taste
- ⅔ cup sun-dried tomatoes, chopped
- 1 teaspoon onion powder
- 10 eggs
- 2 teaspoons olive oil

Directions:

Heat a pan with the oil over medium-high heat, add the sausage and brown for 5 minutes. Add the garlic and the tomatoes, stir, cook for 5 minutes and take off heat. In a bowl, mix the eggs with the salt, pepper, onion powder, and the sausage mix, stir, divide this into a greased muffin tray, bake in the oven at 400°F for 15 minutes and serve.

Nutrition: Calories - 200, Fat - 4, Fiber - 1, Carbs - 7, Protein - 10

Sweet Potato and Apple Noodle Salad

Preparation time: 10 minutes | Cooking time: 10 minutes | Servings: 3

Ingredients:

-
- 2 teaspoons olive oil
- 1 sweet potato, spiralized
- 1 apple, cored and spiralized

For the salad dressing:

- 1 teaspoon apple cider vinegar
- 2 tablespoons apple juice
- 1 tablespoon almond butter, melted
- 3 tablespoons almonds, toasted and sliced
- Salt, to taste
- 3 cups spinach, torn

- ½ teaspoon ginger, minced
- 1½ teaspoons mustard
- 1 tablespoon olive oil

Directions:

In a bowl, mix the vinegar with the apple juice, almond butter, ginger, mustard and 1 tablespoon oil and whisk really well. Heat a pan with the 2 teaspoons oil over medium-high heat, add the sweet potato noodles, stir, cook for 7 minutes and transfer to a bowl. Add the salt, apple, toasted almonds, spinach, and toss. Add the salad dressing, toss and serve.

Nutrition: Calories - 190, Fat - 2, Fiber - 3, Carbs - 7, Protein - 8

Greek Veggie Salad

Preparation time: 10 minutes | Cooking time: 2 hours | Servings: 4

Ingredients:

-
- 2 tablespoons olive oil
- 1 cup black olives, pitted and halved
- 6 cups cauliflower florets, grated and blanched
- Salt and ground black pepper, to taste
- ¼ cup onion, chopped
- 1 teaspoon fresh mint leaves, chopped
- 1 tablespoon fresh parsley, chopped
- Juice of ½ lemon

Directions:

In a salad bowl, mix the cauliflower with the olives, salt, pepper, onion, mint, parsley, lemon juice and oil, toss well and serve.

Nutrition: Calories - 175, Fat - 12, Fiber - 6, Carbs - 10, Protein - 6

Citrus Lettuce Salad

Preparation time: 10 minutes | Cooking time: 0 minutes | Servings: 3

Ingredients:

-
- 1 orange, peeled and cut into segments
- 2 green onions, chopped
- 1 romaine lettuce head, chopped

For the salad dressing:

- 1 teaspoon mustard
- ¼ cup olive oil
- 2 tablespoons balsamic vinegar

- ¼ cup almonds, roasted and sliced

- Juice of ½ orange
- Salt and black pepper

Directions:

In a bowl, mix the mustard with the oil, vinegar, orange juice, salt and pepper and whisk well. In a salad bowl, mix the lettuce with the almonds, onions and orange segments, toss, add the salad dressing, toss again and serve.

Nutrition: Calories - 100, Fat - 0.2, Fiber - 2, Carbs - 0.4, Protein - 4

Kale and Chicken Soup

Preparation time: 10 minutes | Cooking time: 30 minutes | Servings: 6

Ingredients:

- 1 bunch kale, chopped
- 1 cup chicken meat, shredded
- Salt and ground black pepper, to taste

- 2 quarts chicken stock
- 3 carrots, peeled and chopped

Directions:

In a blender, mix the kale with 2 cups chicken stock, pulse well, pour this into a soup pot, add the rest of the stock and heat everything over medium. Add the chicken, salt, pepper and carrots, stir, cook for 30 minutes, ladle into soup bowls and serve.

Nutrition: Calories - 180, Fat - 7, Fiber - 2, Carbs - 10, Protein - 5

Chicken with Veggies and Ginger Sauce

Preparation time: 10 minutes | Cooking time: 12 minutes | Servings: 4

Ingredients:

-
- 1 garlic clove, peeled and minced
- 1 pound chicken tenders
- 1 tablespoon fresh ginger, grated
- 1 tablespoon water
- Juice of ½ lime
- ¼ cup sunflower butter
- 4 tablespoons coconut aminos
- Salt and ground black pepper, to taste
- 5 tablespoons olive oil
- ½ cup carrot, shredded
- 1 date. chopped
- 2 red bell peppers, seeded and sliced
- 2 zucchinis, spiralized
- 1 tablespoon sesame seeds
- ½ cup fresh cilantro, chopped

Directions:

In a bowl, mix the garlic with the ginger, water, sunflower butter, lime juice, coconut aminos, salt, pepper, 1 tablespoon water, date and 1 tablespoon oil, and whisk. Heat a pan with the 2 tablespoons oil over medium-high heat. Add the chicken, stir, brown for 3 minutes on each side and transfer to a bowl. Heat the same pan with the remaining oil, add the carrots, zucchini, and bell peppers, stir, and cook for 2 minutes. Add the ginger sauce, the cilantro and the chicken, toss, cook for 2 minutes, divide between plates, and serve with sesame seeds on top.

Nutrition: Calories - 230, Fat - 5, Fiber - 3, Carbs - 2, Protein - 11

Cod and Fennel

Preparation time: 10 minutes | Cooking time: 15 minutes | Servings: 4

Ingredients:

-
- 4 cod fillets, boneless
- Salt and ground black pepper, to taste
- Juice of ½ lemon
- 2 fennel bulbs, sliced
- 2 tablespoons olive oil

Directions:

Heat a pan with half of the oil over medium-high heat, add the fennel slices, season with salt and pepper, and brown for 3 minutes on each side. Reduce the heat and cook fennel for 8 minutes. Heat a pan with the remaining olive oil over medium-high heat, add the fish fillets, season with salt and pepper, and cook for 3 minutes on each side. Divide the fish on plates, add the fennel on the side, drizzle the lemon juice all over, and serve.

Nutrition: Calories - 200, Fat - 2, Fiber - 4, Carbs - 10, Protein - 8

Leek and Broccoli Cream

Preparation time: 10 minutes | Cooking time: 25 minutes | Servings: 4

Ingredients:

-
- 4 leeks, chopped
- 2 tablespoons olive oil
- 2 pounds broccoli florets, chopped
- Salt and ground black pepper, to taste
- 2 yellow onions, peeled and chopped
- 1 quart vegetable stock
- 1 teaspoon curry powder
- 1 cup coconut milk

Directions:

Heat a pot with the oil over medium heat, add the leeks and the onions, stir, and cook for 6 minutes. Add the broccoli, stock, salt and pepper, stir, and cook over medium heat for 20 minutes. Add the curry powder, stir, transfer to a blender, pulse well, add the coconut milk, pulse again, divide into bowls and serve.

Nutrition: Calories - 150, Fat - 8, Fiber - 1, Carbs - 10, Protein - 7

Carrots and Cauliflower Soup

Preparation time: 10 minutes | Cooking time: 1 hour | Servings: 4

Ingredients:

-
- 3 pounds cauliflower florets, chopped
- 1 onion, peeled and chopped
- 3 carrots, chopped
- 1 tablespoon olive oil
- Salt and ground black pepper, to taste
- 2 garlic cloves, peeled and crushed
- 2 cups vegetable stock
- 1 cup water
- ½ cup coconut milk
- A handful fresh parsley, chopped

Directions:

Heat a pot with the olive oil over medium-high heat, add the onion, carrots, and garlic, stir, and cook for 5 minutes. Add the cauliflower, the water and stock, stir, bring to a boil, reduce heat, cover, and cook for 55 minutes. Transfer the soup to a blender, add salt and pepper, pulse well, return the soup to pot, add the coconut milk, stir, cook for 2-3 minutes, divide into bowls, sprinkle parsley, and serve.

Nutrition: Calories - 100, Fat - 2, Fiber - 1, Carbs - 10, Protein - 4

Purple Potato and Cauliflower Cream

Preparation time: 10 minutes | Cooking time: 1 hour and 15 minutes | Servings: 6

Ingredients:

- 6 purple potatoes, chopped
- 1 cauliflower head, florets separated
- 1 yellow onion, peeled and chopped
- Salt and ground black pepper, to taste
- 4 garlic cloves, peeled and minced
- 3 tablespoons olive oil
- 1 cup fresh rosemary, chopped
- 2 shallots, peeled and chopped
- 4 cups chicken stock

Directions:

In a bowl, mix the potatoes cauliflower, onion, garlic, salt, pepper, half of the oil and the rosemary, toss, arrange on a lined baking sheet and bake in the oven at 400°F for 45 minutes, stirring every 10 minutes. Heat a pot with the remaining oil over medium-high heat, add the shallots, stir, and cook for 10 minutes. Add the roasted vegetables to the pot, add the stock, bring to a boil, cook for 20 minutes, transfer the soup to a food processor, pulse well, divide into bowls and serve.

Nutrition: Calories - 140, Fat - 8, Fiber - 0, Carbs - 5, Protein - 6

Whole Food Side Dish Recipes

Balsamic Roasted Potato Salad

Preparation time: 10 minutes | Cooking time: 30 minutes | Servings: 4

Ingredients:

-
- 3 sweet potatoes, cut into medium chunks
- 1 tablespoon olive oil
- 4 ounces baby spinach, torn
- A pinch of salt and black pepper
- ½ cup onion, chopped
- 2 tablespoons balsamic vinegar
- 2 tablespoons lemon juice
- 1 avocado, peeled, pitted, and chopped

Directions:

Arrange the potato pieces on a lined baking sheet, season with salt and black pepper, drizzle with the oil, toss, place in the oven at 400°F, bake for 30 minutes, and transfer the potatoes to a salad bowl. Add the spinach, onion, avocado, lemon juice, and vinegar, toss well and serve.

Nutrition: Calories - 185, Fat - 6, Fiber - 6, Carbs - 10, Protein - 3

Winter Squash Salad

Preparation time: 10 minutes | Cooking time: 45 minutes | Servings: 4

Ingredients:

- 1 acorn squash, seeded and sliced into medium pieces
- Salt, to taste
- 4 cups kale, chopped

For the salad dressing:

- 1½ teaspoons balsamic vinegar
- 1 teaspoon olive oil
- 1 tablespoon olive oil
- 3 tablespoons pomegranate seeds
- ¼ cup walnuts, toasted
- ½ teaspoon mustard
- A pinch of salt

Directions:

Arrange the squash on a lined baking sheet, add half of the oil and salt, toss, bake in the oven at 400°F for 40 minutes, and transfer to a bowl. In another bowl, mix the kale with the rest of the oil, toss to coat and add to the squash. Add the pomegranate seeds and the walnuts to this salad and toss. In a separate bowl, mix the balsamic vinegar with 1-teaspoon oil, mustard and a pinch of salt, whisk well, add to the salad, toss and serve.

Nutrition: Calories - 300, Fat - 12, Fiber - 11, Carbs - 30, Protein - 8

Moroccan Roasted Potatoes

Preparation time: 10 minutes | Cooking time: 30 minutes | Servings: 4

Ingredients:

- 8 sweet potatoes, chopped
- 1 teaspoon turmeric powder
- 3 tablespoons olive oil
- ½ teaspoon ground ginger
- Salt and ground black pepper, to taste
- 1 bunch fresh parsley, chopped
- Juice of 1 lemon
- 1 garlic clove, peeled and minced

Directions:

In a baking dish, mix the sweet potatoes with the turmeric, oil, ginger, salt, pepper, parsley, lemon juice and garlic, toss and bake in the oven at 400°F for 30 minutes. Divide between plates and serve.

Nutrition: Calories - 230, Fat - 3, Fiber - 6, Carbs - 9, Protein - 10

Herbed Potatoes

Preparation time: 10 minutes | Cooking time: 30 minutes | Servings: 4

Ingredients:

-
- 7 bacon slices, chopped
- 1½ pounds potatoes, cut into rounds
- 2 garlic cloves, peeled and minced
- 1 tablespoon sage, chopped
- 1 tablespoon fresh rosemary, chopped
- Salt and ground black pepper, to taste

Directions:

Put the potatoes in a pot, add water to cover, also add some salt, bring to a boil over medium-high heat, cook for 6 minutes and drain. Heat a pan over medium-high heat, add the bacon, stir, brown for 10 minutes, and transfer to a bowl. Add the potatoes to the pan, and cook for 20 minutes, stirring often. Add the bacon, garlic, salt, pepper, sage and rosemary, stir, cook for a few minutes more, divide between plates and serve.

Nutrition: Calories - 300, Fat - 12, Fiber - 4, Carbs - 20, Protein - 4

Sprouts and Orange Dressing

*Preparation time: 10 minutes | **Cooking time:** 30 minutes | **Servings:** 8*

Ingredients:

- 2¼ pounds Brussels sprouts, halved
- Salt and ground black pepper, to taste

For the dressing:

- 1 tablespoon fresh ginger, grated
- 1 tablespoon olive oil
- 1 shallot, peeled and chopped
- 2 garlic cloves, peeled and minced
- 3 tablespoons coconut aminos

- 3 tablespoons coconut oil, melted

- ⅓ cup orange juice
- 1½ tablespoons balsamic vinegar
- ¼ cup fresh cilantro, chopped
- 1½ tablespoons sesame seeds, toasted

Directions:

In a bowl, mix the sprouts with the coconut oil, salt and pepper, toss, arrange them on a lined baking sheet and bake in the oven at 375°F for 20 minutes. Meanwhile, heat a pan with the olive oil over medium high heat, add the shallot and the ginger, stir and cook for 2 minutes. Add the garlic, stir and cook for 1 minute more. Add the aminos, the orange juice, vinegar and cilantro, stir and cook for 8 minutes. Add sesame seeds, toss and take off heat. Add the roasted Brussels sprouts to this dressing, toss well, leave everything aside for about 5 minutes, divide between plates and serve.

Nutrition: Calories - 200, Fat - 4, Fiber - 4, Carbs - 7, Protein - 6

Creamy Sweet Potatoes

Preparation time: 10 minutes | Cooking time: 35 minutes | Servings: 8

Ingredients:

-
- 5 medium sweet potatoes, peeled and sliced into thin rounds
- A pinch of salt and black pepper
- ¼ teaspoon ground nutmeg
- 1 teaspoon fresh thyme, chopped

- 2 garlic cloves, peeled and minced
- 2 cups coconut cream
- 2 tablespoons olive oil

Directions:

Heat a small pan with the oil over medium heat, add the cream, and garlic, stir, bring to a simmer, and cook for 5 minutes. In a bowl, mix the thyme with salt, pepper and the nutmeg, and stir. Arrange half of the potatoes in a baking dish, sprinkle half of the thyme mix, add the rest of the potatoes, sprinkle the rest of the thyme mix, drizzle the coconut cream mixture all over potatoes and bake covered at 400°F for 15 minutes. Uncover the baking dish, cook for 15 minutes more, divide between plates, and serve.

Nutrition: Calories - 340, Fat - 4, Fiber - 3, Carbs - 20, Protein - 7

Sweet Potato and Cranberry Simple Salad

Preparation time: 10 minutes | Cooking time: 50 minutes | Servings: 4

Ingredients:

-
- 4 sweet potatoes, cubed
- 1½ cups cranberries
- 1 tablespoon extra virgin olive oil

- ½ cup coconut cream
- A pinch of salt and black pepper
- ¼ cup walnuts, crushed

Directions:

Arrange the potato cubes on a baking sheet, drizzle with the oil, season with a pinch of salt and pepper, toss and bake at 350°F for 40 minutes. Heat a pan over medium heat, add the cranberries, and cook for 3-4 minutes stirring often. Add roasted potato cubes, coconut cream and the walnuts, toss well, cook for 3-4 minutes more, divide between plates and serve.

Nutrition: Calories - 223, Fat - 8, Fiber - 5.5, Carbs - 20, Protein - 5

Paprika Squash Mix

Preparation time: 10 minutes | Cooking time: 40 minutes | Servings: 4

Ingredients:

-
    - 2 tablespoons olive oil
    - Salt and ground black pepper, to taste
- 8 cups butternut squash, cubed
- 1 tablespoon sweet paprika

Directions:

In a bowl, mix the squash with the oil, paprika, salt and pepper, toss, arrange on a lined baking sheet and bake at 400°F for 40 minutes. Divide between plates and serve.

Nutrition: Calories - 90, Fat - 3, Fiber - 4, Carbs - 14, Protein - 3

Coconut Squash Mash

Preparation time: 10 minutes | Cooking time: 1 hour | Servings: 4

Ingredients:

- 1 butternut squash, halved
- Salt and ground black pepper, to taste
- 4 eggs, whites and yolks separated
- ½ cup coconut milk

Directions:

Arrange the squash halves on a lined baking sheet, season with a pinch of salt and black pepper, bake in the oven at 350°F for 20 minutes, take the squash out of the oven and scoop the flesh into a blender. Add the salt, pepper, milk and egg yolks, blend well and transfer the mixture to a baking dish. In a bowl, beat egg whites very well, add them to the squash mash, toss, place in the oven at 350°F, bake for 40 minutes, divide between plates and serve.

Nutrition: Calories - 203, Fat - 13, Fiber - 2, Carbs - 16, Protein - 4

Cauliflower Rice and Mushrooms
Preparation time: 10 minutes | Cooking time: 20 minutes | Servings: 8

Ingredients:

-
- 2 cauliflower heads, florets separated
- 1 tablespoon olive oil
- 1 onion, peeled and chopped
- 4 celery stalks, chopped
- 1 garlic clove, peeled and minced
- 3 cups mushrooms, chopped
- 2½ teaspoons dried sage
- ½ cup walnuts, chopped
- Salt and ground black pepper, to taste

Directions:

Put the cauliflower in a food processor and pulse a bit. Heat a pan with the oil over medium-high heat, add the garlic, onions, and celery, stir and cook for 5 minutes. Add the cauliflower and the mushrooms, stir, and cook for 15 minutes. Add salt, pepper, sage, and walnuts, stir, cook for 2 more minutes, divide between plates, and serve.

Nutrition: Calories - 120, Fat - 3, Fiber - 4, Carbs - 4, Protein - 7

Herbed Squash Spaghetti
Preparation time: 10 minutes | Cooking time: 45 minutes| Servings: 4

Ingredients:

- 2 tablespoons olive oil
- 1 spaghetti squash, seedless and halved
- Salt and ground black pepper, to taste
- 2 garlic cloves, peeled and minced
- 1 tablespoon fresh parsley, chopped
- 1 tablespoon fresh basil, chopped
- 3 tablespoons pine nuts

Directions:

Put squash halves on a lined baking sheet, bake in the oven at 350°F for 40 minutes, scrape the squash and put it in a bowl. Heat a pan with the oil over medium-high heat, add the garlic, pine nuts, squash, salt, black pepper, parsley and basil, stir, cook for 4 minutes, divide between plates and serve.

Nutrition: Calories - 162, Fat - 8, Fiber - 2, Carbs - 16, Protein - 4

Zucchini Salad

Preparation time: 10 minutes | Cooking time: 5 minutes | Servings: 4

Ingredients:

-
- 3 zucchinis, spiralized
- 1 cup basil leaves
- A pinch of salt and black pepper
- ½ tablespoon olive oil
- 1 cup spinach
- 2 garlic cloves, peeled and minced
- 1 avocado, pitted and peeled
- ⅓ cup cashews, roasted
- Juice and zest of 1 lime

Directions:

Heat a pan with the oil over medium-high heat, add the zucchini noodles, stir, and cook for 4 minutes. In a food processor, mix the basil with salt, pepper, spinach, garlic, avocado, cashews, lime juice and zest, pulse really well, add over the zucchinis, toss, cook everything for 1 more minute, divide between plates and serve.

Nutrition: Calories - 200, Fat - 4, Fiber - 4, Carbs - 10, Protein - 8

Green Bean and Tomato Mix

Preparation time: 10 minutes | Cooking time: 10 minutes | Servings: 4

Ingredients:

- 4 tomatoes, cored and sliced
- 2 garlic cloves, minced
- ½ cup almonds, toasted and sliced
- 1 pound green beans, trimmed
- 1 tablespoon olive oil
- 1 tablespoon parsley, chopped
- Salt and ground black pepper, to taste

Directions:

Heat a pan with the olive oil over medium-high heat, add the garlic, stir, and cook for 1 minute. Add the green beans, tomatoes, almonds, salt, pepper and the parsley, stir, cook for 10 minutes, divide between plates and serve.

Nutrition: Calories - 140, Fat - 2, Fiber - 6, Carbs - 12, Protein - 6

Oyster Mushrooms and Chives
Preparation time: *10 minutes* | **Cooking time:** *15 minutes* | **Servings:** *4*

Ingredients:

-
- 4 cups oyster mushrooms
- 2 tablespoons olive oil
- Salt and ground black pepper, to taste
- ½ cup fresh tarragon, chopped
- 1 tablespoon cilantro, chopped
- 2 tablespoons fresh chives, minced

Directions:

Heat a pan with oil over medium high heat, add the mushrooms, salt, pepper, chives, cilantro and tarragon, toss, cook for 15 minutes stirring often, divide between plates and serve.

Nutrition: Calories - 200, Fat - 12, Fiber - 7, Carbs - 29, Protein - 14

Egg and Cabbage Mix
Preparation time: *10 minutes* | **Cooking time:** *15 minutes* | **Servings:** *4*

Ingredients:

- 4 cups cabbage, shredded
- 3 teaspoons olive oil
- 4 scallions, chopped
- 1 tablespoon ginger, grated
- 2 eggs, whisked
- 3 garlic cloves, peeled and minced
- Salt and ground black pepper, to taste
- 3 tablespoons coconut aminos

Directions:

Heat a pan with 1 teaspoon oil over medium-high heat, add the eggs, salt and pepper, stir, scramble and transfer to a bowl. Heat the same pan with the rest of the oil over medium heat, add the cabbage, the scallions, ginger, garlic, salt, pepper and the aminos, stir and cook for 10 minutes. Add scrambled eggs, toss well, cook everything for 1 minute more, divide between plates and serve.

Nutrition: Calories - 131, Fat - 7, Fiber - 4, Carbs - 12, Protein - 6

Celeriac Wedges

Preparation time: 10 minutes | Cooking time: 25 minutes | Servings: 4

Ingredients:
- 1 tablespoon olive oil
- 1 celeriac, cut into wedges
- ½ teaspoon sweet paprika
- ½ teaspoon garlic powder
- ½ teaspoon onion powder
- Salt and ground black pepper, to taste

Directions:

In a bowl, mix the celeriac with the oil, paprika, garlic powder, onion powder, salt and pepper, toss, arrange on a lined baking sheet, and bake at 400°F for 25 minutes. Divide between plates and serve.

Nutrition: Calories - 50, Fat - 4, Fiber - 1, Carbs - 5, Protein - 1

Carrot and Rutabaga Mash

Preparation time: 10 minutes | Cooking time: 35 minutes | Servings: 4

Ingredients:
- ¾ pound carrots, peeled and chopped
- ¾ pound rutabaga, chopped
- 2 tablespoons coconut milk
- 1 tablespoon coconut oil, melted
- A pinch of salt and black pepper

Directions:

Put the rutabaga in a pot, add water to cover, add some salt, and cook over medium-high heat for 10 minutes. Add the carrots, boil everything for 20 minutes, drain and mash the mix well, Add salt, pepper, milk and the coconut oil, whisk everything, divide between plates and serve.

Nutrition: Calories - 98, Fat - 4, Fiber - 3, Carbs - 18, Protein - 2

Broccoli Puree

Preparation time: 10 minutes | Cooking time: 20 minutes | Servings: 4

Ingredients:

-
- 2 tablespoons coconut oil, melted
- Salt and ground black pepper, to taste

- 6 cups broccoli florets

Directions:

Put the broccoli in a pot, add water to cover, add some salt as well, bring to a boil over medium heat, cook for 20 minutes, drain, and transfer to a food processor and reserve 1 cup of the cooking liquid. Add the reserved liquid to a food processor, add the oil, salt and pepper, pulse well, divide between plates and serve.

Nutrition: Calories - 91, Fat - 4, Fiber - 3, Carbs - 8, Protein - 4

Lemony Radishes

Preparation time: 10 minutes | Cooking time: 25 minutes | Servings: 4

Ingredients:

- 2 bunches radishes, cut in half
- Salt and ground black pepper, to taste
- 2 tablespoons avocado oil

- Juice of ½ lemon
- Zest of 1 lime

Directions:

In a bowl, mix the radishes with salt, pepper, oil, lemon juice and lemon zest, toss, arrange on a lined baking sheet and bake in the oven at 375°F for 25 minutes. Divide the roasted radishes between plates and serve.

Nutrition: Calories - 89, Fat - 1, Fiber - 2, Carbs - 3.4, Protein – 2

Spinach Puree

Preparation time: 10 *minutes* | *Cooking time:* 10 *minutes* | *Servings:* 4

Ingredients:

- ½ cup homemade mayonnaise
- 6 cups spinach
- Salt, to taste
- 2 tablespoons chicken stock
- ½ teaspoon garlic, minced
- 1 tablespoon lime juice
- ¼ teaspoon cumin
- ¼ teaspoon cayenne pepper

Directions:

Heat a pan over medium heat, add the mayonnaise, salt, stock, garlic, lime juice and cumin, whisk well and cook for 2-3 minutes. Add the spinach, stir well, cook for 4 minutes more, blend using an immersion blender, divide between plates and serve.

Nutrition: Calories - 147, Fat - 8, Fiber - 3, Carbs - 11, Protein - 5

Creamy Potato and Pineapple Mix

Preparation time: 10 *minutes* | *Cooking time:* 40 *minutes* | *Servings:* 4

Ingredients:

- 2 cups pineapple, peeled and cubed
- 4 sweet potatoes, cubed
- 2 teaspoons olive oil
- ¼ cup coconut, shredded
- ⅓ cup macadamia nuts, chopped
- 1 cup coconut cream

Directions:

Arrange the sweet potatoes on a lined baking sheet, drizzle with the olive oil, roast in the oven at 350°F for 40 minutes, transfer them to a salad bowl. Add the pineapple, coconut, nuts and coconut cream, toss, divide between plates and serve.

Nutrition: Calories - 220, Fat - 4, Fiber - 3, Carbs - 7, Protein - 12

Chinese Kale Mix

Preparation time: 10 minutes | Cooking time: 0 minutes | Servings: 4

Ingredients:

-
  - 2 bunches kale, torn
  - 1 tablespoon coconut aminos
  - A pinch of salt and black pepper
  - 3 garlic cloves, peeled and minced
  - ⅓ cup olive oil
  - ¼ cup lemon juice

Directions:

In a bowl, mix the kale with the aminos, salt, pepper, oil, lemon juice and garlic, toss, divide between plates and serve.

Nutrition: Calories - 232, Fat - 3, Fiber - 6, Carbs - 10, Protein - 3

Dijon Sweet Potatoes Mix

Preparation time: 10 minutes | Cooking time: 60 minutes | Servings: 4

Ingredients:

-
  - 4 sweet potatoes, sliced
  - 2 teaspoons olive oil
  - 2 garlic cloves, minced
  - A pinch of salt and black pepper
  - 1 bunch parsley, chopped
  - ⅓ cup coconut cream
  - 1 tablespoon Dijon mustard

Directions:

Arrange the sweet potato slices on a lined baking sheet, drizzle the oil, season with salt and pepper, sprinkle the parsley, toss , bake in the oven at 400°F for 1 hour and transfer to a bowl. Add garlic, cream and mustard, toss well, divide between plates and serve.

Nutrition: Calories - 237, Fat - 5, Fiber - 4, Carbs - 12, Protein - 9

Butternut Squash Mix

Preparation time: 10 minutes | Cooking time: 12 minutes | Servings: 4

Ingredients:

-
- 1 cup onion, chopped
- 1 cup low sodium vegetable stock
- 1 tablespoon olive oil
- A pinch of salt and black pepper
- 3 cups butternut squash, peeled cubed
- 1½ tablespoon sage, chopped
- 1 teaspoon garlic powder
- ½ cup coconut milk
- 3 bacon slices, cooked and crumbled

Directions:

Heat a pan with the oil over medium heat, add the onion, stir, and cook for 5 minutes. Add the squash, the stock, salt, pepper, sage, garlic powder and bacon, stir and cook for 6 minutes more. Add the coconut milk, toss, cook for 4 minutes, divide between plates and serve.

Nutrition: Calories - 200, Fat - 4, Fiber - 3, Carbs - 7, Protein - 12

Thyme Potatoes

Preparation time: 10 minutes | Cooking time: 1 hour | Servings: 4

Ingredients:

- 1½ pounds small potatoes, cut in quarters
- A pinch of salt and black pepper
- ⅛ cup avocado oil
- 3 garlic cloves, peeled and minced
- 2 tablespoons fresh thyme, chopped
- 1 tablespoon chives, chopped

Directions:

In a bowl, mix the potatoes with salt, pepper, oil, garlic, thyme and chives, toss, arrange on a lined baking sheet and bake in the oven at 400°F for 1 hour. Divide between plates and serve.

Nutrition: Calories - 230, Fat - 4, Fiber - 2, Carbs - 8, Protein - 9

Potato Cakes

*Preparation time: 10 minutes | **Cooking time:** 25 minutes | Servings: 8*

Ingredients:

- 4 tablespoons olive oil
- 2 cups potatoes, boiled, peeled, and mashed
- ½ teaspoon garlic powder
- A pinch of salt and black pepper
- ¼ cup almond milk
- 2 eggs

For the sauce:

- ¼ cup fresh basil, chopped
- ½ avocado, pitted, peeled, and chopped
- 2½ tablespoons olive oil
- 6 tablespoons water

- ½ cup almond flour
- 1 green onion bunch, chopped
- 3 tablespoons fresh basil, chopped
- ¼ cup red bell pepper, seeded and chopped

- 1 tablespoon lime juice
- 2 tablespoons cashew cream
- 1 garlic clove, peeled and minced

Directions:

In a bowl, mix the mashed potatoes with 2 tablespoons olive oil, garlic powder, salt, pepper, almond milk, eggs, flour, green onions, 3 tablespoons basil and red bell pepper, stir really well and shape medium cakes out of this mix. Heat a pan with 2 tablespoons oil over medium high heat, add the cakes, cook them for 5 minutes on each side and divide between plates. In a food processor, mix ¼ cup basil with the avocado, 2 and ½ tablespoons oil, water, lime juice, cashew cream and garlic, pulse well, drizzle over the potato cakes and serve.

Nutrition: Calories - 250, Fat - 4, Fiber - 6, Carbs - 7, Protein - 10

Apple and Sprout Salad

Preparation time: 10 minutes | Cooking time: 0 minutes | Servings: 4

Ingredients:

-
- 2 tablespoons lemon juice
- 1 teaspoon Dijon mustard
- 2 tablespoons homemade mayonnaise
- ¼ cup olive oil
- 1 tablespoon lemon zest, grated
- 2 apples, peeled, cored, and chopped
- 2 pounds Brussels sprouts, shredded
- 1 yellow onion, chopped
- A pinch of salt and black pepper
- ¼ cup parsley, chopped

Directions:

In a bowl, combine the sprouts with the apples, onion, salt, pepper, parsley, lemon zest, lemon juice, mustard, mayo and oil, toss well and serve.

Nutrition: Calories - 160, Fat - 4, Fiber - 4, Carbs - 9, Protein - 6

Cinnamon Sweet Potato Mix

Preparation time: 10 minutes | Cooking time: 1 hour | Servings: 4

Ingredients:

- 2 sweet potatoes, peeled and sliced
- ½ cup cashews, soaked for 2 hours and drained
- 1 cup coconut cream
- ¼ teaspoon ground cinnamon
- 2 dates

Directions:

In a food processor, mix the dates with the cashews, milk, and cinnamon and pulse well. Arrange half of the potato slices in a greased baking pan. In a blender, mix the cashews with the cinnamon, cream and dates and pulse well. Spread half of this mix over the potato slices, layer the rest of the potato slices, spread the rest of the cashew and cinnamon cream, place in the oven and bake at 350°F for 1 hour. Divide between plates and serve.

Nutrition: Calories - 200, Fat - 5, Fiber - 3, Carbs - 9, Protein - 12

Simple Roasted Sprouts

Preparation time: 10 minutes | Cooking time: 20 minutes | Servings: 4

Ingredients:

- 1 pound Brussels sprouts, trimmed and halved
- A pinch of salt and black pepper
- 1 tablespoon coconut oil, melted
- ¼ cup vegetable stock
- ¼ cup lemon juice
- 1 teaspoon Dijon mustard

Directions:

In a bowl, mix the Brussels sprouts salt, pepper, oil, lemon juice, stock and mustard, toss really well, spread on a lined baking sheet, place in the oven at 400°F, and roast for 20 minutes. Divide between plates and serve.

Nutrition: Calories - 178, Fat - 4, Fiber - 3, Carbs - 7, Protein - 8

Bell Pepper Salad

Preparation time: 10 minutes | Cooking time: 30 minutes | Servings: 4

Ingredients:

- A pinch of salt and black pepper
- ½ cup avocado oil
- 1 tablespoon red vinegar
- 5 red bell peppers, seeded and cut into strips
- 1 tablespoon orange zest, grated
- 2 teaspoons cumin, ground
- 2 jalapeño chilies, chopped
- ½ cup mint leaves, chopped

Directions:

Arrange the bell pepper strips on a lined baking sheet, add salt, pepper, oil, vinegar, orange zest, cumin, chilies and mint, toss well, and bake in the oven at 400°F for 30 minutes. Divide between plates and serve.

Nutrition: Calories - 221, Fat - 4, Fiber - 3, Carbs - 10, Protein - 8

Cauliflower Rice and Carrots

Preparation time: 10 minutes | Cooking time: 17 minutes | Servings: 6

Ingredients:

- 2 cups carrots, chopped
- 1 cauliflower head, florets grated
- 1 onion, peeled and chopped
- 2 tablespoons olive oil
- A pinch of salt and black pepper
- 1½ teaspoon fresh ginger, grated
- ½ cup coconut aminos
- ½ cup green onions, chopped

Directions:

Heat a pan with the oil over medium heat, the onion and the green onions, stir and cook for 1-2 minutes. Add carrots, cauliflower, salt, pepper, ginger and aminos, toss, cook for 15 minutes more, divide between plates and serve.

Nutrition: Calories - 140, Fat - 2, Fiber - 3, Carbs - 8, Protein - 10

Roasted Carrot Sticks

Preparation time: 10 minutes | Cooking time: 40 minutes | Servings: 4

Ingredients:

- 8 cups mixed carrots peeled and cut in sticks
- A pinch of salt and ground black pepper
- 2 tablespoons avocado oil

Directions:

In a bowl, mix carrot sticks with salt, pepper and the oil, toss, arrange on a lined baking sheet, place in the oven at 400°F, bake for 40 minutes, divide between plates and serve.

Nutrition: Calories - 143, Fat - 1, Fiber - 2, Carbs - 4, Protein - 8

Celery Sauté

Preparation time: 10 minutes | Cooking time: 10 minutes | Servings: 6

Ingredients:

- 2 tablespoons olive oil
- 3 celery stalks, chopped
- 1 onion, peeled and chopped
- ¼ teaspoon dried sage
- ¼ teaspoon dried thyme
- 8 ounces walnuts, chopped
- A pinch of salt and black pepper
- 3 tablespoon fresh parsley, chopped

Directions:

Heat a pan with the oil over medium heat, add the onion, stir and cook for 1-2 minutes. Add the celery, sage, thyme, walnuts, salt and pepper, stir and cook for 8 minutes. Add the parsley, toss, divide between plates and serve.

Nutrition: Calories - 300, Fat - 7, Fiber - 5, Carbs - 9, Protein - 4

Zucchini Wedges

Preparation time: 10 minutes | Cooking time: 20 minutes | Servings: 4

Ingredients:

- 4 zucchinis, cut into wedges
- A pinch of salt and black pepper
- ½ teaspoon chili powder
- ¼ teaspoon onion powder
- ¼ teaspoon garlic powder
- 2 tablespoons avocado oil

Directions:

In a bowl, mix the zucchinis with salt, pepper, chili powder, garlic powder, onion powder and the oil, toss, arrange on a lined baking sheet, bake in the oven at 400°F for 20 minutes, divide between plates and serve.

Nutrition: Calories - 135, Fat - 3, Fiber - 2, Carbs - 6, Protein - 8

Roasted Beets and Carrots
Preparation time: 10 minutes | Cooking time: 35 minutes | Servings: 4

Ingredients:

- 3 beets, peeled and chopped
- 4 carrots, peeled and cut into chunks
- 2 tablespoons chives, chopped
- ½ teaspoon fresh rosemary, chopped
- A pinch of salt and black pepper
- 3 tablespoons avocado oil

Directions:

In a bowl, mix the beets with the carrots, chives, rosemary, salt, pepper and the oil, toss, arrange on a lined baking sheet, bake in the oven at 375°F for 35 minutes, divide between plates and serve.

Nutrition: Calories - 145, Fat - 2, Fiber - 2, Carbs - 7, Protein - 10

Smoked Sweet Potato Patties
Preparation time: 10 minutes | Cooking time: 8 minutes | Servings: 6

Ingredients:

- 3 sweet potatoes, grated
- 2 eggs
- 2 tablespoons olive oil
- 1 onion, minced
- ½ teaspoon smoked paprika
- A pinch of salt and black pepper
- 1 tablespoon coconut flour

Directions:

In a bowl, mix the sweet potatoes with the eggs, onion, paprika, salt, pepper and the flour, stir well and shape 6 patties out of this mix. Heat a pan with oil over medium heat, add the patties, cook them for 4 minutes on each side, divide between plates and serve.

Nutrition: Calories - 179, Fat - 4, Fiber - 3, Carbs - 7, Protein - 8

Green Cabbage and Fennel Mix

Preparation time: 10 minutes | Cooking time: 12 minutes | Servings: 6

Ingredients:

- 1 teaspoon fennel seeds, toasted
- 1 green cabbage head, shredded
- 2 tablespoons olive oil
- 1 onion, peeled and sliced
- 1 tablespoon white vinegar
- ½ small bunch cilantro, chopped
- A pinch of salt and black pepper

Directions:

Heat a pan with the oil over medium heat, add the onion, stir, and cook for 2 minutes. Add the cabbage, toss, and cook for 2 minutes. Add the vinegar, cilantro, salt, pepper and the fennel, stir, cook for 10 minutes, divide between plates and serve

Nutrition: Calories - 97, Fat - 4, Fiber - 3, Carbs - 5, Protein - 2

Garlic Potatoes

Preparation time: 10 minutes | Cooking time: 45 minutes | Servings: 4

Ingredients:

-
- 21 ounces sweet potatoes, cubed
- 2 garlic heads, peeled and divided into cloves
- 1 teaspoon black peppercorns
- 1 tablespoon lemon juice
- 1 teaspoon fresh thyme, chopped
- 10 ounces avocado oil
- A pinch of salt and black pepper

Directions:

In a baking dish, mix the potatoes with the garlic, peppercorns, lemon juice, thyme, oil, salt and pepper, toss, bake in the oven at 360°F for 45 minutes, divide between plates and serve.

Nutrition: Calories - 250, Fat - 10, Fiber - 5, Carbs - 13, proteins 4

Green Bean Sauté

Preparation time: 10 minutes | Cooking time: 10 minutes | Servings: 4

Ingredients:

- 1½ tablespoons sesame seeds paste
- 1½ tablespoons water
- Juice and zest of 1 lemon
- 2 tablespoons olive oil
- 1 garlic clove, peeled and minced
- 1 onion, sliced
- 1 yellow pepper, sliced
- 12 ounces green beans, trimmed
- A pinch of salt and black pepper

Directions:

Heat a pan with the oil over medium high heat, add the onion and the garlic, stir and cook for 2-3 minutes. Add the yellow pepper, green beans, lemon juice, lemon zest, water and the sesame paste, toss, cook for 8 minutes over medium heat, divide between plates and serve.

Nutrition: Calories - 240, Fat - 10, Fiber - 6, Carbs - 13, Protein - 13

Zucchini and Arugula Salad

Preparation time: 10 minutes | Cooking time: 10 minutes | Servings: 2

Ingredients:

- 1 teaspoon sesame seeds
- 1 teaspoon olive oil
- 10 ounces zucchini, sliced
- 1 cup arugula leaves, torn
- Zest of ½ lemon
- A pinch of salt and black pepper

Directions:

Heat a pan with the oil over medium heat, add the zucchini, salt, pepper and sesame seeds, toss gently and cook for about 10 minutes. In a salad bowl, mix the zucchini with the arugula and lemon zest, toss, divide between plates and serve.

Nutrition: Calories - 176, Fat - 7, Fiber - 9, Carbs - 12, Protein - 15

Bell Pepper Mix

Preparation time: 10 minutes | Cooking time: 20 minutes | Servings: 4

Ingredients:

- 3 yellow bell peppers, cut in half and deseeded
- 3 red bell peppers, cut in half and deseeded

For the dressing:

- 2 tablespoons balsamic vinegar
- 6 tablespoons olive oil
- 7 ounces lettuce leaves

- 1 tablespoon fresh ginger, grated

Directions:

Arrange the yellow and red peppers in a baking dish, place in the oven, bake at 400°F for 20 minutes, transfer to a bowl, cover, set aside to cool down. Peel, cut them into strips, put in a bowl, add the lettuce and toss a bit. In a bowl, mix the oil with the vinegar and ginger, whisk well, and add over the bell peppers, toss and serve.

Nutrition: Calories - 123, Fat - 5, Fiber - 6, Carbs - 10, Protein - 12

Roasted Eggplant, Zucchini and Tomatoes

Preparation time: 10 minutes | Cooking time: 45 minutes | Servings: 6

Ingredients:

- 2 eggplants, sliced
- 2 zucchinis, cut into medium chunks
- 4 plum tomatoes, cut in half
- 2 onions, cut into wedges
- 1 tablespoon oregano, chopped
- 5 tablespoons olive oil
- A pinch of salt and black pepper
- 2 garlic cloves, peeled and minced
- 14 ounces canned diced tomatoes

Directions:

In a baking dish, combine the eggplants with the zucchinis, tomatoes, onions, oregano, oil, salt, pepper, garlic and tomatoes, toss a bit, bake in the oven at 375°F for 45 minutes, divide between plates and serve.

Nutrition: Calories - 150, Fat - 3, Fiber - 10, Carbs - 16, Protein - 15

Beet and Tarragon Mix

Preparation time: 10 minutes | Cooking time: 0 minutes | Servings: 5

Ingredients:

- 1 tablespoon mustard
- 1½ tablespoon avocado oil
- 8 ounces beets, baked and sliced
- ½ cup fresh tarragon, chopped
- A pinch of salt and black pepper

Directions:

In a salad bowl, mix the beets with the oil, mustard, tarragon, salt and pepper, toss and serve.

Nutrition: Calories - 150, Fat - 5, Fiber - 7, Carbs - 10, proteins 10

Minty Kale Mix

Preparation time: 10 minutes | Cooking time: 0 minutes | Servings: 6

Ingredients:

- 4 ounces kale, torn
- A bunch of mint leaves, chopped
- A bunch of green onions, chopped
- A pinch of cinnamon powder
- 3 tablespoons olive oil
- Zest and juice of ½ lemon

Directions:

In a salad bowl, mix the kale with the mint, green onions, cinnamon, oil, lemon zest and juice, toss and serve.

Nutrition: Calories - 100, Fat - 3, Fiber - 3, Carbs - 10, Protein - 8

Olive and Cucumber Salad

Preparation time: 5 minutes | Cooking time: 0 minutes | Servings: 4

Ingredients:

- 3 tablespoons olive oil
- 2 tablespoons lemon juice
- A pinch of salt and black pepper
- 2 teaspoon parsley, chopped
- 4 cups cucumbers, cubed
- 1 red onion, chopped
- 2 tablespoons black olives, pitted and chopped

Directions:

In a salad bowl, mix the cucumbers with the onion, black olives, salt, pepper, parsley, lemon juice and oil, toss well and serve cold.

Nutrition: Calories - 89, Fat - 1, Fiber - 3, Carbs - 6, Protein - 5

Mixed Lettuce Salad

Preparation time: 10 minutes | Cooking time: 0 minutes | Servings: 6

Ingredients:

- 1 tablespoon balsamic vinegar
- ¼ cup avocado oil
- 1 teaspoon mustard
- 1 tablespoon lemon juice
- 2 garlic cloves, peeled and minced
- ½ cup Kalamata olives, chopped
- 1 tablespoon cilantro, chopped
- 10 cups mixed lettuce (chicory, radicchio and leaf lettuce)
- 2 endives, sliced
- A pinch of salt and black pepper

Directions:

In a salad bowl, combine all the lettuce leaves with endives, salt, pepper, cilantro, garlic and olives and toss. In another bowl, mix the vinegar with the oil, mustard and lemon juice, whisk well, and add to your salad, toss and serve.

Nutrition: Calories - 75, Fat - 1, Fiber - 3, Carbs - 5, Protein - 2

Tomato, Pepper and Lettuce Salad
Preparation time: 10 minutes | Cooking time: 0 minutes | Servings: 6

Ingredients:
- 1 cucumber, cubed
- 5 tomatoes, cored and chopped
- 1 lettuce head, torn

For the salad dressing:
- ⅓ cup olive oil
- Juice of 1½ limes
- 1 teaspoon sumac
- 1 cup fresh parsley, chopped
- 5 green bell peppers, seeded and chopped
- 5 radishes, sliced

- ¼ teaspoon allspice
- A pinch of salt and black pepper

Directions:
In a bowl, mix the cucumber with the tomatoes, parsley, lettuce, bell peppers and radishes and toss. In another bowl, mix the oil with the lime juice, sumac, allspice, salt and pepper, whisk; add to the salad, toss and serve.

Nutrition: Calories - 120, Fat - 0.3, Fiber - 4, Carbs 7, Protein - 6

Mixed Spicy Peppers
Preparation time: 10 minutes | Cooking time: 35 minutes | Servings: 5

Ingredients:
- 2 tablespoons avocado oil
- 1 onion, peeled and chopped
- 1 celery stalk, chopped
- 2 garlic cloves, peeled and minced
- 1 pound green, yellow and red bell peppers, seeded and chopped
- 1 teaspoon dried oregano
- 1 tablespoon lemon juice
- 2 cups canned tomatoes and green chilies, chopped
- ½ teaspoon hot sauce
- 2 tablespoons fresh parsley, chopped
- A pinch of salt and black pepper

Directions:
Heat a large pot with the oil over medium heat, add the onion, garlic and celery, stir and cook for 5 minutes. Add the mixed peppers, oregano, tomatoes and chilies, salt, pepper, hot sauce and lemon juice, toss, cook over medium heat for 25 minutes, take off heat, add parsley, toss, divide between plates and serve.

Nutrition: Calories - 160, Fat - 2.6, Fiber - 5, Carbs - 8, Protein - 15

Green Bean and Almond Mix

Preparation time: 10 minutes | Cooking time: 25 minutes | Servings: 6

Ingredients:

- 5 tablespoons olive oil
- 3 pounds green beans, trimmed, halved and blanched
- 8 tablespoons almonds, toasted and sliced
- A pinch of salt and black pepper
- 2 onions, peeled and chopped
- 2½ tablespoons cilantro, chopped

Directions:

Heat a pan with the olive oil over medium heat, add the onions, salt and pepper, stir, reduce heat to low, and cook for 20 minutes. Add green beans, almonds and cilantro, toss, cook for 5 minutes more, divide between plates and serve

Nutrition: Calories - 110, Fat - 1, Fiber - 2, Carbs - 7, Protein - 8

Minty Plum Tomatoes Mix

Preparation time: 10 minutes | Cooking time: 0 minutes | Servings: 4

Ingredients:

- ½ bunch mint leaves, chopped
- 6 plum tomatoes, cored and sliced
- 1 teaspoon mustard
- 1 tablespoon rosemary vinegar
- A pinch of salt and ground black pepper

Directions:

In a bowl, mix the tomatoes with the mint, mustard, vinegar, salt and pepper, toss and serve.

Nutrition: Calories - 70, Fat - 2, Fiber - 2, Carbs - 7, Protein - 4

Beets and Asparagus Side Salad

Preparation time: 10 minutes | Cooking time: 4 minutes | Servings: 4

Ingredients:

- 1 tablespoon olive oil
- 1 cup lettuce leaves, chopped
- 2 beets, peeled and chopped
- 1 bunch asparagus, halved
- Juice of 1 lemon
- ½ cup cilantro, chopped
- A pinch of salt and black pepper

Directions:

Put the asparagus and the beets in a pot, add water to cover, bring to a boil over medium heat, cook for 3-4 minutes, drain, and transfer to a salad bowl. Add lettuce leaves, oil, lemon juice, cilantro, salt and pepper, toss and serve.

Nutrition: Calories - 140, Fat - 2, Fiber - 2, Carbs - 6, proteins 10

Tomato and Cucumber Salad

Preparation time: 10 minutes | Cooking time: 0 minutes | Servings: 4

Ingredients:

- 1 tablespoon fresh basil, chopped
- 1 avocado, pitted, peeled, and chopped
- 3 tablespoons olive oil
- 2 cucumbers, peeled and sliced
- 4 assorted tomatoes, cored and cut into chunks
- A pinch of salt and black pepper

Directions:

In a bowl, mix the tomatoes with cucumbers, salt, pepper, avocado, oil and basil, toss and serve.

Nutrition: Calories - 90, Fat - 1, Fiber - 3, Carbs - 4, Protein - 4

Green Bean and Basil Dressing
Preparation time: 15 minutes | Cooking time: 0 minutes | Servings: 4

Ingredients:

- 4 cups green beans, trimmed, steamed, and cut in half
- A pinch of salt and black pepper
- ⅓ cup olive oil
- 1 teaspoon lemon zest
- ¼ cup fresh lemon juice
- 1 tablespoon Dijon mustard
- 1 medium bunch fresh basil, chopped
- ½ teaspoon red pepper flakes

Directions:

In a food processor, mix the oil with the lemon zest, lemon juice, mustard, basil, pepper flakes, salt and pepper, and pulse well. In a salad bowl, mix the green beans with the basil-dressing, toss and serve.

Nutrition: Calories - 76, Fat - 3, Fiber - 2, Carbs - 4, Protein - 5

Cilantro Green Beans
Preparation time: 1 hour and 10 minutes | Cooking time: 10 minutes | Servings: 4

Ingredients:

- 2 tablespoons olive oil
- Juice of 1 lime
- 2 pounds fresh green beans, trimmed
- Zest of 2 limes, grated
- 2 garlic cloves, peeled and minced
- ½ cup fresh cilantro, chopped
- A pinch of salt and black pepper

Directions:

Heat a pan with the oil over high heat, add the green beans, and cook for 10 minutes, tossing often, Add lime juice, lime zest, garlic, cilantro, salt and pepper, toss, cook for 1-2 minutes more, divide between plates and serve.

Nutrition: Calories - 78, Fat - 2, Fiber - 3, Carbs - 8, Protein - 2

Squash Salad

Preparation time: 10 minutes | *Cooking time:* 10 minutes | *Servings:* 6

Ingredients:

- 3 tablespoons olive oil
- 5 small squash, peeled sliced

For the salsa:

- 7 tomatillos
- A pinch of salt and black pepper
- 1 onion, peeled and chopped

- 1 cup pumpkin seeds, toasted

- 2 tablespoons fresh lime juice
- 2 tablespoons fresh cilantro, chopped

Directions:

Heat a kitchen grill over high heat, drizzle the oil over squash slices, grill them for 10 minutes and divide them between plates. In a food processor, mix the tomatillos with salt, pepper, onion, lime juice and cilantro, pulse a bit, divide over the squash and serve with pumpkin seeds sprinkled on top.

Nutrition: Calories - 80, Fat - 2, Fiber - 1, Carbs - 2, Protein - 1

Green Cabbage Mix

Preparation time: 10 minutes | *Cooking time:* 0 minutes | *Servings:* 6

Ingredients:

- 4 cups green cabbage, shredded
- 2 big apples, sliced
- ⅓ cup coconut cream
- 3 tablespoons balsamic vinegar

- ½ teaspoon caraway seeds
- A pinch of salt and black pepper

Directions:

In a bowl, mix the green cabbage with the apples, caraway seeds, salt, pepper, vinegar and cream, toss and serve.

Nutrition: Calories - 130, Fat - 3, Fiber - 6, Carbs - 10, Protein - 3

Celery and Apple Sauce

Preparation time: 10 minutes | Cooking time: 30 minutes | Servings: 6

Ingredients:

- 3 bunches celery, halved
- 1 celery root, cubed
- 2 tablespoons olive oil
- A pinch of salt and black pepper
- 2 cups natural apple juice
- ¼ cup fresh parsley, chopped
- ¼ cup walnuts, chopped

Directions:

In a baking dish, mix the celery with the celery root cubes, oil, salt, pepper, apple juice, parsley and walnuts, toss, bake in the oven at 350°F for 30 minutes, divide between plates and serve.

Nutrition: Calories - 130, Fat - 2, Fiber - 2, Carbs - 3, Protein - 6

Green Onions and Thyme

Preparation time: 10 minutes | Cooking time: 40 minutes | Servings: 8

Ingredients:

- 15 green onions
- A pinch of salt and black pepper
- 1 teaspoon fresh thyme, chopped
- 1 tablespoon coconut oil, melted

Directions:

Put the onions in a baking dish, add salt, pepper, thyme and the coconut oil, toss, bake in the oven at 350°F for 40 minutes, divide between plates and serve.

Nutrition: Calories - 70, Fat - 2, Fiber - 2, Carbs - 7, Protein - 2

Micro Greens Salad

Preparation time: 10 minutes | Cooking time: 0 minutes | Servings: 6

Ingredients:

- 12 ounces micro greens
- 2 tablespoons lime juice
- 6 radishes, sliced
- A pinch of sea salt and black pepper
- 4 tablespoons olive oil

Directions:

In a bowl, combine the micro greens with the radishes, lime juice, salt, pepper and the oil, toss and serve.

Nutrition: Calories - 110, Fat - 3, Fiber - 2, Carbs - 6, Protein - 2

Mediterranean Tomato Mix

Preparation time: 10 minutes | Cooking time: 0 minutes | Servings: 4

Ingredients:

- ½ cup Kalamata olives, pitted and sliced
- 1 cup cherry tomatoes, cut in half
- 4 tomatoes, cored and chopped

For the salad dressing:

- 1 teaspoon coconut sugar
- 2 tablespoons balsamic vinegar
- ¼ cup olive oil
- 1 onion, peeled and chopped
- 2 tablespoons oregano, chopped
- 1 tablespoon mint leaves, chopped

- 1 garlic clove, peeled and minced
- 1 teaspoon coconut aminos
- Ground black pepper, to taste

Directions:

In a salad bowl, mix the cherry tomatoes with the onion, tomatoes, mint and oregano and toss. In another bowl, mix the coconut sugar with the vinegar, oil, garlic, aminos and black pepper, whisk well, and add over the salad, toss and serve.

Nutrition: Calories - 110, Fat - 2, Fiber - 3, Carbs - 4, Protein - 7

Whole Food Snack and Appetizer Recipes

Cucumber Bites
Preparation time: 10 minutes | Cooking time: 0 minutes | Servings: 1

Ingredients:

- 2 eggs, hard boiled, peeled and sliced
- 1 cucumber, cut into medium slices
- 1 tablespoon fresh dill, chopped
- ¼ teaspoon sweet paprika
- Salt and ground black pepper, to taste

Directions:

Arrange the cucumber slices on a plate, add the egg slices on top, season with salt and pepper, sprinkle the paprika and the dill on top and serve.

Nutrition: Calories - 170, Fat - 5, Fiber - 1, Carbs - 2, Protein - 14

Peach, Chive and Turkey Wraps
Preparation time: 10 minutes | Cooking time: 0 minutes | Servings: 2

Ingredients:

- 6 chives, 2 of them chopped
- 4 ounces turkey breast, cooked and cut into 8 pieces
- 1 peach, cut into 8 wedges

Directions:

Roll 2 peach wedges and some of the minced chives in 2 slices of turkey. Wrap this roll in 1 chive, tie in a knot, place on a platter, repeat with the rest of the ingredients and serve.

Nutrition: Calories - 180, Fat - 2, Fiber - 5, Carbs - 23, Protein - 17

Plantain Chips and Salsa Dip

Preparation time: 10 minutes | Cooking time: 6 minutes | Servings: 4

Ingredients:

- 4 green plantains, peeled and thinly sliced
- 4 cups coconut oil, melted

For the mango salsa:

- 1 avocado, pitted, peeled, and cubed
- 2 cups mango, cubed
- ¼ cup fresh cilantro, chopped
- ½ cup onion, chopped
- Salt

- 2 tablespoons olive oil
- Salt and ground black pepper, to taste
- Juice of 1 lime
- A pinch of red pepper flakes

Directions:

Heat a pan with the coconut oil over medium-high heat, add the plantain chips, cook them for about 6 minutes, drain excess grease on paper towels and divide them into bowls. In a bowl, mix the avocado with the mango, cilantro, onion, 2 tablespoons oil, salt, pepper, lime juice and pepper flakes, toss and serve the plantain chips with this mix.

Nutrition: Calories - 200, Fat - 3, Fiber - 9, Carbs - 8, Protein - 12

Roasted Kale Snack

Preparation time: 10 minutes | Cooking time: 1 hour and 30 minutes | Servings: 10

Ingredients:

- 1 bunch kale, trimmed and leaves separated
- Salt and ground black pepper, to taste
- 3 tablespoons olive oil

- Juice of 1 lemon
- ⅔ cup jarred roasted peppers
- ¼ teaspoon chili powder
- ½ teaspoon garlic powder

Directions:

In a food processor, mix the roasted pepper with the oil, salt, pepper, lemon juice, chili powder and garlic powder and pulse really well. Arrange the kale on a lined baking sheet, add the pepper mix, toss and cook in the oven at 400°F for 1 hour, flip, cook the chips for 30 minutes, arrange them on a platter and serve cold.

Nutrition: Calories - 126, Fat - 7, Fiber - 2, Carbs - 9, Protein - 5

Green Bean Snack

Preparation time: 10 minutes | Cooking time: 8 hours | Servings: 8

Ingredients:

- ⅓ cup olive oil
- 5 pounds green beans, trimmed
- A pinch of salt and black pepper
- 1 teaspoon garlic powder
- 1 teaspoon onion powder

Directions:

In a bowl, mix the beans with salt, pepper, garlic powder, onion powder and the oil, toss well. Transfer the beans to a dehydrator and dry them for 8 hours at 135°F. Serve them as a snack.

Nutrition: Calories - 50, Fat - 3, Fiber - 4, Carbs - 10, Protein - 3

Stuffed Dates

Preparation time: 10 minutes | Cooking time: 0 minutes | Servings: 1

Ingredients:

- 2 medjool dates, cut on one side
- 5 pistachios, raw and chopped
- 1 teaspoon coconut, shredded

Directions:

Stuff each date with the pistachios and coconut, divide into bowls and serve them as a snack.

Nutrition: Calories - 60, Fat - 1, Fiber - 0, Carbs - 0.2, Protein - 1

Coffee Balls

Preparation time: 1 hour | Cooking time: 0 minutes | Servings: 12

Ingredients:

- 3 cups brewed coffee, cold
- 1 cup raw almonds
- 2 tablespoons cocoa powder
- 10 dates
- 2 teaspoons instant coffee

Directions:

In a bowl, mix the almonds with the coffee, set aside for about 1 hour, drain the almonds, transfer them to a food processor, add cocoa powder, dates and the instant coffee. Pulse well, shape small balls out of the mixture and serve them cold.

Nutrition: Calories - 50, Fat - 2, Fiber - 3, Carbs - 8, Protein - 1

Roasted Nut and Fruit Bowls

Preparation time: 10 minutes | Cooking time: 12 minutes | Servings: 8

Ingredients:

- 1 cup dried fruits
- 1 cup dates, pitted and dried
- 1 cup mixed nuts

Directions:

Arrange nuts on a lined baking sheet and roast in the oven at 350°F for 12 minutes. Leave the nuts to cool down, add dates and dried fruits, toss, divide into small bowls and serve.

Nutrition: Calories - 200, Fat - 7, Fiber - 4, Carbs - 41, Protein - 4

Nori Chips

Preparation time: 10 minutes | Cooking time: 15 minutes | Servings: 6

Ingredients:

- 12 nori sheets
- 1 tablespoon olive oil
- ¼ cup water
- Salt and ground black pepper, to taste
- 3 garlic cloves, peeled and minced

Directions:

Place 6 nori sheets on a lined baking sheet, brush with water, top them with the other 6 sheets and cut them all into thin strips. Brush the seaweed chips with the oil, add garlic, salt and pepper, and toss a bit, place in the oven at 275 ° F, and bake for 15 minutes. Serve cold as a snack.

Nutrition: Calories - 42, Fat - 2.3, Fiber - 1, Carbs - 3, Protein - 2.1

Garlic Baby Spinach Snack

Preparation time: 10 minutes | Cooking time: 10 minutes | Servings: 3

Ingredients:

- 2 cups baby spinach, washed
- Salt and ground black pepper, to taste
- 2 teaspoons garlic, minced
- ½ tablespoon olive oil

Directions:

In a bowl, mix the garlic with salt, pepper and the oil and whisk well. Arrange the baby spinach on a lined baking sheet, brush them with the garlic and oil mix, place in the oven and bake at 400° F for 10 minutes. Serve as a snack.

Nutrition: Calories - 75, Fat - 4, Fiber - 1.5, Carbs - 2.4, Protein – 2

Easy Chicken Bake

Preparation time: 10 minutes | Cooking time: 50 minutes | Servings: 4

Ingredients:

- 1 pound chicken meat, cooked and shredded
- ½ cup mayonnaise

For the sauce:

- 15 ounces tomato sauce
- 4 teaspoons mustard
- ¼ cup apple cider vinegar
- 2 teaspoons chili powder
- 3 tablespoons cilantro, chopped
- 1 onion, peeled and chopped
- Salt and ground black pepper, to taste
- 2 teaspoons onion powder

Directions:

Heat a small pot over medium heat, add the tomato sauce, vinegar, mustard, chili powder, onion powder, salt, and pepper, stir, bring to a boil, cook for 20 minutes, take off the heat and transfer to a baking dish. Add chicken, mayo, cilantro and the onion, toss, bake in the oven at 350°F for 20 minutes, and serve warm.

Nutrition: Calories - 130, Fat - 2, Fiber - 4, Carbs - 12, Protein - 9

Zucchini Spread

Preparation time: 10 minutes | Cooking time: 20 minutes | Servings: 6

Ingredients:

- 2 zucchinis, chopped
- Salt and ground black pepper, to taste
- 1 tablespoon olive oil
- 4 garlic cloves, peeled and chopped
- ½ cup sesame seeds paste
- 2 tablespoons lemon juice
- 4 ounces roasted bell peppers, chopped

Directions:

Arrange the zucchini on a baking sheet, drizzle the oil, add the salt and pepper, toss to coat, bake in the oven at 400°F for 20 minutes, cool them down, and transfer to a food processor. Add the garlic, lemon juice, sesame seeds paste and roasted peppers, blend well and serve.

Nutrition: Calories - 140, Fat - 1, Fiber - 2, Carbs - 6, Protein – 8

Beef Nachos

Preparation time: 10 minutes | Cooking time: 14 minutes | Servings: 4

Ingredients:

For the Nachos:

- 1½ tablespoons tomato paste
- ¾ pound ground beef
- 1 small onion, peeled and chopped
- 4 ounces canned green chilies, chopped
- 1½ tablespoons taco seasoning
- ½ cup salsa
- ½ cup guacamole
- 2 tablespoons coconut oil
- ¼ cup black olives, pitted and chopped
- 4 cups plantain chips
- 2 green onions, chopped, for serving
- 2 tablespoons fresh cilantro, chopped

Directions:

Heat a pan with the oil over medium-high heat, add the onions and chilies, stir, and cook for 4 minutes. Add the meat and taco seasoning, stir, and cook for 10 minutes. Add to the tomato paste, salt and pepper, stir, cook for 2 minutes, and take off the heat. Spread the plantain chips on a plate, add a layer of beef, then guacamole, olives, salsa, green onions, and cilantro, and serve.

Nutrition: Calories - 223, Fat - 12, Fiber - 1, Carbs - 5, Protein - 21

Chicken and Dip

Preparation time: 10 minutes | *Cooking time:* 20 minutes | *Servings:* 6

Ingredients:

- 2 chicken breast, cut into thin strips
- 1 cup coconut flour
- ½ cup coconut, shredded
- 1 teaspoon dry mustard
- 1 teaspoon garlic powder
- 2 eggs

- 1 teaspoon sweet paprika
- 2 tablespoons sesame seeds
- Salt and ground black pepper, to taste
- 3 tablespoons olive oil

For the dip:

- Zest and juice from 1 lemon
- 4 mint sprigs, chopped
- 1 small garlic clove, minced

- Salt and ground black pepper, to taste

Directions:

In a bowl, whisk the eggs well. In a second bowl, whisk the flour with the coconut, paprika, mustard, salt, pepper, and sesame seeds and stir. Dip the chicken in the egg and then in almond mix, arrange the strips on a lined baking sheet, drizzle the olive oil over them, and bake in the oven at 400°F for 15 minutes. In a bowl, mix the lemon juice with lemon zest, mint, garlic, salt and pepper, whisk well and serve the chicken with this mix.

Nutrition: Calories - 300, Fat - 12, Fiber - 8, Carbs - 11, Protein – 25

Eggplant Appetizer

Preparation time: 10 minutes | Cooking time: 25 minutes | Servings: 6

Ingredients:

- 2 eggplants, sliced
- ½ cup coconut flour
- 3 egg whites, whisked
- 2 teaspoons olive oil
- ¼ teaspoon sweet paprika
- Salt and ground black pepper, to taste
- 16 ounces chorizo, cooked and diced
- 3 garlic cloves, peeled and minced
- 1 onion, peeled and chopped
- 1 tomato, cored and chopped
- ¼ cup fresh basil, chopped

Directions:

In a bowl, mix flour with the salt, pepper, and paprika. Put the egg white in a second bowl. Dip eggplant slices in the egg white, then in the flour mixture, place them on a lined baking sheet, drizzle the oil over them, cook at 350°F for 25 minutes and arrange them on a platter. In another bowl, mix the chorizo with the tomato, onion, garlic, basil, salt, and pepper, divide the mix on each eggplant slice and serve.

Nutrition: Calories - 160, Fat - 3, Fiber - 6, Carbs - 12, Protein - 7

Potato and Egg Bites

Preparation time: 10 minutes | Cooking time: 20 minutes | Servings: 3

Ingredients:

- 1 potato, sliced
- 2 bacon slices, cooked and crumbled
- 1 small avocado, pitted and cubed
- A drizzle of olive oil
- 4 eggs, hard boiled, peeled and sliced

Directions:

Arrange the potato slices on a lined baking sheet, drizzle the oil, bake in the oven at 350°F for 20 minutes, arrange them on a platter, top each with an egg slice, avocado and bacon and serve.

Nutrition: Calories - 140, Fat - 4, Fiber - 1, Carbs - 8, Protein - 9

Stuffed Eggs

Preparation time: 10 minutes | Cooking time: 0 minutes | Servings: 12

Ingredients:

-
- 6 eggs, hard boiled, peeled and cut into halves lengthwise and yolks separated
- 1 teaspoon mustard
- Salt and ground black pepper, to taste
- ¼ cup homemade mayonnaise
- 1 teaspoon white vinegar
- 1 avocado, pitted, peeled, and chopped
- 3.5 ounces smoked salmon, flaked
- A handful fresh cilantro, chopped

Directions:

In a bowl, mix the egg yolks with mustard, salt, pepper, mayonnaise, vinegar, avocado, salmon and cilantro and stir well. Stuff egg halves with this mixture and serve.

Nutrition: Calories - 89, Fat - 5, Fiber - 1, Carbs - 1, Protein - 5

Mushroom Bites

Preparation time: 10 minutes | Cooking time: 25 minutes | Servings: 12

Ingredients:

-
- 1 pound pork sausage, chopped
- 1 tablespoon olive oil
- 1 red bell pepper, seeded and chopped
- 1 onion, peeled and chopped
- 2 pounds button mushrooms caps
- 3 garlic cloves, peeled and minced
- 2 cups spinach, chopped
- Salt and ground black pepper, to taste
- ¼ cup fresh cilantro, chopped

Directions:

Heat a pan with the oil over medium heat, add the bell pepper and onion, stir, and cook for 3 minutes. Add the garlic, cilantro, spinach, salt, and pepper, stir, cook for 1-2 minutes more, take off the heat, and set aside to cool down. Add the chorizo and stir everything. Stuff each mushroom with this mixture, arrange them on a lined baking sheet, bake them in the oven at 350ºF for 20 minutes, arrange on a platter and serve.

Nutrition: Calories - 200, Fat - 8, Fiber - 1, Carbs - 20, Protein - 9

Sesame Seed Dip

Preparation time: 10 minutes | Cooking time: 0 minutes | Servings: 6

Ingredients:

- 1 cup sesame seed paste
- Salt and ground black pepper, to taste
- 1 cup vegetable stock
- ½ cup lemon juice
- 3 garlic cloves, peeled and chopped
- 2 tablespoons cilantro, chopped

Directions:

In a food processor, mix the sesame seed paste with salt, pepper, stock, lemon juice and garlic, pulse well, add cilantro, stir, divide into bowls and serve.

Nutrition: Calories - 150, Fat - 12, Fiber - 2, Carbs - 7, Protein - 5

Sweet Potato Bites

Preparation time: 10 minutes | Cooking time: 55 minutes | Servings: 6

Ingredients:

-
- 5 bacon slices, cooked and chopped
- 1 tablespoon fresh rosemary, chopped
- 3 onions, peeled and chopped
- Salt and ground black pepper, to taste
- 3 dates, pitted and chopped
- 2 sweet potatoes, sliced
- 1 tablespoons olive oil + a drizzle

Directions:

Heat a pan with a drizzle of oil over medium heat, add the onions, stir, reduce the temperature to medium-low, and cook for 15 minutes. Add the dates, rosemary, salt, and pepper, stir, cook for 15 minutes more, take off the heat, combine with the bacon and stir. Arrange the potato slices on a baking sheet, add 1 tablespoon oil, toss to coat, bake in the oven at 425°F for 25 minutes, arrange the potato sliced on a platter, top with the bacon mix and serve.

Nutrition: Calories - 198, Fat - 12, Fiber - 2, Carbs - 17, Protein - 5

Beets and Vinaigrette

Preparation time: 1 hour and 10 minutes | Cooking time: 30 minutes | Servings: 4

Ingredients:

- 2 beets, sliced
- ⅓ cup white vinegar
- A pinch of ground black pepper
- 1 cup olive oil
- 1 teaspoon green tea powder

Directions:

Put the vinegar in a small pot, heat over medium heat, add tea powder, stir well, bring to a simmer, take off the heat, and cool down completely. Add half of the oil, some black pepper, whisk well and leave aside for 1 hour. Add the beets, toss everything, arrange the beets on a lined baking sheet, add the rest of the oil, toss and bake in the oven at 350°F and bake for 30 minutes. Arrange on a platter and serve.

Nutrition: Calories - 100, Fat - 2, Fiber - 2, Carbs - 3, Protein - 2

Cabbage and Carrot Salad

Preparation time: 10 minutes | Cooking time: 0 minutes | Servings: 4

Ingredients:

- 2 carrots, peeled and grated
- 1 green cabbage head, shredded
- 10 strawberries, cored and cut in half
- A pinch of salt and black pepper
- 2 tablespoons white wine vinegar
- 1 tablespoon Dijon mustard
- ¼ cup lemon juice
- ¾ cup olive oil

Directions:

In a bowl, mix the carrots with the cabbage and the strawberries and toss. Add salt, pepper, vinegar, mustard, lemon juice and the oil, toss and serve as an appetizer.

Nutrition: Calories - 100, Fat - 1, Fiber - 2, Carbs - 2, Protein - 4

Pineapple and Chicken Bites
Preparation time: 10 minutes | Cooking time: 10 minutes | Servings: 4

Ingredients:

- 20 ounces pineapple slices
- 2 teaspoons olive oil
- 1 tablespoon sweet paprika
- 3 cups chicken thighs, boneless, skinless, and cut into medium pieces
- 1 tablespoon parsley, chopped

Directions:

Heat a pan over medium-high heat, add the pineapple slices, grill them for 2 minutes on each side, cool them and cut into medium cubes. Heat a pan with the oil over medium-high heat, add the chicken, season with the paprika, cook them for 5 minutes on each side, arrange on a platter, top each of the chicken pieces with a pineapple cube, prick with toothpicks and serve.

Nutrition: Calories - 120, Fat - 3, Fiber - 1, Carbs - 5, Protein - 2

Lemon Tea Mushroom Mix
Preparation time: 1 day and 10 minutes | Cooking time: 10 minutes | Servings: 6

Ingredients:

- 8 lemon tea bags
- 6 Portobello mushroom caps
- 3 tablespoons cilantro, chopped
- A pinch of salt and black pepper
- 1 cup hot water
- 1 cup avocado oil

Directions:

In a bowl, mix the water with the tea bags, cover, leave aside for 10 minutes and strain the tea into another bowl. Add the cilantro, the oil, salt and pepper and whisk. Add the mushrooms and toss them. Heat a kitchen grill over medium-high heat, add the mushrooms, grill them for 5 minutes on each side, slice and serve right away.

Nutrition: Calories - 150, Fat - 3, Fiber - 1, Carbs - 5, Protein - 3

Zucchini Paste

Preparation time: 10 minutes | Cooking time: 5 minutes | Servings: 6

Ingredients:

- 2 tablespoons olive oil
- 2 tablespoons lime juice
- 2 tablespoons mint leaves, chopped
- Ground black pepper, to taste
- 2 garlic cloves, peeled and minced
- 4 zucchinis, chopped
- ½ cup coconut cream

Directions:

Heat a pan with the oil over medium-high heat, add the zucchini and the garlic, stir, cook for 5 minutes, take off the heat, cool down, transfer to a food processor, add coconut cream, lime juice, mint and black pepper, pulse well, divide into bowls and serve.

Nutrition: Calories - 130, Fat - 4, Fiber - 5, Carbs - 7, Protein - 8

Arugula and Mushroom Mix

Preparation time: 10 minutes | Cooking time: 10 minutes | Servings: 4

Ingredients:

- 1 pound cremini mushrooms, halved
- 4 tablespoons olive oil
- Ground black pepper, to taste
- 4 bunches arugula
- 2 tablespoons balsamic vinegar
- 8 sun-dried tomatoes, chopped
- 2 tablespoons parsley, chopped

Directions:

Heat a pan with 2 tablespoons olive oil over medium-high heat, add the mushrooms and black pepper, stir, and cook for 8 minutes. Add the rest of the oil and the vinegar, stir, cook for 2 minutes more, transfer to a salad bowl, add arugula, tomatoes and parsley, toss and serve.

Nutrition: Calories - 90, Fat - 2, Fiber - 3, Carbs - 6, Protein - 7

Basil Mushroom Salad

Preparation time: 10 minutes | Cooking time: 7 minutes | Servings: 4

Ingredients:

- ½ pound mushrooms, sliced
- 1 tablespoon olive oil
- 3 garlic cloves, peeled and minced
- 2 teaspoons basil, dried
- Ground black pepper, to taste
- 3 tablespoons lime juice
- ½ cup water
- 1 tablespoons parsley, chopped

Directions:

Heat a pan with the oil over medium heat, add the mushrooms, stir, cook for 4 minutes, add basil, garlic, black pepper, lime juice, water and parsley, toss, cook for 3 minutes more, divide into small bowls and serve.

Nutrition: Calories - 90, Fat - 2, Fiber - 4, Carbs - 6, Protein - 6

Tomato Bites

Preparation time: 10 minutes | Cooking time: 0 minutes | Servings: 8

Ingredients:

- 1 small watermelon, cut into 32 cubes
- ¼ cup balsamic vinegar
- 32 basil leaves
- 16 cherry tomatoes, cut in half
- 2 tablespoon olive oil

Directions:

Place one watermelon cube on the tip of a skewer. Add a basil leaf and then a tomato piece. Repeat with the rest of the ingredients, arrange the skewers on a platter, drizzle the olive oil and balsamic vinegar all over and serve.

Nutrition: Calories – 87, Fat - 1, Fiber - 3, Carbs - 5, Protein - 6

Stuffed Cherry Tomatoes

Preparation time: 10 minutes | Cooking time: 5 minutes | Servings: 24 pieces

Ingredients:

- 24 cherry tomatoes, cored and flesh scooped
- 1 tablespoon extra virgin olive oil
- A pinch of salt
- ¼ teaspoon red pepper flakes
- 1 tablespoon black olive paste
- 1 tablespoon water
- ¼ cup mint leaves, torn

Directions:

In a bowl, mix tomato flesh with salt, pepper flakes, tomato paste, water and mint and stir well. Stuff the tomatoes with this mix, arrange them on a lined baking sheet, drizzle the oil, place under preheated broiler, and broil for 5 minutes, arrange on a platter and serve.

Nutrition: Calories - 120, Fat - 2, Fiber - 3, Carbs - 6, Protein - 7

Tomato and Dragon Fruit Platter

Preparation time: 10 minutes | Cooking time: 0 minutes | Servings: 4

Ingredients:

- 4 tomatoes, cored and sliced thin
- 1 tablespoon lemon juice
- 1 dragon fruit, skinless and cubed
- 1 teaspoon lemon zest
- 1 tablespoon balsamic vinegar
- A pinch of salt
- 1 tablespoon mint, chopped
- 4 tablespoons olive oil

Directions:

Arrange the tomatoes on a platter and top with the dragon fruit cubes. In a bowl, mix lemon zest with lemon juice, vinegar, salt, oil and mint, whisk well, drizzle over the tomatoes and dragon fruit and serve.

Nutrition: Calories - 98, Fat - 1, Fiber - 2, Carbs - 3, Protein - 6

Mango and Tomato Salad

Preparation time: 10 minutes | Cooking time: 0 minutes | Servings: 6

Ingredients:

- 4 tomatoes, cored, seeded, and chopped
- A pinch of salt and black pepper
- ⅓ cup onion, chopped
- 1 mango, peeled, seedless, and chopped
- 2 jalapeño peppers, chopped
- ¼ cup fresh cilantro, chopped
- 3 tablespoons lime juice

Directions:

In a bowl, mix the tomatoes with onion, mango, jalapeno, cilantro, lime juice, salt and pepper, toss and serve.

Nutrition: Calories - 67, Fat - 1, Fiber - 2, Carbs - 4, Protein - 7

Tuna Cucumber Rounds

Preparation time: 10 minutes | Cooking time: 0 minutes | Servings: 6

Ingredients:

- 1 cucumber, sliced
- 1 tablespoon fresh cilantro, chopped
- 6 ounces canned tuna, drained and flaked
- 1 teaspoon lemon juice

Directions:

In a bowl, mix the tuna with lemon juice and cilantro and mash well. Spoon this mixture on each cucumber slice and serve.

Nutrition: Calories - 120, Fat - 1, Fiber - 2, Carbs - 5, Protein - 6

Tuna Salad

Preparation time: 10 minutes | Cooking time: 0 minutes | Servings: 2

Ingredients:

- 8 ounces canned tuna, drained and flaked
- 2 teaspoons olive oil
- 2 tablespoons shallots, chopped
- 4 lettuce leaves, torn
- 1 tablespoon capers, drained
- 2 tablespoons red bell pepper, seeded and chopped
- 1 tablespoon arugula leaves, torn
- 2 tablespoons hard boiled egg, peeled and chopped
- A pinch of salt and black pepper
- Juice of ½ lemon

Directions:

In a bowl, mix the tuna with oil, shallots, lettuce leaves, capers, bell pepper, arugula, eggs, salt, pepper and lemon juice, toss and serve cold.

Nutrition: Calories - 120, Fat - 2, Fiber - 3, Carbs - 6, Protein - 8

Tuna and Carrot Salad

Preparation time: 10 minutes | Cooking time: 0 minutes | Servings: 4

Ingredients:

- ¼ red onion, peeled and chopped
- 4 carrots, cut into thin sticks
- 1 tablespoon avocado oil
- 6 ounces canned tuna, drained and flaked
- 1 tablespoon Dijon mustard
- 1 tablespoon red vinegar
- A pinch of salt and black pepper
- 1 tablespoon lemon juice

Directions:

In a large bowl, mix the onion with the carrots, tuna, oil, mustard, vinegar, salt, pepper and lemon juice, toss well and serve cold.

Nutrition: Calories - 140, Fat - 3, Fiber - 3, Carbs - 6, Protein - 8

Shrimp and Lobster Platter

Preparation time: 10 minutes | *Cooking time:* 0 minutes | *Servings:* 2

Ingredients:

- 1 tablespoon shallots, chopped
- ¼ cup white vinegar
- A pinch of salt and black pepper
- 2 tablespoons cucumber, diced
- 1 tablespoon horseradish
- ⅓ cup tomato paste, unsweetened
- ¼ teaspoon orange zest
- 4 shrimp, peeled, deveined, and steamed
- 1 lobster tail, steamed and cut in half

Directions:

In a bowl, mix the shallots with the vinegar, salt, pepper, horseradish, tomato paste and orange zest and whisk really well. Arrange the lobster and the shrimp on a platter; add the sauce you have just made and serve.

Nutrition: Calories - 176, Fat - 4, Fiber - 4, Carbs - 6, Protein - 8

Olive and Anchovy Spread

Preparation time: 10 minutes | *Cooking time:* 0 minutes | *Servings:* 4

Ingredients:

- 1 garlic clove, peeled and chopped
- 1 cup green olives, pitted
- 3 tablespoons capers, drained
- 5 anchovy fillets, chopped
- 2 teaspoons lemon juice

Directions:

In a food processor, mix the olives with the garlic, capers, anchovy and lemon juice, pulse well and serve cold.

Nutrition: Calories - 100, Fat - 2, Fiber - 3, Carbs - 6, Protein - 8

Beef and Caper Tartar

Preparation time: 45 minutes | Cooking time: 0 minutes | Servings: 2

Ingredients:

- 3 tablespoons olive oil
- 8 ounces beef tenderloin, julienned
- 1 egg yolk
- 3 tablespoons capers, soaked in water, drained and rinsed
- 1 onion, minced
- 2 tablespoons fresh parsley, minced
- A pinch of sea salt and black pepper
- 1 Serrano chili pepper, minced
- 1 teaspoon Dijon mustard
- 1 teaspoon balsamic vinegar

Directions:

Put the meat on a cutting board, dice finely, put it in a bowl and keep it in the fridge for 45 minutes. In a bowl, mix the egg yolk with the oil and whisk well. Add the parsley, chili pepper, capers, onion, salt, pepper, the beef and the vinegar and stir really well. Transfer to plates and serve with the Dijon mustard on top.

Nutrition: Calories - 140, Fat - 3, Fiber - 3, Carbs - 6, Protein - 8

Shrimp Spread

Preparation time: 10 minutes | Cooking time: 10 minutes | Servings: 8

Ingredients:

- 1 pound shrimp, cooked, peeled, deveined and chopped
- 2 tablespoons coconut cream
- A pinch of salt and black pepper

Directions:

In a bowl, mix the shrimp with the coconut cream, salt and pepper, stir well, divide into bowls and serve.

Nutrition: Calories - 110, Fat - 1, Fiber - 3, Carbs - 6, Protein - 8

Salmon Bites

Preparation time: 10 minutes | Cooking time: 0 minutes | Servings: 14

Ingredients:

- 1 cucumber, peeled and sliced thin into 42 pieces
- 2 teaspoons lemon juice
- 4 ounces coconut cream
- 1 teaspoon lemon zest
- A pinch of salt and ground black pepper
- 2 teaspoons fresh dill, chopped
- 4 ounces smoked salmon, cut into 42 strips

Directions:

In a bowl, mix the coconut cream with lemon zest, lemon juice, salt and pepper and stir well. Arrange the cucumber slices on a platter, top each with the salmon strips, add coconut mixture over the salmon, sprinkle the dill and serve.

Nutrition: Calories - 165, Fat - 4, Fiber - 5, Carbs - 7, Protein - 10

Tuna Platter

Preparation time: 10 minutes | Cooking time: 0 minutes | Servings: 2

Ingredients:

- 7 ounces tuna, sliced thin
- 1 tomato, cored and chopped
- 1 teaspoon lime juice
- 1 teaspoon fresh parsley, chopped
- 1 avocado, pitted and chopped
- 1 teaspoon olive oil
- A pinch of salt and black pepper

Directions:

In a bowl, mix the tomato with the lime juice, parsley, avocado, oil, salt and pepper and toss. Arrange the tuna on a platter, top the slices with the tomato mix and serve.

Nutrition: Calories - 120, Fat - 2, Fiber - 3, Carbs - 6, Protein - 8

Tuna Cube Salad

Preparation time: 10 minutes | Cooking time: 0 minutes | Servings: 3

Ingredients:

- 7 ounces sashimi-grade tuna, cubed
- 4 cherry tomatoes, cubed
- ⅓ cucumber, cubed
- 1 teaspoon fresh cilantro, minced
- 4 tablespoons olive oil
- A pinch of salt and ground black pepper
- 3 tablespoons white vinegar
- 1 teaspoons lemon juice

Directions:

In a bowl, mix the tomatoes with the cucumber, cilantro, half of the oil, salt, pepper, vinegar and half of the lemon juice and toss well. In a separate bowl, mix the tuna cubes with the rest of the oil and remaining lemon juice, toss and arrange them on a platter. Add the tomato mix on the side and serve.

Nutrition: Calories - 150, Fat - 5, Fiber - 4, Carbs - 5, Protein - 6

Eggplant Spread

Preparation time: 10 minutes | Cooking time: 35 minutes | Servings: 8

Ingredients:

- 2 tablespoons olive oil+ a drizzle
- 4 pounds eggplants, cut in half
- 2 shallots, peeled and chopped
- 1 pound tomatoes, peeled and chopped
- 4 garlic cloves, peeled and minced
- A pinch of salt and ground black pepper
- 2 tablespoons lemon juice

Directions:

Put the eggplant halves in a baking dish, brush them with a drizzle of olive oil, place in the oven at 350°F, bake for 30 minutes, cool them down, peel the flesh and put in a blender. Heat a pan with the rest of the oil over medium high heat, add the shallots and the garlic, stir and cook them for 5 minutes. Transfer this to the blender as well, add the tomatoes, salt, pepper and the lemon juice, pulse well, divide into bowls and serve as a dip.

Nutrition: Calories - 150, Fat - 4, Fiber - 5, Carbs - 6, Protein - 7

Olive and Roasted Pepper Tapenade

Preparation time: 10 minutes | Cooking time: 0 minutes | Servings: 8

Ingredients:

- 2 tablespoons olive oil
- ½ cup bottled roasted peppers, chopped
- ½ cup Kalamata and black olives, pitted and chopped
- 1 tablespoon lemon juice
- 1 teaspoon red pepper flakes
- A pinch of salt and black pepper
- ½ tablespoon mint leaves, chopped
- ½ tablespoon fresh parsley, chopped
- ½ tablespoon fresh oregano, chopped
- ½ tablespoon fresh basil, chopped

Directions:

In a bowl, mix the bell peppers with the olives, lemon juice, pepper flakes, salt, pepper, mint, parsley, oregano, basil and the oil, toss and serve cold.

Nutrition: Calories - 140, Fat - 4, Fiber - 4, Carbs - 7, Protein - 9

Chinese Tuna Skewers

Preparation time: 30 minutes | Cooking time: 10 minutes | Servings: 16

Ingredients:

- 2 tablespoons coconut aminos
- 1 pound tuna steaks, cut in 16 cubes
- 2 tablespoons balsamic vinegar
- A pinch of salt and black pepper
- 1 tablespoon sesame seeds
- 2 tablespoons olive oil
- 16 pieces pickled ginger

Directions:

In a bowl, mix the aminos with the vinegar and tuna, toss to coat, cover the bowl, and keep in the refrigerator for 30 minutes. Pat dry the tuna and season with the salt and black pepper, and sprinkle the sesame seeds. Heat a pan with the oil over medium heat, add the tuna pieces, cook them for 2 minutes on each side and transfer them to a plate. Thread one ginger slice on each of the 16 skewers, continue with the tuna, arrange everything on a platter and serve.

Nutrition: Calories - 150, Fat - 4, Fiber - 4, Carbs - 6, Protein - 8

Smoked Salmon Platter

Preparation time: 10 minutes | Cooking time: 0 minutes | Servings: 4

Ingredients:

- 2 tablespoons scallions, chopped
- 2 tablespoons onion, peeled and chopped
- 1½ teaspoons lime juice
- 1 tablespoon fresh chives, minced
- 1 tablespoon olive oil
- ½ pound smoked salmon fillet, skinless and diced
- 12 cherry tomatoes, cut in half
- A pinch of salt and black pepper
- 1 tablespoon parsley, chopped

Directions:

In a bowl, mix the salmon with the scallions, onion, lime juice, chives, oil, tomatoes, salt, pepper and parsley, toss, arrange on a platter and serve.

Nutrition: Calories - 170, Fat - 3, Fiber - 4, Carbs - 6, Protein - 7

Carrot Spread

Preparation time: 10 minutes | Cooking time: 12 minutes | Servings: 6

Ingredients:

- 3 carrots, peeled and grated
- ¼ cup olive oil
- ⅓ cup pine nuts
- A pinch of salt and black pepper
- 2 cups coconut yogurt
- 1 shallot, minced

Directions:

Heat a pan with the oil over medium-high heat, add the carrots and the shallot, stir, and cook for 6 minutes. Add the salt, pepper and pine nuts, reduce the heat, cook for 6 minutes more. Transfer this to a bowl, add the coconut yogurt, whisk and serve.

Nutrition: Calories - 140, Fat - 2, Fiber - 3, Carbs - 7, Protein - 8

Veggies and Pomegranate Salad

Preparation time: 10 minutes | Cooking time: 0 minutes | Servings: 6

Ingredients:

- 3 garlic cloves, peeled and minced
- 2 tablespoons olive oil
- ½ teaspoon red pepper flakes
- A pinch of salt and black pepper
- 2 teaspoon pomegranate seeds
- 2 tomatoes, cored and chopped
- 2 cucumbers, cubed
- 2 scallions, chopped
- 1 onion, peeled and chopped
- 1 green bell pepper, and chopped
- ½ cup cilantro, chopped
- ¼ cup mint leaves, chopped

Directions:

In a bowl, mix the tomatoes with the cucumber, garlic, scallions, onion, bell pepper, cilantro and mint and toss. Add the oil, pepper flakes, salt, pepper and the pomegranate seeds, toss and serve.

Nutrition: Calories - 120, Fat - 2, Fiber - 3, Carbs - 4, Protein - 7

Fresh Tomato Salad

Preparation time: 40 minutes | Cooking time: 0 minutes | Servings: 6

Ingredients:

- 1 pound tomatoes, cubed
- ¾ pound cucumbers, chopped
- 1 green bell pepper, seeded and chopped
- 1 onion, sliced thin
- ¼ cup fresh parsley, chopped
- 2 tablespoons mint leaves, chopped
- A pinch of salt and black pepper
- 3 tablespoons olive oil
- 3 tablespoons lemon juice
- 10 black olives, pitted and chopped

Directions:

In a salad bowl, mix the tomatoes with the cucumbers, bell pepper, onion, parsley, mint, salt, pepper, oil, lemon juice and olives, toss and serve.

Nutrition: Calories - 120, Fat - 2, Fiber - 3, Carbs - 5, Protein - 5

Zucchini and Green Onion Salad

Preparation time: 10 minutes | Cooking time: 0 minute | Servings: 4

Ingredients:

- 4 zucchinis, spiralized
- 4 green onions, chopped
- Juice of 1 lime
- 1 tablespoon olive oil
- ½ cup fresh parsley, chopped
- ¾ cup almonds, chopped
- A pinch of salt and black pepper

Directions:

In a salad bowl, mix zucchini with the green onions, lime juice, oil, almonds, parsley, salt and pepper, toss and serve.

Nutrition: Calories - 90, Fat - 4, Fiber - 2, Carbs - 5, Protein - 7

Curry Cabbage Slaw

Preparation time: 1 hour | Cooking time: 0 minutes | Servings: 4

Ingredients:

- 1 green cabbage head, chopped
- ⅓ cup coconut, shaved
- ¼ cup avocado oil
- 2 tablespoons lemon juice
- 3 tablespoons sesame seeds
- ½ teaspoon curry powder
- ⅓ teaspoon turmeric powder

Directions:

In a bowl, mix the cabbage with the coconut, oil, lemon juice, curry powder, turmeric and sesame seeds, toss and serve after keeping the mix in the fridge for 1 hour.

Nutrition: Calories - 100, Fat - 2, Fiber - 5, Carbs - 5, Protein - 6

Papaya and Cabbage Slaw
Preparation time: 10 minutes | Cooking time: 0 minutes | Servings: 4

Ingredients:

- 2 cups green papaya, peeled and grated
- ¼ cup carrots, grated
- 2 tablespoons coconut aminos
- ¼ cup green cabbage, shredded
- 10 cherry tomatoes, cut in half
- 1 teaspoon olive oil
- 2 red chilies, chopped
- 2 garlic cloves, peeled and minced
- 1 teaspoon lemon juice
- 2 tablespoons walnuts, chopped
- A pinch of salt and black pepper

Directions:

In a salad bowl, mix the papaya with the carrots, tomatoes, cabbage, chilies, garlic, walnuts, salt and pepper. Add the lemon juice, oil and the aminos, toss and serve cold.

Nutrition: Calories - 140, Fat - 3, Fiber - 2, Carbs - 6, Protein - 8

Apple and Celery Appetizer Salad
Preparation time: 1 hour | Cooking time: 0 minutes | Servings: 4

Ingredients:

-
- 3 apples, cored and chopped
- 1 celery stalk, chopped

For the salad dressing:

- 1 tablespoon lemon juice
- 2 garlic cloves, peeled and minced
- ¼ cup homemade mayonnaise
- 1 tablespoon balsamic vinegar
- 2 carrot, grated
- ¼ cup cashews, chopped

- 2 tablespoons water
- 3 tablespoons olive oil
- 1 tablespoon fresh parsley, chopped
- A pinch of sea salt

Directions:

In a bowl, mix the apples with the carrots, celery and cashews and toss. In another bowl, mix the garlic with the lemon juice, mayonnaise, vinegar, oil, parsley, salt and water, whisk well, pour over the salad, toss and serve cold.

Nutrition: Calories - 100, Fat - 3, Fiber - 4, Carbs - 5, Protein - 6

Radish Slaw

Preparation time: 10 minutes | Cooking time: 0 minutes | Servings: 4

Ingredients:

- 16 radishes, sliced
- 2 tablespoons raisins
- Juice of 2 lemons
- 1 tablespoon fresh chives, minced
- 1 tablespoon fresh parsley, chopped
- 1 tablespoon sesame seeds
- 4 handfuls spinach leaves, torn
- 4 tablespoons olive oil
- A pinch of salt and black pepper

Directions:

In a salad bowl, mix the radishes with the raisins, chives, parsley, lemon juice, spinach, sesame seeds, oil, salt and pepper, toss and serve cold.

Nutrition: Calories - 90, Fat - 2, Fiber - 2, Carbs - 4, Protein - 6

Oregano Tomatoes Mix

Preparation time: 10 minutes | Cooking time: 0 minutes | Servings: 4

Ingredients:

-
- ½ cup olive oil
- 2 pints cherry tomatoes, cut in half
- A pinch of salt and black pepper
- 1 red onion, peeled and chopped
- 3 tablespoons red vinegar
- 1 garlic clove, peeled and minced
- 1 bunch oregano, chopped

Directions:

In a bowl, mix the tomatoes with salt, pepper, onion, garlic, oregano, vinegar and oil, toss and serve cold.

Nutrition: Calories - 100, Fat - 1, Fiber - 2, Carbs - 2, Protein - 5

Tomato and Avocado Salad
Preparation time: 10 minutes | Cooking time: 0 minutes | Servings: 4

Ingredients:
- 1 pound tomatoes, cored and chopped
- 2 avocados, pitted and chopped
- 1 small onion, chopped
- 2 tablespoons olive oil
- 2 tablespoons lemon juice
- ¼ cup cilantro, diced
- A pinch of sea salt and black pepper

Directions:
In a bowl, mix the tomatoes with the avocados, onion, oil, lemon juice, cilantro, salt and pepper, toss and serve as an appetizer.

Nutrition: Calories - 120, Fat - 2, Fiber - 2, Carbs - 3, Protein - 4

Cucumber, Fennel and Chive Slaw
Preparation time: 10 minutes | Cooking time: 0 minutes | Servings: 4

Ingredients:
- 4 cucumbers, chopped
- ¾ cup fennel, sliced
- 2 tablespoons fresh chives, minced
- ½ cup walnuts, chopped
- 2 tablespoons lemon juice
- 4 tablespoons olive oil
- A pinch of salt and black pepper

Directions:
In a bowl, mix the cucumbers with the fennel, chives, walnuts, lemon juice, oil, salt and pepper, toss and serve cold.

Nutrition: Calories - 70, Fat - 1, Fiber - 1, Carbs - 1, Protein - 5

Endive Appetizer Salad

Preparation time: 10 minutes | Cooking time: 0 minutes | Servings: 4

Ingredients:

- 2 tablespoons lemon juice
- ¼ cup olive oil
- A pinch of salt and black pepper
- 1 teaspoon Dijon mustard
- 4 endives, shredded
- ½ cup almonds, chopped
- 2 tablespoons cilantro, chopped

Directions:

In a salad bowl, mix the endives with almonds, cilantro, lemon juice, oil, salt, pepper and mustard, toss and serve cold.

Nutrition: Calories - 100, Fat - 0, Fiber - 1, Carbs - 0, Protein - 6

Ginger Cilantro Dip

Preparation time: 10 minutes | Cooking time: 0 minutes | Servings: 6

Ingredients:

- ½ cup ginger, grated
- 2 bunches fresh cilantro
- 3 tablespoons balsamic vinegar
- ½ cup olive oil
- 2 tablespoons coconut aminos

Directions:

In a blender mix cilantro with the oil, aminos, vinegar and ginger, pulse well, divide into bowls and serve.

Nutrition: Calories - 89, Fat - 2, Fiber - 2, Carbs - 6, Protein - 8

Roasted Beet Spread

Preparation time: 3 hours and 10 minutes | Cooking time: 1 hour | Servings: 6

Ingredients:

- 3 beets
- 1 cup coconut cream
- A pinch of salt and black pepper
- 2 tablespoons mint leaves, chopped
- 2 teaspoons balsamic vinegar
- A drizzle of olive oil

Directions:

Place beets in a baking dish, add some hot water on the bottom of the pan, add a pinch of salt and pepper, cover the pan, place in the oven at 450°F and bake for 1 hour. Let the beets cool down, peel, chop, and transfer to a bowl. Add cream, salt, pepper, mint, vinegar and the oil, pulse using an immersion blender and serve cold after 3 hours.

Nutrition: Calories - 130, Fat - 4, Fiber - 5, Carbs - 8, Protein - 9

Red Bell Pepper Hummus

Preparation time: 10 minutes | Cooking time: 10 minutes | Servings: 4

Ingredients:

- 1 garlic clove, peeled and minced
- 3 red bell peppers, deseeded and cut into quarters
- A pinch of salt and black pepper
- 1½ tablespoons olive oil
- ¼ cup coconut cream
- 2 green onions, sliced

Directions:

Place the peppers on preheated grill over medium-high heat, cook for 8 minutes, transfer to a bowl, cover, leave aside for a few minutes. Peel, transfer to a food processor, add garlic, salt, pepper, oil and the cream, pulse well, divide into bowls, sprinkle the green onions on top and serve.

Nutrition: Calories - 176, Fat - 3, Fiber - 2, Carbs - 6, Protein - 7

Whole Food Seafood and Fish Recipes

Shrimp and Asparagus Mix
Preparation time: 10 minutes | Cooking time: 10 minutes | Servings: 4

Ingredients:

- 1 pound shrimp, peeled and deveined
- 2 tablespoons olive oil
- 2 tablespoons lemon juice
- 1 bundle asparagus, trimmed and halved
- Salt and ground black pepper, to taste
- 4 garlic cloves, peeled and minced
- ½ teaspoon ginger, grated
- ⅔ cup vegetable stock

Directions:

Heat a pan with the oil over medium-high heat, add the garlic, ginger, salt and pepper, stir and cook for 2 minutes. Add the asparagus and the lemon juice, toss and cook for 3 minutes more. Add the shrimp and the stock, stir, cook for 4 minutes more, divide between plates and serve.

Nutrition: Calories - 240, Fat - 10, Fiber - 3, Carbs - 8, Protein - 20

Shrimp, Avocado and Tomato Mix
Preparation time: 10 minutes | Cooking time: 0 minutes | Servings: 2

Ingredients:

- 2 green onions, chopped
- 1 tomato, cored and chopped
- 1 avocado, pitted, peeled, and cut into medium chunks
- 2 tablespoons fresh cilantro, chopped
- 1 cup shrimp, cooked, peeled and deveined
- Salt and ground black pepper, to taste

Directions:

In a salad bowl, mix the onions with the tomato, cilantro, avocado, shrimp, salt and pepper, toss and serve cold.

Nutrition: Calories - 130, Fat - 2, Fiber - 3, Carbs - 10, Protein - 3

Lime Shrimp Mix

Preparation time: 10 minutes | Cooking time: 7 minutes | Servings: 2

Ingredients:

- 1 pound shrimp, peeled and deveined
- 1½ tablespoons chili powder
- 1 cup coconut flakes
- Zest of 3 limes
- 1 egg
- Juice from 2 limes
- 3 tablespoons olive oil

Directions:

In a bowl, mix the coconut flakes with the chili powder, and lime zest and stir. Put the egg in a second bowl. Coat the shrimp in egg, then in coconut mixture. Heat a pan with the oil over medium-high heat, add the shrimp, cook for 3 minutes on each side, divide between plates, drizzle the lime juice all over and serve.

Nutrition: Calories - 300, Fat - 5, Fiber - 1, Carbs - 20, Protein - 20

Citrus Calamari Mix

Preparation time: 10 minutes | Cooking time: 5 minutes | Servings: 4

Ingredients:

- 1 lime, sliced
- 1 lemon, sliced
- 2 pounds calamari tubes and tentacles, sliced
- Salt and ground black pepper, to taste
- ¼ cup olive oil
- 2 garlic cloves, peeled and minced
- 3 tablespoons lemon juice
- 1 orange, sliced
- 2 tablespoons fresh parsley, chopped

Directions:

In a bowl, mix the calamari salt, pepper, lime slices, lemon slices, orange slices, garlic, oil, parsley, and lemon juice and toss. Heat a pan over medium-high heat, add the calamari and the citrus mix, cook for 5 minutes, divide between plates, and serve.

Nutrition: Calories - 250, Fat - 2, Fiber - 1, Carbs - 31, Protein - 30

Mussels Curry
Preparation time: 10 minutes | Cooking time: 10 minutes | Servings: 4

Ingredients:

- 2½ pounds mussels, debearded and scrubbed
- 14 ounces coconut milk
- 3 tablespoons red curry paste
- 1 tablespoon olive oil
- Salt and ground black pepper, to taste
- ½ cup chicken stock
- Juice of 1 lime
- Zest of 1 lime
- ¼ cup fresh cilantro, chopped
- 3 tablespoons parsley, chopped

Directions:

Heat a pan with the oil over medium-high heat, add the curry paste, stir, and cook for 2 minutes. Add the mussels, coconut milk, salt, pepper, stock, lime juice and lime zest, toss and cook for 7 minutes. Discard unopened mussels, add cilantro and the parsley, toss, divide into bowls and serve.

Nutrition: Calories - 400, Fat - 12, Fiber - 2, Carbs - 20, Protein - 30

Sriracha Lobster Tails
Preparation time: 6 minutes | Cooking time: 10 minutes | Servings: 4

Ingredients:

- ¼ cup olive oil
- 4 lobster tails, cut halfway and opened
- 1 tablespoon fresh chives, minced
- Salt and ground black pepper, to taste
- 2 tablespoons Sriracha sauce
- 1 tablespoon lime juice
- A handful cilantro, chopped

Directions:

In a bowl, mix the Sriracha sauce with the oil, salt, pepper, chives, and lime juice, stir. Stuff the lobster tails with this mix, place on a preheated grill pan over medium-high heat, cook for 4 minutes on each side, divide between plates, sprinkle cilantro on top and serve.

Nutrition: Calories - 270, Fat - 12, Carbs - 5, Fiber - 1, Protein - 20

Veggie and Salmon Bake
Preparation time: 10 minutes | Cooking time: 60 minutes | Servings: 4

Ingredients:

- 8 sweet potatoes, sliced
- 4 cups salmon, cooked and flaked
- 1 onion, peeled and chopped
- 2 carrots, peeled and chopped
- Salt and ground black pepper, to taste
- 2 cups coconut milk
- 3 tablespoons olive oil
- 2 tablespoons fresh chives, minced
- 2 garlic cloves, diced

Directions:

Heat a pan with the oil over medium heat, add the garlic, stir, and cook for 1 minute. Add the coconut milk, salt, and pepper, stir, cook for a couple more minutes and take off heat. In a bowl, mix the carrots with the salmon, chives, onion, salt, and pepper and stir. Arrange a layer of potatoes in a baking dish, drizzle half of the coconut milk, layer half of the salmon mix, layer the rest of the potatoes and top with the rest of the sauce. Bake in the in the oven at 375°F, bake for 1 hour, divide between plates, and serve.

Nutrition: Calories - 280, Fat - 9, Carbs - 14, Fiber - 10, Protein - 12

Scallops and Vegetable Sauce
Preparation time: 10 minutes | Cooking time: 15 minutes | Servings: 4

Ingredients:

- 12 scallops
- 3 garlic cloves, peeled and minced
- Salt and ground black pepper, to taste
- 2 cups cauliflower florets, chopped
- 2 tablespoons olive oil
- 2 cups sweet potatoes, chopped
- 2 rosemary sprigs
- ¼ cup pine nuts, toasted
- 2 cups vegetable stock
- 2 tablespoons chives, diced

Directions:

In a pot, mix the stock with the cauliflower and potatoes, stir, bring to a boil, reduce heat, simmer for 10 minutes, drain, transfer to a blender. Add salt and pepper and pulse well. Heat a pan with the oil over medium-high heat, add the rosemary and garlic, stir, and cook for 1 minute. Add the scallops, some salt and pepper, cook them for 2 minutes, and divide between plates. Add the vegetable sauce all over, sprinkle chives and pine nuts all over and serve.

Nutrition: Calories - 150, Fat - 10, Fiber - 1, Carbs - 5, Protein - 20

Salmon and Tomato Salsa

Preparation time: 10 minutes | Cooking time: 20 minutes | Servings: 4

Ingredients:

- 4 salmon fillets, boneless
- 1 teaspoon cumin
- 1 teaspoon sweet paprika
- 1 teaspoon onion powder

For the salsa:

- 2 tomatoes, chopped
- 1 garlic clove, peeled and minced
- Juice of lime
- Salt and ground black pepper, to taste

- 1 teaspoon chili powder
- ½ teaspoon garlic powder
- Salt and ground black pepper, to taste

- 1 onion, peeled and chopped
- 1 tablespoon olive oil
- 1 tablespoon fresh cilantro, chopped

Directions:

Mix paprika with the cumin, onion powder, garlic powder, chili powder, salt, and pepper. Add the salmon pieces, toss to coat, and keep in the refrigerator for 10 minutes. Put the salmon on your preheated grill over medium high heat, cook for 3 minutes on each side and divide between plates. In a bowl, mix the tomatoes with the garlic, lime juice, salt, pepper, onion, oil and cilantro, toss, add next to the salmon and serve.

Nutrition: Calories - 150, Fat - 10, Carbs - 8, Fiber - 6, Protein - 20

Tilapia And Pico de Gallo Tortillas
Preparation time: 10 minutes | Cooking time: 10 minutes | Servings: 4

Ingredients:

- 4 tilapia fillets, cut into pieces
- ¼ cup coconut flour
- 2 eggs
- 1 cup tapioca starch
- ¼ cup sparkling water

For the Pico de Gallo:

- 2 tomatoes, cored and chopped
- 2 tablespoons lime juice
- 2 tablespoons jalapeño, chopped

- 2 cups coconut oil, melted
- 2 cups cabbage, shredded
- Salt and ground black pepper, to taste
- 2 limes, cut into wedges
- Cauliflower tortillas

- 6 tablespoons onion, chopped
- 1 tablespoon cilantro, diced
- Salt, to taste

Directions:

In a bowl, mix almost all of the tapioca starch with the coconut flour, sparkling water, salt, pepper, and eggs and whisk well. Coat the fish with the tapioca starch, and dip each piece in eggs mixture. Heat a pan with the coconut oil over medium-high heat, add the fish, cook for 2 minutes on each side and transfer to a bowl. In a bowl, mix the tomatoes with the lime juice, jalapeno, onion, cilantro and salt and stir well. Divide the fish on the cauliflower tortillas, also divide the Pico de Gallo, wrap and serve.

Nutrition: Calories - 240, Fat - 9, Fiber - 5, Carbs - 12, Protein - 13

Salmon and Cucumber Salad

Preparation time: 10 minutes | Cooking time: 0 minutes | Servings: 2

Ingredients:

- 2 cups cherry tomatoes, cut in half
- 1 onion, sliced thin
- 8 ounces smoked salmon, sliced thin
- 3 cucumber, chopped
- 6 tablespoons extra virgin olive oil
- ½ teaspoon garlic, minced
- 2 tablespoons lemon juice
- Salt and ground black pepper, to taste
- 1 teaspoon balsamic vinegar
- 1 tablespoon oregano, chopped

Directions:

In a bowl, mix the smoked salmon with the tomatoes, onion, cucumbers, garlic, oil, lemon juice, salt, pepper, vinegar and oregano, toss and serve cold.

Nutrition: Calories - 159, Fat - 23, Fiber - 3, Carbs - 4, Protein - 14

Cod and Parsley Bake

Preparation time: 10 minutes | Cooking time: 20 minutes | Servings: 4

Ingredients:

- ¼ cup olive oil
- 4 medium cod fillets, skinless and boneless
- 2 garlic cloves, peeled and chopped
- Salt and ground black pepper, to taste
- 1 tablespoon fresh parsley, diced
- 1 teaspoon Dijon mustard
- 1 shallot, peeled and chopped
- 3 tablespoons prosciutto, chopped
- 2 tablespoons lemon juice

Directions:

Mix the parsley with half of the oil, mustard, garlic, shallot, prosciutto, salt, pepper, and lemon juice and toss. Heat a pan with the rest of the oil over medium-high heat, add the fish, cook for 4 minutes on each side, spread the parsley mix all over and bake in the oven at 425°F for 10 minutes. Divide between plates and serve.

Nutrition: Calories - 138, Fat - 4, Fiber - 1, Carbs - 6, Protein - 23

Cod, Peaches and Vinaigrette

Preparation time: 10 minutes | Cooking time: 10 minutes | Servings: 4

Ingredients:

- 4 cod fillets, skinless and boneless
- Salt and ground black pepper, to taste
- 1 tablespoon balsamic vinegar
- 1 teaspoon fresh thyme, chopped
- 1 tablespoon fresh ginger, grated
- 3 tablespoons olive oil
- 2 onions, cut into medium wedges
- 3 peaches, pitted and cut into medium wedges

Directions:

Season the cod with salt and pepper, place on heated grill over medium-high heat, cook for 4 minutes on each side and divide between plates. Place the peaches and onions on grill, cook for 4 minutes on each side as well and divide next to the fish. In a bowl, mix the vinegar, with thyme, ginger and oil, whisk well, drizzle over the fish and the peaches and serve.

Nutrition: Calories - 300, Fat - 3, Fiber - 3, Carbs - 23, Protein - 30

Lemony Salmon

Preparation time: 10 minutes | Cooking time: 20 minutes | Servings: 8

Ingredients:

- 3 pounds salmon fillet, skinless
- Salt and ground black pepper, to taste
- 1 tablespoon extra virgin olive oil
- 1 lemon, sliced thin
- 2 tablespoons thyme, chopped

Directions:

Grease a baking dish with the oil, add salmon, salt, pepper, thyme and top with the lemon slices. Place in the oven at 375°F, bake for 20 minutes, divide everything between plates and serve.

Nutrition: Calories - 400, Fat - 10, Fiber - 2, Carbs - 5, Protein - 30

Green Onion and Shrimp Soup

Preparation time: 10 minutes | Cooking time: 12 minutes | Servings: 8

Ingredients:

- 46 ounces chicken stock
- 3 cups shrimp, peeled and deveined
- A pinch of salt and black pepper
- 1 teaspoon dill, chopped
- 2 tablespoons green onions, chopped

Directions:

Put the stock in a pot, heat over medium heat, add shrimp, salt, pepper and the green onions, stir, cook for 10 minutes, add the dill, toss, cook for 1-2 minutes more, ladle into bowls and serve.

Nutrition: Calories - 90, Fat - 1, Fiber - 2, Carbs - 2, Protein - 8

Shrimp and Oyster Sauce

Preparation time: 10 minutes | Cooking time: 7 minutes | Servings: 4

Ingredients:

- 1½ pounds shrimp, peeled and deveined
- 1 tablespoon olive oil
- 1 teaspoon sesame seeds
- 24 ounces broccoli florets
- 1 green onion, chopped
- 2 tablespoons oyster sauce
- 3 tablespoons soy sauce
- 1 tablespoon balsamic vinegar
- 2 garlic cloves, peeled and minced
- 1 tablespoon fresh ginger, grated
- 1 teaspoon sesame oil
- 1 teaspoon arrowroot powder

Directions:

In a bowl, mix the oyster sauce with the aminos, vinegar, and garlic, ginger, and sesame oil and arrowroot powder and whisk well. Heat a pan with the olive oil over medium high heat, add the shrimp, toss and cook for 3 minutes. Add the sesame seeds, broccoli and the green onions, toss; cook for 2-3 minutes more, divide between plates and serve with the oyster sauce mix drizzled all over.

Nutrition: Calories - 265, Fat - 2, Fiber - 1, Carbs - 10, Protein - 20

Simple Shrimp Pan
Preparation time: 10 minutes | Cooking time: 10 minutes | Servings: 4

Ingredients:

- 2 tablespoons olive oil
- 1½ pounds shrimp, peeled and deveined
- A pinch of salt and black pepper
- Juice of 1 lemon
- 5 garlic cloves, peeled and minced
- ¼ cup vegetable stock
- 2 tablespoons cilantro, chopped

Directions:

Heat a pan with the oil over medium-high heat, add the shrimp, salt and pepper, stir, cook for 3 minutes, and transfer to a bowl. Heat the same pan again over medium heat, add the garlic, stir, and cook for 1 minute. Add the lemon juice stock, stir, bring to a simmer, and cook for 2 minutes. Return the shrimp to pan, add the cilantro, stir, cook for a few seconds, divide between plates, and serve.

Nutrition: Calories - 254, Fat - 4, Fiber - 1, Carbs - 3, Protein - 14

Coconut Shrimp Mix
Preparation time: 10 minutes | Cooking time: 0 minutes | Servings: 2

Ingredients:

- 6 shrimp, cooked, peeled, and deveined
- 1 tablespoon coconut cream
- ¼ teaspoon jalapeño sauce
- ½ teaspoon lime juice
- 1 tablespoon fresh parsley, chopped
- A pinch of ground black pepper

Directions:

In a bowl, mix the shrimp with the cream, jalapeno sauce, lime juice, parsley and black pepper, toss, divide into bowls and serve.

Nutrition: Calories - 123, Fat - 1, Fiber - 3, Carbs - 7, Protein - 9

Baked Shrimp

Preparation time: 10 minutes | Cooking time: 10 minutes | Servings: 4

Ingredients:

- 1 tablespoon fresh parsley, chopped
- 2 pounds shrimp, peeled and deveined
- 2 tablespoons olive oil
- A pinch of salt and ground black pepper
- 3 garlic cloves, peeled and minced
- 1 tablespoon fresh chives, minced
- Lemon wedges, for serving

Directions:

In a baking dish, mix the shrimp with the parsley, oil, salt, pepper, garlic and chives, toss and bake in the oven at 400°F for 10 minutes. Divide between plates and serve with the lemon wedges on the side.

Nutrition: Calories - 150, Fat - 2, Fiber - 3, Carbs - 5, Protein - 8

Salmon and Balsamic Mushrooms

Preparation time: 10 minutes | Cooking time: 10 minutes | Servings: 4

Ingredients:

- 8 ounces salmon fillets, boneless
- Salt and ground black pepper, to taste
- 2 ounces dried morel mushrooms, rehydrated
- ½ small shallot, sliced thin
- ¼ cup balsamic vinegar
- 2 teaspoons Dijon mustard
- Salt and ground black pepper, to taste
- ½ cup extra virgin olive oil+ a drizzle
- 3 tablespoons cilantro, chopped

Directions:

In a bowl, mix the shallot with the vinegar, mustard, salt, and pepper and stir well. Slowly add olive oil, the mushrooms and cilantro, stir again, and set aside. Brush the salmon with a drizzle of olive oil and season with salt and pepper, place on heated grill, and cook for 3 minutes on each side over medium heat. Divide the fish between plates, top with the mushroom mix and serve.

Nutrition: Calories - 300, Fat - 4, Fiber - 10, Carbs - 16, Protein - 20

Yam and Clams Soup

Preparation time: 10 minutes | Cooking time: 20 minutes | Servings: 4

Ingredients:

- 3 cups yams, cubed
- 4 cod fillets, boneless, skinless and cubed
- 1 cup celery, chopped
- 1 cup onion, chopped
- Salt and ground black pepper, to taste

- 2 tablespoons garlic, minced
- 2 tablespoons olive oil
- 2 tablespoons tomato paste
- 4 cups vegetable stock
- 1½ cups tomatoes, chopped
- 1½ teaspoons dried thyme

Directions:

Heat a pot with the oil over medium heat, add to the tomato paste, celery, onion, and garlic, stir, and cook for 5 minutes. Add the stock, the tomatoes, potatoes, salt, and pepper, stir, bring to a boil, reduce heat, and cook for 10 minutes. Add the thyme and the cod, stir, cook for 5 minutes more, divide into bowls, and serve.

Nutrition: Calories - 250, Fat - 6, Fiber - 5, Carbs - 34, Protein - 23

Fruity Salmon Mix

Preparation time: 10 minutes | Cooking time: 15 minutes | Servings: 4

Ingredients:

- 2 pounds salmon steaks, boneless
- 1 tablespoon olive oil
- 1 teaspoon cumin
- 1 teaspoon garlic powder
- 1 teaspoon chili powder
- Salt and ground black pepper, to taste
- 1 teaspoon paprika

- 2 tablespoons strawberries, diced
- 2 tablespoons peaches, diced
- 2 tablespoons blueberries, diced
- 1 tablespoon fresh cilantro, chopped
- 3 tablespoons lime juice
- ¼ onion, peeled and chopped

Directions:

Heat a pan with the oil over medium heat, add the salmon, salt, pepper, chili powder, cumin, garlic powder, and paprika, toss to coat, cook for 5 minutes on each side and divide between plates. In a bowl, mix the strawberries with the peaches, blueberries, cilantro, onion, lime juice, salt, and pepper and stir. Add this over the salmon steaks, and serve.

Nutrition: Calories - 300, Fat - 12, Fiber - 4, Carbs - 23, Protein - 34

Mackerel Patties

Preparation time: 10 *minutes* | *Cooking time:* 6 *minutes* | *Servings:* 4

Ingredients:

- 8 ounces Spanish mackerel, cooked and flaked
- Salt and ground black pepper, to taste
- Juice of ½ lime
- 1 teaspoon sriracha sauce
- 1 egg white
- 1 green onion, chopped
- 2 tablespoons coconut flour
- A drizzle of olive oil

Directions:

In a bowl, mix the mackerel with the salt, pepper, lime juice, sriracha sauce, onion, egg white, and coconut flour, stir well and shape medium patties out of this mix, Heat a pan with the oil over medium-high heat, add the patties, cook for 3 minutes on each side, transfer them to paper towels, drain the excess grease, and serve hot.

Nutrition: Calories - 279, Fat - 19, Fiber - 0, Carbs - 8, Protein - 18

Cinnamon and Paprika Salmon

Preparation time: 10 *minutes* | *Cooking time:* 10 *minutes* | *Servings:* 2

Ingredients:

- 2 salmon fillets, boneless and skin-on
- Salt and ground black pepper, to taste
- 1 tablespoon ground cinnamon
- 1 tablespoon sweet paprika
- 1-tablespoon olive oil

Directions:

Heat a pan with the oil over medium heat, add the salt, pepper, paprika and cinnamon and stir well. Add the salmon, skin side up, cook for 5 minutes on each side, divide between plates and serve.

Nutrition: Calories - 300, Fat - 12, Fiber - 4, Carbs - 15, Protein - 19

Scallops Ceviche

Preparation time: 2 hours | Cooking time: 6 minutes | Servings: 2

Ingredients:

-
  - 4 ounces scallops
  - ½ cup Pico de gallo
  - ½ cup strawberries, chopped
- 1 tablespoon lemon juice
- Salt and ground black pepper, to taste

Directions:

Heat a pan over medium heat, add the scallops, cook for 3 minutes on each side, and transfer to a plate. In a bowl, mix the strawberries with the lemon juice, Pico de gallo, salt, and pepper and toss to coat. Heat a pan over medium high heat, add scallops, cook them for 3 minutes on each side, add them to the chevice, toss and serve cold after 2 hours.

Nutrition: Calories - 169, Fat - 2, Fiber - 2, Carbs - 12, Protein - 23

Wrapped Scallops

Preparation time: 10 minutes | Cooking time: 6 minutes | Servings: 12

Ingredients:

- 2 pounds scallops
- 1 pound bacon slices, halved
- A drizzle of avocado oil
- 2 lemons cut in wedges
- A pinch of salt and black pepper

Directions:

Wrap each scallop with a bacon piece, season with salt and pepper, drizzle the oil all over, place them on preheated kitchen grill, cook over medium high heat for 3 minutes on each side, divide between plates and serve with lemon wedges on the side.

Nutrition: Calories - 190, Fat - 2, Fiber - 3, Carbs - 6, Protein - 8

Stuffed Oysters

Preparation time: 10 minutes | Cooking time: 20 minutes | Servings: 3

Ingredients:

- 6 fresh oysters, top shells discarded
- A pinch of salt and black pepper
- 1 teaspoon fresh parsley, chopped
- ½ teaspoon mustard
- 1 tablespoon coconut oil, melted
- 2 slices bacon, cooked and chopped
- Lemon wedges, for serving

Directions:

In a bowl, mix the parsley, salt, pepper, mustard, and coconut oil and whisk well. Stuff the oysters with this mix, sprinkle the bacon on top. Arrange all of the oysters on a lined baking sheet, bake in the oven at 450°F for 10 minutes, divide them between plates and serve with lemon wedges on the side.

Nutrition: Calories - 200, Fat - 4, Fiber - 4, Carbs - 6, Protein - 8

Salmon and Beet Salad

Preparation time: 10 minutes | Cooking time: 7 minutes | Servings: 4

Ingredients:

- 2 tablespoons apple cider vinegar
- 4 golden beets, peeled, baked and cut into wedges
- 2 tablespoons olive oil
- A pinch of salt and black pepper
- 1 teaspoon mustard
- 6 cups curly kale, stemmed
- 12 ounces canned, skinless and boneless salmon, drained
- ¼ cup almonds, toasted and sliced

Directions:

In a small bowl, mix the vinegar with the oil, mustard, salt, pepper and whisk well. Add the kale and beets, toss and divide between plates. Top with the salmon and almonds and serve.

Nutrition: Calories - 200, Fat - 3, Fiber - 5, Carbs - 9, Protein - 7

Seafood Salad

Preparation time: 10 minutes | Cooking time: 15 minutes | Servings: 4

Ingredients:

-
- 8 ounces squid, cubed
- 8 ounces shrimp, peeled and deveined
- 1 onion, sliced
- 1 cucumber, chopped
- 2 tomatoes, cored and cut into wedges
- 2 tablespoons fresh cilantro, chopped
- 1 hot jalapeño pepper, chopped
- 3 tablespoons balsamic vinegar
- 3 tablespoons olive oil
- A pinch of salt and black pepper

Directions:

In a bowl, mix the onion with the cucumber, tomatoes, pepper, cilantro, shrimp, and squid and toss. Transfer this to a baking dish, add the oil, vinegar, salt and pepper and bake in the oven at 400°F for 15 minutes. Divide everything between plates and serve.

Nutrition: Calories - 178, Fat - 2, Fiber - 3, Carbs - 6, Protein - 7

Tuna Frittata

Preparation time: 10 minutes | Cooking time: 5 minutes | Servings: 2

Ingredients:

- 6 ounces canned tuna, drained
- A pinch of sweet paprika
- 3 eggs
- A drizzle of olive oil
- ¼ cup coconut milk
- Salt and ground black pepper, to taste
- 1 tomato, cored and sliced
- 3 green onions, chopped
- 2 tablespoons fresh parsley, chopped

Directions:

In a bowl, mix the eggs with the tuna, paprika, milk, salt, pepper, tomato, green onions and parsley and whisk well. Heat a pan with the oil over medium high heat, add the eggs and tuna mix, spread well, cook for 2 minutes, flip, cook for 3 minutes more, slice, divide between plates and serve.

Nutrition: Calories - 212, Fat - 2, Fiber - 3, Carbs - 5, Protein - 8

Tuna Kabobs

Preparation time: 10 minutes | Cooking time: 5 minutes | Servings: 12

Ingredients:

- 2 tablespoons red vinegar
- 3 tablespoons Dijon mustard
- 3 tablespoons olive oil
- 2 tablespoons coconut aminos
- 1 teaspoon hot pepper sauce
- 1 pound tuna steaks, cut into 30 cubes
- Salt and ground black pepper, to taste
- 2 green onions, chopped

Directions:

In a bowl, mix the vinegar with the mustard, aminos, pepper sauce, half of the olive oil, salt and pepper and whisk well. Add the tuna, toss, thread the pieces on skewers and brush them with the rest of the oil. Place the kabobs on preheated grill over medium high heat, cook for 2 minutes, flip, cook for 3 minutes more, divide between plates and serve.

Nutrition: Calories - 200, Fat - 3, Fiber - 3, Carbs - 5, Protein - 8

Cod Cakes

Preparation time: 10 minutes | Cooking time: 6 minutes | Servings: 4

Ingredients:

- 28 ounces cod, skinless, boneless and minced
- 1¼ cup coconut flour
- 1 large egg, whisked
- 1 tablespoon coconut aminos
- ¼ cup capers, drained
- Sea salt and black pepper, to taste
- 2 tablespoons fresh parsley, chopped
- 2 tablespoons extra virgin olive oil
- 1 tablespoon lemon juice

Directions:

In a bowl, mix the cod with 1 cup flour, egg, aminos, capers, salt, pepper and the parsley. Stir and shape medium cakes out of this mix. Heat a pan with the oil over medium heat, coat the cakes in the remaining flour, add them to the pan, cook for about 3 minutes on each side, divide them between plates, drizzle the lemon juice all over and serve.

Nutrition: Calories - 242, Fat - 3, Fiber - 2, Carbs - 5, Protein - 9

Coconut Salmon with Cauliflower

Preparation time: 10 minutes | Cooking time: 15 minutes | Servings: 6

Ingredients:

- 1 tablespoon lemon zest
- 1 tablespoon lime juice
- 1 lemon, cut into wedges
- A pinch of salt and black pepper
- 1 cup coconut cream
- 1 pound cauliflower florets
- 6 medium salmon fillets, skinless and boneless

Directions:

Put some water in a pot, add a pinch of salt, bring to a boil over medium heat, add the cauliflower, cook for 5 minutes, drain and put in a bowl. Heat the same pot again over medium heat, add the salmon, cook for 5 minutes, drain, and set aside as well. Put the coconut cream in a pan, heat over medium, add lemon zest, lime juice, salt and pepper and cook for 2-3 minutes. Add the salmon and the cauliflower, toss, cook for 2 minutes more, divide between plates and serve.

Nutrition: Calories - 264, Fat - 4, Fiber - 5, Carbs - 7, Protein - 8

Salmon and Tomato Mix
Preparation time: 10 minutes | Cooking time: 20 minutes | Servings: 4

Ingredients:

- 4 medium salmon fillets, boneless
- 1 tablespoon olive oil
- 8 ounces, tomatoes, chopped
- 1 onion, peeled and chopped
- ¼ cup Kalamata olives, pitted and chopped
- 1 tablespoon capers, drained
- 1 tablespoon lemon juice
- Salt and ground black pepper, to taste

Directions:

Heat a pan with the oil over medium-high heat, add the salmon, season with salt and pepper, cook for 3 minutes on each side and transfer to a plate. Heat the same pan over medium heat, add the onion, stir, and cook for 5 minutes. Add to the tomatoes, olives, lemon juice, salt, pepper and capers, stir, bring to a boil, and cook for 6 minutes and divide between plates. Add the salmon fillets next to the tomato mix and serve.

Nutrition: Calories - 233, Fat - 4, Fiber - 1, Carbs - 4, Protein - 10

Minty Salmon Fillets
Preparation time: 10 minutes | Cooking time: 20 minutes | Servings: 2

Ingredients:

-
- 2 medium salmon fillets
- 1 tablespoon fresh basil, chopped
- 1 tablespoon lemon juice
- Sea salt and black pepper, to taste
- 1 cup coconut cream
- 2 teaspoons curry powder
- 1 garlic clove, peeled and minced
- 1 teaspoon mint leaves, chopped

Directions:

Place each salmon fillet on a medium parchment sheet, do 3 splits into each, stuff with the basil, season with salt and pepper, drizzle the lemon juice, seal the edges and bake in the oven at 400°F for 20 minutes. In a bowl, mix the coconut cream with salt, pepper, garlic, curry and mint and whisk. Divide the salmon between plates, drizzle the mint sauce all over and serve.

Nutrition: Calories - 222, Fat - 3, Fiber - 4, Carbs - 5, Protein - 10

Baked Salmon and Celery

Preparation time: 10 minutes | Cooking time: 15 minutes | Servings: 4

Ingredients:

- ¼ cup extra virgin olive oil
- 4 medium salmon fillets, skinless and boneless
- 2 cups onions, peeled and chopped
- 1 teaspoon fresh thyme, chopped
- Salt and ground black pepper, to taste
- 1 tablespoon garlic, minced
- 3 cups celery, chopped
- 1½ cups vegetables stock
- 2 tablespoons tomato paste
- 2 tablespoons red vinegar

Directions:

Heat a pan with the oil over medium high heat, add the onions, stir and sauté for 5 minutes, Add the thyme, salt, pepper, garlic, celery, vinegar, tomato paste and stock, stir and simmer for 15 minutes. Add the salmon, place the pan in the oven at 450°F and bake for 7 minutes. Divide eveyrthing between plates and serve.

Nutrition: Calories - 182, Fat - 3, Fiber - 3, Carbs - 5, Protein - 10

Simple Salmon and Veggie Salsa

Preparation time: 10 minutes | Cooking time: 25 minutes | Servings: 2

Ingredients:

- 2 medium salmon fillets
- Salt and ground black pepper, to taste
- 2 teaspoons olive oil
- 1 garlic clove, peeled and minced
- 3 ounces carrots, chopped
- 3 ounces tomato, chopped
- 3 ounces cucumber, chopped
- 3 ounces chicory, chopped
- 1 small mango, pitted and chopped
- 1 red chili pepper, chopped
- 1 small ginger piece, grated
- Juice of 1 lime

Directions:

Put the salmon fillets on a baking dish, season with salt and pepper, rub with the oil and garlic, bake in the oven at 350°F for 25 minutes and divide between plates. In a bowl, mix the carrots with the tomato, cucumber, chicory, mango, chili, ginger and lime juice, toss, add next to the salmon and serve.

Nutrition: Calories - 121, Fat - 3, Fiber - 4, Carbs - 5, Protein - 10

Salmon with Cabbage and Blackberry Slaw
Preparation time: 10 minutes | Cooking time: 35 minutes | Servings: 4

Ingredients:

- 2 teaspoons olive oil
- 1 onion, peeled and chopped
- 1 head red cabbage, shredded
- Salt and ground black pepper, to taste
- 2 tablespoons balsamic vinegar
- ½ cup blackberries
- 4 salmon fillets, skinless
- 1 tablespoon cilantro, chopped

Directions:

Heat a pan with the oil over medium-high heat, add the onion, stir, and cook for 3 minutes. Add the cabbage, the vinegar, salt, and pepper, stir, and cook over medium heat for 25 minutes. Add the blackberries, toss and take off heat. Season the salmon with salt and pepper, place in a baking pan and broil under preheated broiler over medium heat, and cook for 7 minutes. Divide between plates and serve with the cabbage slaw on the side and with cilantro sprinkled on top.

Nutrition: Calories - 210, Fat - 3, Fiber - 2, Carbs - 6, Protein - 10

Cod with Olive Sauce
Preparation time: 5 minutes | Cooking time: 15 minutes | Servings: 4

Ingredients:

- 4 cod fillets, skinless and boneless
- Salt and ground black pepper, to taste
- ¼ cup water
- 1 cup coconut cream
- ¼ cup green olives, pitted and chopped
- ¼ cup fresh chives, minced
- 1 tablespoon olive oil
- 1 tablespoon lime juice

Directions:

Arrange the cod in a baking dish, season with the salt and black pepper, add the water, place under preheated broiler, cook over medium high heat for 8 minutes, and leave aside. In a bowl, mix the coconut cream with the chives, olives, lime juice, olive oil, salt, and black pepper, whisk well, drizzle over the cod and serve.

Nutrition: Calories - 210, Fat - 3, Fiber - 3, Carbs - 6, Protein - 8

Tuna and Lettuce Salad

Preparation time: 10 minutes | Cooking time: 0 minutes | Servings: 4

Ingredients:

- ⅓ cup olive oil
- 1 tablespoon mustard
- 3 tablespoons apple vinegar
- A pinch of salt and black pepper
- 10 ounces canned tuna, drained and flaked
- 1 bunch radishes, sliced
- 1 head romaine lettuce, chopped

Directions:

In a bowl, mix the tuna with the radishes and the lettuce and toss, add the oil, mustard, apple vinegar, salt and pepper, toss and serve cold.

Nutrition: Calories - 190, Fat - 3, Fiber - 3, Carbs - 6, Protein - 9

Cod in Orange Sauce

Preparation time: 10 minutes | Cooking time: 15 minutes | Servings: 4

Ingredients:

- 2 tablespoons olive oil
- A pinch of salt and black pepper
- 4 cod fillets, boneless
- ¼ teaspoon fresh tarragon, chopped
- ¼ cup orange juice
- 1 teaspoon shallots, chopped

Directions:

Heat a pan with the oil over medium high heat, add the cod, season with salt and pepper, toss and cook for 4 minutes on each side. Add the tarragon, shallots and orange juice, toss, cover the pan, cook everything for 3 minutes more, divide between plates and serve.

Nutrition: Calories - 200, Fat - 10, Fiber - 1, Carbs - 2, Protein - 2

Ginger, Broccoli and Shrimp Salad

Preparation time: 10 minutes | Cooking time: 0 minutes | Servings: 4

Ingredients:

- 3 cups broccoli florets, steamed
- 4 sun-dried tomatoes, chopped
- A pinch of salt and black pepper
- 1 tablespoon ginger, grated
- 2 tablespoons olive oil
- 1 pound shrimp, deveined and peeled

Directions:

In a bowl, mix the broccoli with the tomatoes, salt, pepper, ginger, shrimp and oil, toss, divide between plates and serve.

Nutrition: Calories - 150, Fat - 4, Fiber - 3, Carbs - 9, Protein - 2

Shrimp and Zucchini Salad

Preparation time: 10 minutes | Cooking time: 0 minutes | Servings: 4

Ingredients:

- 1 pound shrimp, cooked, peeled and deveined
- ½ chili pepper, chopped
- A pinch of salt and black pepper
- 2 tablespoons olive oil
- 1 zucchini, spiralized
- 1 red bell pepper, cut into thin strips
- 1 onion, peeled and chopped
- 2 tablespoons lime juice
- ¼ cup fresh cilantro, chopped

Directions:

In a salad bowl, mix the shrimp with chili pepper, zucchini, bell pepper, onion, cilantro, lime juice, salt, pepper and oil, toss and serve cold.

Nutrition: Calories - 140, Fat - 3, Fiber - 3, Carbs - 7, Protein - 9

Chinese Tuna Steaks

Preparation time: 30 minutes | Cooking time: 11 minutes | Servings: 4

Ingredients:

- ¼ cup orange juice
- 1 garlic clove, peeled and minced
- 1 tablespoon coconut aminos
- 1 tablespoon lemon juice
- 2 tablespoons olive oil
- A pinch of salt and black pepper
- 2 tablespoons fresh parsley, chopped
- 4 medium tuna steaks

Directions:

Heat a pan with the oil over medium high heat, add the tuna steaks, season with salt and pepper and cook for 2-3 minutes on each side. Add the garlic, the orange juice, aminos, lemon juice, salt and pepper, toss gently, cook for 5 minutes more, divide between plates, sprinkle the parsley on top and serve.

Nutrition: Calories - 210, Fat - 4, Fiber - 2, Carbs - 5, Protein - 8

Mexican Tuna Steaks

Preparation time: 34 minutes | Cooking time: 4 minutes | Servings: 4

Ingredients:

- 4 tuna steaks
- 4 tablespoons olive oil
- 2 green onions, chopped
- 1 cucumber, chopped
- 1 tomato, cored and chopped
- ½ red chili pepper, chopped
- 2 tablespoons fresh parsley, chopped
- 1 tablespoon lemon juice
- A pinch of salt and black pepper

Directions:

Put the tuna steaks in a bowl, add the 3 tablespoons olive oil, toss to coat, and set aside for 30 minutes. Heat a kitchen grill pan over medium high heat, add the tuna steaks, cook them for 2 minutes on each side and divide between plates. In a bowl, mix the cucumber with onions, tomato, chili pepper, parsley, lemon juice, salt, pepper and the rest of the oil, toss well, add next to the tuna and serve.

Nutrition: Calories - 190, Fat - 4, Fiber - 3, Carbs - 6, Protein - 9

Basil Cod Mix

Preparation time: 10 minutes | Cooking time: 20 minutes | Servings: 2

Ingredients:

- 2 medium cod fillets, boneless
- 1 tablespoon basil, chopped
- 2 medium tomatoes, cored and sliced
- 1 tablespoon avocado oil
- A pinch of salt and black pepper

Directions:

Put the cod in a baking dish, drizzle the oil all over, add basil, tomatoes, salt and pepper, place in the oven and bake at 375°F for 20 minutes. Divide between plates and serve.

Nutrition: Calories - 360, Fat - 4, Fiber - 7, Carbs - 9, Protein - 11

Orange and Ginger Salmon

Preparation time: 10 minutes | Cooking time: 10 minutes | Servings: 4

Ingredients:

- Juice of 1 orange
- 2 tablespoons coconut aminos
- 1 tablespoon olive oil
- 2 garlic cloves, peeled and minced
- 4 salmon fillets, boneless
- 1 teaspoon fresh ginger, grated
- A pinch of salt and black pepper
- 1 tablespoon parsley, chopped

Directions:

In a bowl, mix the orange juice with the ginger, aminos, oil, garlic, salt and pepper and whisk well. Add the salmon, toss, place the fish on preheated kitchen grill and cook over medium heat for 5 minutes on each side. Divide between plates and serve with a side salad.

Nutrition: Calories - 230, Fat - 4, Fiber - 2, Carbs - 6, Protein - 8

Salmon Curry

Preparation time: 10 minutes | Cooking time: 15 minutes | Servings: 2

Ingredients:

- 2 medium salmon fillets, skinless, boneless and cubed
- A drizzle of olive oil
- 1 tablespoon fresh basil, chopped
- 1 tablespoon lemon juice
- A pinch of sea salt and black pepper
- 1 cup coconut cream
- 2 teaspoons curry powder
- 1 garlic clove, peeled and minced
- ½ teaspoon fresh parsley, chopped
- ½ teaspoon mint leaves, chopped

Directions:

Heat a pan with the oil over medium high heat, add the salmon cubes and cook for 2 minutes on each side. Add the basil, lemon juice, salt, pepper, curry powder, garlic, cream, parsley and mint, toss, cook for 10 minutes more, divide into bowls and serve.

Nutrition: Calories - 130, Fat - 3, Fiber - 3, Carbs - 7, Protein - 9

Cod and Cucumber Salad

Preparation time: 10 minutes | Cooking time: 8 minutes | Servings: 4

Ingredients:

- 4 medium cod fillets, skinless and boneless
- 1 tablespoon fresh tarragon, chopped
- 3 tablespoons olive oil
- A pinch of salt and black pepper
- 1 small onion, sliced
- 5 cucumbers, sliced
- 2 tablespoons lemon juice

Directions:

Heat a pan with 2 tablespoon olive oil over medium high heat, add the cod, season with salt and pepper, cook for 4 minutes on each side and divide between plates. Meanwhile, in a bowl, mix the cucumbers with the rest of the oil, tarragon, salt, pepper, onion and lemon juice, toss, divide next to the cod and serve.

Nutrition: Calories - 278, Fat - 10, Fiber - 1, Carbs - 5, Protein - 13

Greek Shrimp Mix

Preparation time: 10 minutes | Cooking time: 6 minutes | Servings: 4

Ingredients:

- 1 pound shrimp, deveined and peeled
- 2 teaspoons olive oil
- 6 tablespoons lemon juice
- 3 tablespoons fresh dill, chopped
- 1 tablespoon fresh oregano, chopped
- 2 garlic cloves, peeled and minced
- Ground black pepper, to taste
- ¾ cup coconut cream
- ½ pounds cherry tomatoes

Directions:

Heat a pan with the oil over medium high heat, add the shrimp, season with some black pepper and cook for 2 minutes. Add the lemon juice, dill, oregano, garlic, cream and cherry tomatoes, toss, cook for 4 minutes more, divide between plates and serve.

Nutrition: Calories - 253, Fat - 6, Fiber - 6, Carbs - 10, Protein - 11

Cod Soup

Preparation time: 10 minutes | Cooking time: 16 minutes | Servings: 4

Ingredients:

- 1 carrot, peeled and grated
- 2 sweet potatoes, peeled and cut in half
- 3½ cups vegetable stock
- A pinch of salt and black pepper
- 1 onion, peeled and chopped
- 10 ounces cod fillets, cubed
- 1 tablespoon coconut cream
- 3 tablespoons fresh dill, chopped

Directions:

Put the stock in a pot, heat over medium high heat, add the carrot, sweet potatoes, salt, pepper and the onion, stir and cook for 10 minutes. Add the cod, the cream and the dill, cook for 5-6 minutes, ladle into bowls and serve.

Salmon Stew

Preparation time: 10 minutes | Cooking time: 30 minutes | Servings: 4

Ingredients:

- 2 tablespoons fresh parsley, chopped
- 2 tomatoes, peeled and grated
- 1 tablespoon lemon juice
- 2 tablespoons fresh cilantro, chopped
- 2 garlic cloves, peeled and minced
- ½ teaspoon sweet paprika
- ½ cup vegetable stock
- A pinch of salt and black pepper

- 4 salmon fillets, boneless, skinless and cubed
- ¼ cup olive oil
- 3 carrots, peeled and sliced
- 1 red bell pepper, seeded and cut into thin strips
- 3 sweet potatoes, peeled and cubed
- ½ cup black olives, pitted and sliced
- 1 onion, sliced

Directions:

Heat a pot with the oil over medium high heat, add the garlic and the onion, stir and cook for 2 minutes. Add the tomatoes, paprika, stock, carrots, bell pepper, olives and sweet potatoes, stir and cook for 7-8 minutes more. Add the lemon juice, salmon, salt and pepper, stir and cook for 10 minutes. Add parsley and cilantro, toss, divide into bowls and serve.

Nutrition: Calories - 340, Fat - 10, Fiber - 8, Carbs - 23, Protein - 14

Tomato and Shrimp Soup

Preparation time: 10 minutes | Cooking time: 12 minutes | Servings: 4

Ingredients:

- 3 cups tomato juice
- 3 jarred roasted red bell peppers, chopped
- 2 tablespoons olive oil
- 2 tablespoons vinegar
- 1 garlic clove, peeled and minced
- A pinch of salt and ground black pepper
- ½ teaspoon cumin
- ¾ pounds shrimp, peeled and deveined
- 1 teaspoon fresh parsley, chopped

Directions:

Heat a pot with the oil over high heat, add the shrimp, stir, and cook for 2 minutes. Add the tomato juice, bell peppers, vinegar, garlic, salt, pepper and cumin, stir and simmer over medium heat for 10 minutes. Add the parsley, toss, ladle into bowls and serve.

Nutrition: Calories - 200, Fat - 4, Fiber - 10, Carbs - 20, Protein - 14

Coconut and Tomato Shrimp Soup

Preparation time: 10 minutes | Cooking time: 20 minutes | Servings: 4

Ingredients:

- 2 pounds tomatoes, cored, seeded, and cut in half
- 3 tablespoons olive oil
- ½ cup onion, diced
- 2 tablespoons tomato paste
- A pinch of salt and black pepper
- ¼ cup coconut cream
- 3 cups vegetable stock
- 1 pound shrimp, peeled, deveined and chopped

Directions:

Heat a pot with the oil over medium-high heat, add the onion and tomatoes, stir, and cook for 7 minutes. Add the tomato paste, stock, and salt, and pepper, stir, bring to a boil, reduce heat to medium, and simmer for 10 minutes. Add the cream, blend the soup with an immersion blender, heat everything up over medium low heat, add the shrimp, cook for 3 minutes, ladle into bowls and serve.

Nutrition: Calories - 240, Fat - 4, Fiber - 5, Carbs - 8, Protein - 9

Shrimp and Bacon Cold Mix

Preparation time: 1 hour | Cooking time: 0 minutes | Servings: 4

Ingredients:

- 4 tomatoes, cored and cut in wedges
- ½ pound shrimp, peeled, deveined, and cooked
- A pinch of salt and black pepper
- 2 spring onions, chopped
- 1 jalapeño, chopped
- 2 garlic cloves, peeled and minced
- ¼ cup lemon juice
- 1 teaspoon lemon zest
- ¼ cup fresh parsley, chopped
- ⅓ cup olive oil
- 5 bacon slices, cooked and crumbled

Directions:

In a bowl, mix the shrimp with the tomatoes, spring onions, garlic, jalapeno, salt, pepper, lemon juice, lemon zest, bacon, parsley and oil toss and keep in the fridge for 1 hour before serving.

Nutrition: Calories - 200, Fat - 3, Fiber - 4, Carbs - 8, Protein - 10

Fish and Veggie Soup

Preparation time: 10 minutes | Cooking time: 30 minutes | Servings: 6

Ingredients:

- 6 tomatoes, peeled and chopped
- 2 tablespoons olive oil
- 1 onion, peeled and chopped
- 2 celery stalks, chopped
- 1 carrot, peeled and chopped
- 1 jalapeño, chopped
- 1 red bell pepper, seeded and chopped
- 2 garlic cloves, peeled and minced
- 3 white fish fillets, skinless, boneless, and cubed
- 4 cups vegetable stock
- A pinch of salt and black pepper
- A drizzle of balsamic vinegar
- ½ cup fresh parsley, chopped

Directions:

Heat a pot with the oil over medium-high heat, add the onion, jalapeno and the garlic, stir and cook for 5 minutes. Add the celery, the bell pepper and the carrot, stir and cook for 5 minutes more. Add the tomatoes, the stock, salt and pepper, bring to a simmer, reduce heat to medium and cook everything for 10 minutes. Add the fish, simmer the soup for 8 more minutes. Ladle into bowls, drizzle some vinegar all over and serve with the parsley sprinkled on top.

Nutrition: Calories - 240, Fat - 4, Fiber - 4, Carbs - 8, Protein - 12

Shrimp and Crab Salad

Preparation time: 10 minutes | Cooking time: 0 minutes | Servings: 6

Ingredients:

- 6 sweet potatoes, peeled, cut into medium-sized chunks and boiled
- 15 ounces shrimp, peeled, deveined, cooked, and chopped
- 4 eggs, hard boiled, peeled and chopped
- 2 shallots, peeled and chopped
- 15 ounces canned crab meat, drained
- 1 tablespoon fresh cilantro, chopped
- 1 tablespoon green onions, chopped
- ½ cup lime juice
- 2 tablespoons coconut cream
- A pinch of salt and black pepper

Directions:

In a salad bowl, mix the potatoes with the shrimp, eggs, shallots, crabmeat, cilantro, green onions, lime juice, cream, salt and pepper, toss and serve cold.

Nutrition: Calories - 200, Fat - 5, Fiber - 8, Carbs - 10, Protein - 12

Salmon Carpaccio and Sauce

Preparation time: 1 day and 10 minutes | Cooking time: 0 minutes | Servings: 4

Ingredients:

For the Carpaccio:

- 1 teaspoon black peppercorns, toasted
- 1 teaspoon white peppercorns, toasted
- A pinch of sea salt
- A drizzle of olive oil

For the sauce:

- 1 tablespoon white vinegar
- 2 tablespoons mustard
- 3 tablespoons avocado oil
- 1 teaspoon coriander seeds
- 1 pound salmon fillet, thinly sliced
- 1 cup fresh dill, chopped

- A pinch of salt
- 2 tablespoons fresh dill, chopped

Directions:

In a bowl, mix the peppercorns with salt, coriander, oil and 1 cup dill and toss. Rub the salmon with this mix, put in a bowl, cover and keep in the fridge for 24 hours. In a bowl, mix the vinegar with the mustard, oil, salt and 2 tablespoons dill and whisk well. Arrange the salmon slices on a platter, drizzle the sauce all over and serve.

Nutrition: Calories - 245, Fat - 7, Fiber - 8, Carbs - 10, Protein - 7

Mackerel and Chicory Salad

Preparation time: 15 minutes | Cooking time: 0 minutes | Servings: 8

Ingredients:

-
  - 7 ounces smoked mackerel fillets, skinless, boneless, and flaked
  - Juice and zest of ½ lemon
  - 4 tablespoons coconut cream
  - Ground black pepper, to taste

  - A small bunch of chives diced
  - 1 radicchio, chopped
  - ½ cup fresh dill, chopped
  - 2 chicory heads, chopped

Directions:

In a bowl, mix the mackerel with lemon juice, lemon zest, chives, radicchio, chicory, dill, black pepper and the cream, toss and serve cold.

Nutrition: Calories - 190, Fat - 5, Fiber - 4, Carbs - 8, Protein - 10

Spicy Clam Soup

Preparation time: 1 hour | Cooking time: 10 minutes | Servings: 4

Ingredients:

- 2 pounds clams, scrubbed
- 3 cups vegetable stock
- 1 jalapeño pepper, sliced

- 1 garlic clove, peeled and sliced
- 1 red chili pepper, sliced
- ½ scallion sliced thin

Directions:

Put the clams in a large bowl, add enough water to cover, set them aside for 1 hour, and then drain. Heat a pot with the stock over medium heat, add the clams, jalapeno, chili, scallion and garlic, toss, cook for 10 minutes, discard unopened clams, ladle the soup into bowls and serve.

Nutrition: Calories - 200, Fat - 3, Fiber - 3, Carbs - 7, Protein - 9

Shrimp and Bell Pepper Salsa
Preparation time: 10 minutes | Cooking time: 4 minutes | Servings: 4

Ingredients:

- 1 pound shrimp, peeled and deveined
- 2 tablespoons lime juice
- 4 teaspoons coconut aminos
- 1 jalapeño pepper, chopped
- 1 teaspoon fresh ginger, grated
- 1 garlic clove, peeled and minced
- 1 tablespoon olive oil+ a drizzle
- 3 red bell peppers, seeded and cut into strips
- A pinch of salt and black pepper
- 1 tablespoon parsley, chopped

Directions:

Heat a pan with 1 tablespoon oil over medium high heat, add the shrimp, season with salt and black pepper, also add the aminos, cook for 2 minutes on each side and divide between plates. In a bowl, mix the bell peppers with lime juice, jalapeno, ginger, garlic, a drizzle of oil and parsley, toss, add next to the shrimp and serve.

Nutrition: Calories - 281, Fat - 6, Fiber - 8, Carbs - 10, Protein - 18

Rosemary Shrimp Mix
Preparation time: 10 minutes | Cooking time: 10 minutes | Servings: 2

Ingredients:

- 17 ounces shrimp, peeled and deveined
- 4 garlic cloves, peeled and minced
- 2 tablespoons olive oil
- 1 tablespoon rosemary, chopped
- A pinch of salt and black pepper
- 1 tablespoon lime juice
- 2 tomatoes, cored and chopped
- 1 tablespoon parsley, chopped

Directions:

Heat a pan with the oil over medium high heat, add the shrimp and cook for 2 minutes on each side. Add the garlic, rosemary, salt, pepper, lime juice, tomatoes and parsley, toss, cook for 5 minutes more, divide into bowls and serve.

Nutrition: Calories - 243, Fat - 4, Fiber - 7, Carbs - 12, Protein - 6

Fish Soup

Preparation time: 10 minutes | Cooking time: 30 minutes | Servings: 4

Ingredients:

- 9 ounces small fish, without heads
- ½ teaspoon lemon zest
- Juice of ½ lemon
- 3 tablespoons olive oil
- A pinch of salt and black pepper
- 3 cups hot water
- 1 celery stalk, chopped
- 3 tomatoes, cored and chopped
- 2 onions, peeled and chopped
- 2 tablespoons fresh parsley, chopped
- 2 tablespoons fresh cilantro, chopped

Directions:

Heat a pot with the water over medium high heat, add lemon zest, lemon juice, salt, pepper and the oil and whisk really well. Add the fish and cook for 15 minutes. Add celery, tomatoes and onions, toss, and cook for 15 minute more, ladle into bowls and serve with parsley and cilantro sprinkled on top.

Nutrition: Calories - 200, Fat - 3, Fiber - 5, Carbs - 9, Protein - 10

Halibut and Parsley Sauce

Preparation time: 10 minutes | Cooking time: 15 minutes | Servings: 4

Ingredients:

- 1½ pounds halibut boneless, cubed
- ½ teaspoon cumin seeds, ground
- A pinch of salt and black pepper
- ½ teaspoon sweet paprika
- ½ teaspoon coriander seeds
- Juice of ½ lime
- 2 garlic cloves, peeled and minced
- 1 onion, sliced
- 2 tablespoons olive oil
- 1 cup coconut cream
- 1 tablespoon fresh parsley, chopped
- 1 tablespoon fresh dill, chopped
- 1 tablespoon mint leaves, chopped

Directions:

Heat a pan with the oil over medium high heat, add coriander seeds, cumin seeds, garlic, onion, salt and pepper, stir and cook for 5 minutes. Add the halibut and the lime juice and cook for 5 minutes more. Add the cream, mint, dill and parsley, toss, cook for another 5 minutes, divide between plates and serve.

Nutrition: Calories - 240, Fat - 4, Fiber - 4, Carbs - 8, Protein - 10

Cod and Endives Mix

Preparation time: 10 minutes | Cooking time: 20 minutes | Servings: 4

Ingredients:

- 4 cod fillets, skinless and boneless
- A pinch of salt and black pepper
- Juice of 1 small lemon
- 2 endives, shredded
- 1 tablespoon coconut oil, melted
- 1 tablespoon olive oil

Directions:

Heat a pan with the coconut oil over medium-high heat, add the endives, salt, pepper and half of the lemon juice, toss, cook them for 10 minutes and divide between plates. Heat another pan with the olive oil over medium high heat, add the cod, salt and pepper, cook for 4 minutes on each side, add next to the endives, drizzle the rest of the lemon juice all over and serve.

Nutrition: Calories - 200, Fat - 2, Fiber - 4, Carbs - 7, Protein - 8

Shrimp, Tomato and Avocado Mix

Preparation time: 10 minutes | Cooking time: 6 minutes | Servings: 6

Ingredients:

-
- 1 pound shrimp, deveined and peeled
- A drizzle of olive oil
- 2 cups cherry tomatoes, cut in half
- 1 cucumber, chopped
- 1 avocado, pitted, peeled, and chopped
- ½ cup fresh cilantro, chopped
- A pinch of salt and black pepper
- 2 tablespoon vegetable stock
- 2 tablespoons lime juice
- ½ teaspoon lime zest, grated

Directions:

Heat a pan with the oil over medium high heat, add the shrimp, some salt and pepper and cook for 2 minutes. Add the tomatoes, the cucumber, the avocado, cilantro, stock, lime juice and lime zest, toss, cook for 4 minutes more, divide into bowls and serve.

Nutrition: Calories - 156, Fat - 3, Fiber - 5, Carbs - 8, Protein - 12

Veggie and Snapper Warm Salad

Preparation time: 10 minutes | Cooking time: 25 minutes | Servings: 2

Ingredients:

- 1 red bell pepper, chopped
- 3 summer squash, peeled and chopped
- 1 baby eggplant, chopped
- ½ sweet potato, chopped
- 1 tablespoon olive oil
- 1 onion, cut into wedges
- 1 teaspoon hot paprika

- 2 teaspoons cumin
- A pinch of salt and ground black pepper
- 2 snapper fillets, boneless and skinless
- 4 cups baby spinach leaves

For the salad dressing:

- 2 tablespoons fresh cilantro, chopped
- ¼ cup lime juice

- ¼ cup coconut oil, melted

Directions:

Put the bell peppers in a baking dish, add the squash, eggplant, sweet potato, onion and the olive oil, toss to coat, place in the oven at 400°F, bake for 15 minutes, transfer to a salad bowl, add the spinach and leave aside. Put the snapper in another baking dish, season with salt, pepper, paprika and cumin, bake in the oven at 400°F for 10 minutes, take out of the oven, flake and add it over the veggies. In a bowl, mix the cilantro with salt, pepper, coconut oil, and lime juice, whisk well, add over the salad, toss and serve.

Nutrition: Calories - 250, Fat - 4, Fiber - 4, Carbs - 7, Protein - 12

Simple Sea Bass Mix

Preparation time: 10 minutes | Cooking time: 12 minutes | Servings: 4

Ingredients:

- 3 garlic cloves, peeled and minced
- 1 pound fresh sea bass, diced
- A pinch of salt and black pepper
- ¼ cup fresh cilantro, chopped
- ¾ cup lime juice

- 1 jalapeño pepper, chopped
- 1 onion, peeled and sliced
- 1 cup cherry tomatoes, cut in half
- 1 tablespoon olive oil
- 1 avocado, pitted, peeled, and chopped

Directions:

Heat a pan with the oil over medium high heat, add the sea bass and cook for 4 minutes on each side. Add garlic, salt, pepper, cilantro, lime juice, jalapeno, onion, cherry tomatoes and avocado, toss, cook for 5 minutes more, divide between plates and serve.

Nutrition: Calories - 200, Fat - 3, Fiber - 3, Carbs - 7, Protein – 10

Sardines with Tapenade

Preparation time: 10 minutes | Cooking time: 10 minutes | Servings: 4

Ingredients:

For the olive tapenade:

- 1 tablespoon lemon, chopped
- 3 garlic cloves, peeled and minced
- 1 cup green olives, pitted and chopped
- 1 shallot, peeled and chopped
- 2 teaspoons lemon juice
- 1 teaspoon red pepper flakes

- 3 tablespoons fresh parsley, chopped
- 1 cup olive oil
- 3 tablespoons fresh chives, minced
- 3 tablespoons fresh thyme, chopped

For the sardines:

- 12 fresh sardines
- 2 tablespoons olive oil
- ½ bunch fresh parsley, chopped

- 2 garlic cloves, peeled and minced
- 1 cup frisee
- 2 radishes, shaved

Directions:

In a bowl, mix the olives with the lemon, garlic, shallot, lemon juice, pepper flakes, parsley, 1 cup oil, chives and thyme and whisk well. Spread this over the sardines, toss well, put them on your preheated kitchen grill and cook for 5 minutes on each side over medium high heat. In a bowl, mix the radishes with the frisee, 2 garlic cloves, ½ bunch parsley and 2 tablespoons oil and toss well. Divide this between plates, top with the sardines and serve.

Nutrition: Calories - 300, Fat - 5, Fiber - 9, Carbs - 8, Protein - 12

Shrimp and Veggie Salad

Preparation time: 10 minutes | Cooking time: 6 minutes | Servings: 4

Ingredients:

-
  - 1 pound shrimp, peeled and deveined
  - 8 Kalamata olives, pitted and chopped
  - 1 tablespoon capers, chopped
  - 3 tablespoons balsamic vinegar
- A pinch of salt and black pepper
- 3 tablespoons olive oil
- 3 tomatoes, cored and chopped
- ¼ cup onion, chopped
- ¼ cup fresh basil, chopped

Directions:

Heat a pan with the oil over medium high heat, add the shrimp, salt and pepper and cook for 2 minutes. Add the olives, capers, vinegar, tomatoes, onion and basil, toss a bit, cook for 3-4 minutes more, divide between plates and serve warm.

Nutrition: Calories - 190, Fat - 4, Fiber - 7, Carbs - 8, Protein – 9

Greek Sardine Salad

Preparation time: 10 minutes | Cooking time: 0 minutes | Servings: 4

Ingredients:

- 3 tablespoons lime juice
- 2 tablespoons olive oil
- 2 teaspoons dried basil
- 1 garlic clove, peeled and minced
- A pinch of ground black pepper
- 3 tomatoes, cored and cut into chunks
- ¼ cup onion, sliced
- 2 tablespoons Kalamata olives, pitted, peeled, and sliced
- 8 ounces canned sardines, drained

Directions:

In a bowl, mix the sardines with black pepper, oil, lime juice, basil, garlic, tomatoes, onion and olives, toss and serve cold.

Nutrition: Calories - 140, Fat - 1, Fiber - 3, Carbs - 7, Protein - 9

Fish, Shrimp and Veggie Soup

Preparation time: 10 minutes | Cooking time: 4 hours | Servings: 4

Ingredients:

- 1 onion, peeled and chopped
- 2 garlic cloves, peeled and minced
- 14 ounces canned diced tomatoes
- 28 ounces vegetable stock
- 8 ounces canned tomato sauce
- 2½ ounces mushrooms, sliced
- ¼ cup black olives, pitted and sliced
- ½ cup orange juice
- 1 teaspoon dried basil
- ¼ teaspoon fennel seeds, crushed
- A pinch of ground black pepper
- 1 pound shrimp, deveined and peeled
- 1 pound cod fillets, skinless, boneless, and cubed

Directions:

In your Crockpot, mix the onion with the garlic, tomatoes, stock, tomato sauce, mushrooms, olives, orange juice, basil, fennel and black pepper, cover and cook on Low for 3 hours and 30 minutes. Add the shrimp and the cod, cover, cook on Low for 30 minutes more, ladle into bowls and serve.

Nutrition: Calories - 230, Fat - 4, Fiber - 5, Carbs - 7, Protein - 10

Herbed Shrimp Mix

Preparation time: 10 minutes | Cooking time: 6 minutes | Servings: 4

Ingredients:

- ⅓ cup lemon juice
- 1 teaspoon lemon zest
- 3 tablespoons olive oil
- 2 tablespoons fresh oregano, chopped
- 2 tablespoons fresh sage, chopped
- 2 tablespoons fresh chives, minced
- A pinch of salt and black pepper
- 12 cherry tomatoes, cut in half
- 1 cup celery, chopped
- 1 pound shrimp, peeled and deveined

Directions:

Heat a pan with the oil over medium high heat, add the shrimp, salt and pepper, toss and cook for 2 minutes. Add the lemon juice, lemon zest, sage, oregano, chives, tomatoes and celery, toss, cook for 4 minutes more, divide into bowls and serve.

Nutrition: Calories - 150, Fat - 3, Fiber - 4, Carbs - 7, Protein - 8

Asian Shrimp Salad

Preparation time: 10 minutes | Cooking time: 20 minutes | Servings: 4

Ingredients:

- 2 pounds Asian eggplants
- ¼ pound shrimp, peeled, deveined, and poached
- 4 eggs, hard boiled, peeled and cut into quarters
- 2 shallots, peeled and sliced
- 2 tablespoons coconut aminos
- 3 tablespoons lime juice
- 1 tablespoon parsley, chopped
- 3 Serrano chilies, sliced

Directions:

Arrange the eggplants on a lined baking dish, place in the oven, and bake at 450 ° F for about 20 minutes. Allow to cool, peel, cut into medium chunks, and transfer to a bowl. Add shrimp, eggs, shallots, aminos, lime juice, chilies and the parsley, toss and serve.

Nutrition: Calories - 200, Fat - 5, Fiber - 7, Carbs - 10, Protein – 12

Cod and Mustard Sauce

Preparation time: 10 minutes | Cooking time: 20 minutes | Servings: 4

Ingredients:

- ¼ cup olive oil+ 2 tablespoons
- 4 medium cod fillets, skinless and boneless
- 2 garlic cloves, peeled and minced
- A pinch of salt and black pepper
- 1 tablespoon fresh cilantro, minced
- 1 teaspoon Dijon mustard
- 1 shallot, peeled and chopped
- 2 tablespoons lemon juice

Directions:

Heat a pan with 2 tablespoons oil over medium-high heat, add the fish, season with salt and pepper, cook for 4 minutes on each side and transfer to a baking dish. In a bowl, mix the rest of the oil with the garlic, salt, pepper, cilantro, mustard, shallot and lime juice, whisk well, pour over the fish, bake in the oven at 425°F for 10 minutes, divide between plates, and serve.

Nutrition: Calories - 145, Fat - 2, Fiber - 1, Carbs - 10, Protein - 16

Whole Food Poultry Recipes

Chicken and Pineapple Kabobs

Preparation time: 60 minutes | Cooking time: 15 minutes | Servings: 4

Ingredients:

-
- ½ onion, peeled and chopped
- 10 dates, chopped
- 1 tablespoon olive oil
- 2 tablespoons orange juice
- 2 teaspoons garlic, minced
- ¾ cup coconut aminos
- 2 tablespoons white vinegar
- A pinch of salt and black pepper
- 2 chicken breasts, cubed
- ½ pineapple, cubed

Directions:

Heat a pan with the oil over medium heat, add the onion, stir, and cook for 3 minutes. Add the garlic, orange juice, dates, coconut aminos, salt, pepper and vinegar, stir, bring to a boil, simmer for 5 minutes, transfer to a blender and pulse well. In a bowl, mix the chicken with the orange sauce, toss to coat, and set aside for 1 hour. Arrange the pineapple cubes and chicken on skewers; place them on preheated grill pan over medium-high heat, cook for 5 minutes on each side, divide between plates and serve.

Nutrition: Calories - 500, Fat - 6, Fiber - 2, Carbs - 10, Protein - 7

Duck and Plum Sauce

Preparation time: 10 minutes | Cooking time: 4 hours and 20 minutes | Servings: 6

Ingredients:

- 1 duck, scored
- Salt and ground black pepper, to taste
- 1 onion, peeled and chopped
- 1 tablespoon olive oil
- 1 small ginger piece, peeled and chopped
- 4 garlic cloves, peeled and minced
- 21 ounces plums, pitted and chopped
- 6 tablespoons coconut aminos
- 1 tablespoon balsamic vinegar
- 4 tablespoons sriracha

Directions:

Season the duck with salt and pepper, place on a roasting pan and put in the oven at 300°F, and roast for 3 hours and 50 minutes. Heat a pan with the oil over medium heat, add the onion, stir, and cook for 5 minutes. Add the garlic, the ginger, the plums, aminos, sriracha, and vinegar, stir, bring to a simmer, cook for 20 minutes. Transfer the sauce to a blender, pulse a few times and brush the duck with this mix. Cook the duck for 10 minutes, carve, and serve with the sauce drizzled all over.

Nutrition: Calories - 380, Fat - 8, Fiber - 4, Carbs - 42, Protein - 22

Chicken and Peach Sauce

Preparation time: 10 minutes | Cooking time: 45 minutes | Servings: 6

Ingredients:

- 6 chicken thighs
- Salt and ground black pepper, to taste
- 1 tablespoon olive oil
- Zest from 1 lime
- 1½ teaspoons chipotle peppers in adobo sauce
- 1 cup peach, sliced
- 1 tablespoon lime juice

Directions:

Heat a pan with the oil over medium-high heat, add the chicken, season with salt and pepper, brown for 4 minutes on each side. Place the pan in the oven and bake at 375ºF for 20 minutes. In a food processor, mix the peaches with the chipotle, lime zest, and lime juice, blend well, pour this sauce over the chicken, bake for 10 minutes, and serve right away.

Nutrition: Calories - 349, Fat - 6, Fiber - 4, Carbs - 16, Protein – 5

Chicken Tenders and Lemon Sauce

Preparation time: 10 minutes | Cooking time: 20 minutes | Servings: 6

Ingredients:

- 1¾ pounds chicken tenders
- ⅓ cup cassava flour
- Salt and ground black pepper, to taste
- ¼ cup olive oil
- 1 cup chicken stock
- Juice of 1 lemon
- 1 lemon, sliced
- ½ cup fresh parsley, chopped

Directions:

In a bowl, mix the flour with salt and pepper, add the chicken pieces, and toss to coat. Heat a pan with the oil over medium high heat, add the chicken tenders and brown for 5 minutes on each side. Add the stock, lemon juice, lemon slices and the parsley, toss, cook for 10 minutes more, divide between plates and serve.

Nutrition: Calories - 225, Fat - 12, Fiber - 3, Carbs - 20, Protein - 23

Turkey and Potato Mix

Preparation time: 10 minutes | Cooking time: 1 hour and 15 minutes | Servings: 3

Ingredients:

- 2 tablespoons olive oil
- 2 garlic cloves, peeled and minced
- 2 sweet potatoes, poked with a fork
- Salt and ground black pepper, to taste
- ½ onion, peeled and chopped
- 1 pound ground turkey
- 1 teaspoon garlic powder
- 2 tablespoons hot sauce
- ¼ cup tomato paste
- 6 cups spinach

Directions:

Wrap the potatoes in aluminum foil, place in the oven at 425°F, and bake for 1 hour, cool them down, peel and cut them into medium cubes. Heat a pan with the oil over medium high heat, add the garlic and the onion, some salt and pepper, toss and cook for 5 minutes. Add the potatoes, turkey, garlic powder, hot sauce and tomato paste, toss, cook for 10 minutes and take off heat. Add the spinach, toss, cover the pan, leave it aside for 5 minutes, divide everything into bowls and serve.

Nutrition: Calories - 340, Fat - 12, Fiber - 3, Carbs - 32, Protein - 28

Chicken with Cauliflower Rice

Preparation time: 10 minutes | Cooking time: 30 minutes | Servings: 2

Ingredients:

For the sauce:
- 1 teaspoon garlic, minced
- 1½ teaspoons ginger, minced
- 2½ teaspoons coconut oil
- ½ teaspoon habanero pepper, minced
- ½ tablespoon coconut aminos
- ¾ cup mango juice
- 1 teaspoon tapioca flour

For the chicken:
- 2 tablespoons coconut oil
- 8 ounces chicken breast, cubed
- 3 tablespoons tapioca flour
- Salt and ground black pepper, to taste

For the cauliflower rice:
- 3 cups cauliflower, grated
- 2 tablespoons coconut flakes
- 2 teaspoons coconut oil
- ½ mango, cubed, for serving
- Fresh cilantro, chopped, for serving
- Green onions, chopped for serving
- Toasted sesame seeds

Directions:

Heat a pan with 2 and ½ teaspoons coconut oil over medium high heat, add the garlic, ginger, habanero, aminos, mango juice and 1 teaspoon tapioca flour, stir, bring to a simmer, cook over medium heat for 10 minutes and take off heat. Heat a pan with 2 tablespoons coconut oil over medium high heat, coat the chicken in 3 tablespoons tapioca flour, season with salt and pepper, add it to the pan, cook for 4 minutes on each side and transfer to a bowl.

Heat the pan with the sauce over medium heat, add the chicken, toss, cook for 5 minutes more and divide this mix between plates.

Heat another pan with 2 teaspoons oil over medium high heat, add the cauliflower, stir and cook for 1-2 minutes. Add the coconut, mango, cilantro, green onions and sesame seeds, toss, cook for 5 minutes more, add next to the chicken and serve.

Nutrition: Calories - 500, Fat - 32, Fiber - 6, Carbs - 43, Protein - 35

Duck Breasts with Berry Sauce
Preparation time: 10 minutes | Cooking time: 25 minutes | Servings: 2

Ingredients:

-
- 1 shallot, peeled and chopped
- 2 duck breasts, boneless
- A pinch of salt and black pepper
- 2 garlic cloves, peeled and minced
- ⅓ cup balsamic vinegar
- 1 cup chicken stock
- 2 tablespoons olive oil
- 2 cups raspberries

Directions:

Heat a pan with half of the oil over medium-high heat, add the duck breasts skin side down, season with salt and pepper, cook for 3 minutes, bake in the oven at 325°F for 10 minutes and divide between plates. Heat the pan with the rest of the oil over medium-high heat, add the shallot and garlic, stir, and cook for 3 minutes. Add the vinegar, stock, raspberries, salt and black pepper, stir, cook for 5 minutes, drizzle over the duck breasts and serve.

Nutrition: Calories - 400, Fat - 6, Fiber - 3, Carbs - 30, Protein - 7

Chicken and Veggie Curry
Preparation time: 10 minutes | Cooking time: 4 hours | Servings: 4

Ingredients:

- 2 potatoes, chopped
- 3 chicken breasts, boneless, skinless, and cubed
- 1 red bell pepper, seeded and chopped
- 1 onion, peeled and chopped
- 2 cups coconut cream
- 2 cups chicken stock
- 2 tablespoons cilantro, chopped
- 3 tablespoons curry powder
- Salt and black pepper to taste

Directions:

In a slow cooker, mix the chicken with the bell pepper, onion, potatoes, stock, curry powder, salt, pepper and coconut cream, toss a bit, cover, cook on High for 4 hours. Divide into bowls, sprinkle the cilantro on top and serve.

Nutrition: Calories - 430, Fat - 23, Fiber - 1, Carbs - 5, Protein - 29

Chicken and Cilantro Marinade
Preparation time: 1 hour | Cooking time: 30 minutes | Servings: 4

Ingredients:
- 4 garlic cloves, peeled and minced
- 2 pounds chicken thighs, skinless and boneless
- 4 tablespoons olive oil
- 4 tablespoons fresh cilantro, chopped
- 2 tablespoons lime juice
- Salt and ground black pepper, to taste
- 1 teaspoon cumin
- 2 tablespoons parsley, chopped
- 1 teaspoon red chili flakes

Directions:
In a bowl, mix the olive oil with the cilantro, salt, pepper, garlic, lime juice, cumin, and chili flakes, whisk well. Add the chicken, toss to coat, and set aside for 1 hour. Heat a pan over medium-high heat, add the chicken, cook for 4 minutes on each side. Place in the oven and bake at 375°F for 20 minutes more. Divide the chicken between plates, sprinkle the parsley on top and serve.

Nutrition: Calories - 200, Fat - 10, Fiber - 1, Carbs - 5, Protein - 24

Ground Turkey Mix
Preparation time: 5 minutes | Cooking time: 15 minutes | Servings: 6

Ingredients:
- ¾ cup onion, chopped
- 2 garlic cloves, peeled and minced
- 1 tablespoon olive oil
- Salt and ground black pepper, to taste
- 1 tablespoon chili powder
- ½ cup tomato sauce, unsweetened
- ½ teaspoon sweet paprika
- 1 pound ground turkey
- 1 teaspoon cumin
- ½ cup chicken stock

Directions:
Heat a pan with the oil over medium-high heat, add the onion, stir, and cook for 2 minutes. Add the garlic, turkey, salt, and pepper, stir, and cook for 5 minutes. Add the stock, chili powder, and paprika, cumin, and tomato sauce. Stir, reduce heat, simmer for 7 minutes more, divide into bowls and serve.

Nutrition: Calories - 105, Fat - 5, Fiber - 1, Carbs - 4, Protein - 10

Rosemary and Chilli Chicken Thighs

Preparation time: 10 minutes | Cooking time: 35 minutes | Servings: 2

Ingredients:

- 14 ounces chicken thighs, bone-in
- 1 tablespoon lemon juice
- 1 teaspoon chili powder
- ½ tablespoon ginger, minced
- ½ tablespoon garlic, minced
- 1 tablespoon olive oil
- 4 onions, peeled and chopped
- 2 rosemary sprigs, chopped
- Salt and ground black pepper, to taste

Directions:

In a bowl, mix the chili powder with the lemon juice, ginger and garlic, stir, add the chicken, and rub the pieces well with this mix and leave aside for 10 minutes. Heat a pan with the oil over medium-high heat, add the chicken pieces, cook for 2 minutes on each side, reduce the heat. Add the rosemary, onions, salt, and pepper, cover the pan, cook for 25 minutes, divide between plates and serve.

Nutrition: Calories - 400, Fat - 12, Fiber - 4, Carbs - 20, Protein - 22

Chicken Balls and Hot Sauce

Preparation time: 10 minutes | Cooking time: 30 minutes | Servings: 6

Ingredients:

-
- 1 teaspoon olive oil
- 1½ tablespoons ground chicken
- 3 garlic cloves, peeled and minced
- 2 tablespoons coconut flour

For the sauce:

- ½ cup chicken stock
- ½ cup hot sauce
- 2 tablespoons coconut aminos
- Salt and ground black pepper, to taste
- 1 onion, peeled and chopped
- 2 tablespoons hot sauce
- 1 tablespoon parsley, chopped

- A pinch of salt and black pepper
- 1 teaspoon garlic powder
- 2 teaspoons tapioca flour

Directions:

In a bowl, mix the chicken with the garlic, coconut flour, salt, pepper, onion, 2 tablespoons hot sauce, parsley and the egg, stir and shape medium meatballs out of this mix. Heat a pan with 1 teaspoon oil over medium high heat, add the meatballs, cook for 3 minutes on each side and transfer them to a bowl. Heat a pan with the stock over medium high heat, add ½ cup hot sauce, aminos, salt, pepper, garlic powder and tapioca flour. Stir, bring to a simmer over medium heat, cook for 10 minutes, add the meatballs, cook for 5 minutes more, divide everything between plates and serve.

Nutrition: Calories - 245, Fat - 4, Fiber - 10, Carbs - 9, Protein - 8

Turkey and Zoodles

Preparation time: *10 minutes* | **Cooking time:** *20 minutes* | **Servings:** *4*

Ingredients:

- 1 pound ground turkey
- Salt and ground black pepper, to taste
- 1 tablespoon garlic, minced
- 2 tablespoons olive oil
- 28 ounces canned tomatoes, crushed
- 2 tablespoons tomato paste
- ½ cup onion, chopped
- 3 zucchinis, spiralized

Directions:

Heat a pan with the oil over medium high heat, add the onion and the garlic, stir and cook for 1-2 minutes. Add the turkey meat, salt, pepper tomato paste and tomatoes, toss and cook for 15 minutes more. Add the zoodles, toss, cook for 1-2 minutes, divide everything into bowls and serve.

Nutrition: Calories - 340, Fat - 12, Fiber - 4, Carbs - 26, Protein – 30

Turkey Chilli

Preparation time: *10 minutes* | **Cooking time:** *1 hour and 20 minutes* | **Servings:** *6*

Ingredients:

- 3 teaspoons olive oil
- 1 green bell pepper, seeded and chopped
- 1 pound ground turkey
- 1 tablespoons garlic, minced
- 1 onion, peeled and chopped
- 1 teaspoon ancho chilies, ground
- 1 tablespoon chili powder
- 2 teaspoons cumin, ground
- 8 ounces canned green chilies and juice, chopped
- 8 ounces tomato paste
- 15 ounces canned diced tomatoes
- 2 cups beef stock
- Salt and ground black pepper, to taste

Directions:

Heat a pan with 2 teaspoons oil over medium heat, add the turkey, stir, brown well on all sides, and transfer to a pot. Heat the pan with the rest of the oil over medium heat, add the onion and green bell pepper, stir, and cook for 3 minutes. Add the garlic, chili powder, ancho chilies, salt, pepper, and cumin, stir, cook for a couple of minutes more, transfer this to the pot with the turkey, add the green chilies and juice, tomato sauce, chopped tomatoes and stock, stir, cover the pot, bring to a boil and cook for 1 hour. Divide between bowls, and serve.

Nutrition: Calories - 250, Fat - 8, Fiber - 4, Carbs - 19, Protein - 20

Chicken Burgers
Preparation time: 10 minutes | Cooking time: 10 minutes | Servings: 4

Ingredients:

- 1¼ pounds chicken, ground
- Salt and ground black pepper, to taste
- 1 sweet potato, peeled and diced
- ½ cup spinach, chopped
- ½ teaspoon onion powder
- A drizzle of olive oil
- ½ teaspoon garlic powder

Directions:

In a bowl, mix the chicken with salt, pepper, potato, spinach, garlic powder and onion powder, stir well and shape medium burgers out of this mix. Heat a pan with a drizzle of oil over medium high heat, add the burgers, cook for 5 minutes on each side, divide between plates and serve.

Nutrition: Calories - 210, Fat - 12, Fiber - 1, Carbs - 0, Protein - 24

Italian Chicken Mix
Preparation time: 10 minutes | Cooking time: 15 minutes | Servings: 4

Ingredients:

- Salt and ground black pepper, to taste
- 4 chicken breasts, skinless and boneless and cubed
- 2 garlic cloves, peeled and minced
- 3 tablespoons olive oil
- 1 cup chicken stock
- 2 tablespoons fresh parsley, chopped
- ¼ cup tomato juice
- 2 tablespoons capers, drained
- Juice of 1 lemon
- Zest of 1 lemon

Directions:

Heat a pan with the oil over medium high heat, add the chicken, some salt and pepper and brown for 4 minutes on each side. Add the garlic, stock, capers, tomato juice, capers, lemon juice and lemon zest, toss, cook for 10 minutes more, divide into bowls, sprinkle the parsley on top and serve.

Nutrition: Calories - 300, Fat - 12, Fiber - 3, Carbs - 13, Protein - 20

Chicken Casserole

Preparation time: 10 minutes | Cooking time: 1 hour | Servings: 4

Ingredients:

- 4 cups broccoli florets
- 1 onion, peeled and chopped
- Salt and ground black pepper, to taste
- 8 ounces mushrooms, sliced
- ¼ cup olive oil
- 3 cups chicken, cooked and shredded
- 1 cup chicken stock
- ½ teaspoon ground nutmeg
- 2 eggs

Directions:

Heat a pan with half of the olive oil over medium heat, add the onions, mushrooms, salt, and pepper, stir, and cook for 10 minutes. Grease a baking dish with the rest of the oil. Add the mushroom mixture, chicken, and broccoli to the baking dish. In a bowl, mix the stock, eggs, nutmeg, coconut oil, salt, and pepper, whisk, pour this over the chicken, cook in the oven at 350°F for 40 minutes, slice and serve.

Nutrition: Calories - 345, Fat - 12, Fiber - 3, Carbs - 12, Protein - 30

Chicken Salad

Preparation time: 10 minutes | Cooking time: 15 minutes | Servings: 4

Ingredients:

- 4 bacon slices, chopped
- 2 sweet potatoes, baked, flesh chopped
- 1 onion, peeled and chopped
- 12 ounces mushrooms, chopped
- 2 garlic cloves, peeled and minced
- ½ teaspoon dried thyme
- 3 cups chicken, cooked and shredded
- 2 cups spinach
- Salt and ground black pepper, to taste
- A drizzle of balsamic vinegar
- A drizzle of olive oil

Directions:

Heat a pan over medium-high heat, add the bacon, brown for 5 minutes. Add the onion, potato flesh, garlic, mushrooms, thyme, spinach, salt, pepper and chicken, stir, cook for 10 minutes, divide into bowls, drizzle olive oil and vinegar all over and serve.

Nutrition: Calories - 100, Fat - 2, Fiber - 8, Carbs - 7, Protein - 10

Whole Chicken Roast
Preparation time: 10 minutes | Cooking time: 1 hour | Servings: 8

Ingredients:
- 1 whole chicken, washed, patted dry, and giblets removed
- Salt and black pepper to taste
- 2 tablespoons olive oil
- 1 shallot, peeled and chopped
- 2 teaspoons Dijon mustard
- 1 cup chicken stock
- 2 teaspoons lemon juice
- 2 teaspoons fresh cilantro, chopped

Directions:
Place the chicken in a roasting tin, season with salt and black pepper and rub well. Brush chicken with the oil and the mustard and tie the legs with kitchen twine. Add shallots, stock, lemon juice and cilantro, place in the oven and roast at 425°F for 60 minutes. Carve the chicken, divide it and the cooking juices from the pan between plates and serve.

Nutrition: Calories - 300, Fat - 4, Fiber - 4, Carbs - 29, Protein - 27

Chicken Thighs, Beets and Artichokes Mix
Preparation time: 10 minutes | Cooking time: 40 minutes | Servings: 6

Ingredients:
- 6 chicken thighs
- 1 tablespoon olive oil
- 1 onion, peeled and chopped
- 7 garlic cloves, peeled
- 1 cup chicken stock
- Juice of 1 lemon
- Zest of 1 lemon
- Salt and ground black pepper, to taste
- 1 beet, peeled and chopped
- 6 artichoke hearts, chopped

Directions:
Heat a pan with the oil over medium heat, add the onion and garlic, stir, and cook for 5 minutes. Add the chicken pieces, season with salt and pepper and cook for 5 minutes on each side. Add the stock and lemon zest, artichoke hearts, lemon juice and beets, toss, cover, and bake in the oven at 425°F for 30 minutes. Divide between plates and serve.

Nutrition: Calories - 250, Fat - 5, Fiber - 8, Carbs - 12, Protein - 22

Chicken with Mango Chutney

Preparation time: 10 minutes | Cooking time: 8 minutes | Servings: 4

Ingredients:

- 4 chicken breast halves, skinless and boneless
- 1 tablespoon coconut aminos
- 2 tablespoons lime juice
- 2 tablespoons olive oil
- 2 tablespoons mango chutney
- ½ teaspoon fresh ginger, grated
- A pinch of salt and black pepper

Directions:

In a bowl, mix the chicken breasts with the oil, chutney, salt, pepper, lime juice, ginger, and coconut aminos, toss to coat, and set aside for a few minutes. Heat a kitchen grill over medium-high heat, add the chicken, reserve some of the chutney mix, cook for 4 minutes on each side, leave to cool down, divide between plates and serve with the reserved chutney mix on top.

Nutrition: Calories - 160, Fat - 3, Fiber - 4, Carbs - 8, Protein - 9

Chicken and Green Salad

Preparation time: 10 minutes | Cooking time: 0 minutes | Servings: 4

Ingredients:

- 2 chicken breast halves, cooked and shredded
- 4 green onions, chopped
- A pinch of salt and black pepper
- 3 tablespoons mustard
- ¼ cup mint leaves, chopped
- 2 and ½ cups baby spinach
- 1 tablespoon lemon juice
- 2 garlic cloves, peeled and minced

Directions:

In a bowl, mix the chicken with the green onions, salt, pepper, mustard, mint, spinach, garlic and lemon juice, toss and serve.

Nutrition: Calories - 130, Fat - 4, Fiber - 4, Carbs - 8, Protein - 10

Chicken Soup

Preparation time: 10 minutes | Cooking time: 20 minutes | Servings: 6

Ingredients:

- 2 chicken breasts, cut into strips
- 1 onion, peeled and chopped
- 2 tablespoons olive oil
- 1 garlic clove, peeled and minced
- 12 ounces pumpkin, peeled and cubed
- 2 sweet potatoes, cubed
- 2 carrots, peeled and chopped
- ½ teaspoon fresh ginger, grated
- 1 teaspoon turmeric powder
- A pinch of salt and black pepper
- 14 ounces coconut milk
- 14 ounces vegetable stock

Directions:

Heat a pot with the oil over medium-high heat, add the onion and garlic, stir, and cook for 5 minutes. Add the chicken, salt and pepper, toss and brown for 2-3 minutes. Add the pumpkin, sweet potatoes, carrots, ginger, turmeric, salt, pepper, milk and stock, toss, bring to a simmer over medium heat, cook for 15 minutes, ladle the soup into bowls and serve.

Nutrition: Calories - 129, Fat - 5, Fiber - 5, Carbs - 9, Protein - 10

Dill Chicken Soup

Preparation time: 10 minutes | Cooking time: 1 hour and 15 minutes | Servings: 6

Ingredients:

- 1 whole chicken, cut into medium pieces
- ½ cup green onions, chopped
- 1 pound potatoes, chopped
- 1 cup onion, chopped
- Salt and ground black pepper, to taste
- 1 tablespoon fresh dill, chopped

Directions:

Put the chicken in a pot, add the water to cover, bring to a boil over medium heat, cook for 1 hour, transfer to a cutting board. Discard the bones, strain the soup, return it to the pot, add the chicken and heat everything over medium heat again. Add the potatoes, green onions, onion, salt and pepper, simmer the soup for 15 minutes more, ladle into bowls, sprinkle the dill all over and serve.

Nutrition: Calories - 232, Fat - 4, Fiber - 4, Carbs - 8, Protein - 12

Chicken and Vegetable Soup

Preparation time: 10 minutes | Cooking time: 1 hour | Servings: 6

Ingredients:

- 1 whole chicken
- Salt and ground black pepper, to taste
- 1 onion, peeled
- 1 tablespoon black peppercorns
- 4 parsnips, peeled and sliced
- 1 cup celery, chopped
- 2 tablespoons fresh parsley, chopped
- 4 carrots, peeled and sliced

Directions:

Put the chicken, peppercorns, and onion in a pot, add the water to cover, bring to a boil over high heat, reduce temperature to medium, simmer for 40 minutes. Transfer the chicken to a cutting board, discard the bones and shred the meat. Discard the onion and the peppercorns from pot, return it to medium heat, add the parsnips, carrots, and celery, bring to a boil over medium heat and simmer for 15 minutes. Return the chicken to the soup, season with salt and pepper, stir, ladle into bowls, and serve.

Nutrition: Calories - 250, Fat - 7, Fiber - 3, Carbs - 12, Protein - 9

Mexican Chicken Soup

Preparation time: 10 minutes | Cooking time: 40 minutes | Servings: 4

Ingredients:

- 4 chicken thighs, skin and bone in
- ¾ cup fresh parsley, chopped
- 1 chili pepper, minced
- 4 and ¼ cups vegetable stock
- 2 garlic cloves, peeled and minced
- 2 tablespoons olive oil
- ½ red bell pepper, seeded and chopped
- ½ onion, peeled and chopped
- A pinch of salt and black pepper
- 1 lime, cut in wedges

Directions:

Heat a pot with the olive oil over medium-high heat, add the chicken thighs, cook for 5 minutes on each side and transfer to a bowl. Return the pot to medium heat, add the onion, stir, and cook for 5 minutes. Return the chicken, also add the chili pepper, garlic, bell pepper, salt, pepper and the stock, toss, bring to a simmer and cook for 35 minutes. Ladle into bowls and serve with lime wedges on the side.

Nutrition: Calories - 291, Fat - 5, Fiber - 8, Carbs - 10, Protein - 12

Chicken and Leek Soup

Preparation time: *10 minutes* | **Cooking time:** *1 hour and 10 minutes* | **Yield:** *4*

Ingredients:

- 1 whole chicken
- A pinch of salt and black pepper
- 12 cups water
- 2 leeks, cut in quarters
- 1 carrot, peeled and cut into quarters
- 2 cups onion, chopped
- 2 eggs, whisked
- ½ cup lemon juice

Directions:

Put the chicken in a pot, add the water, some salt and pepper, bring to a boil over medium heat, skim the foam, add the carrot, the onion and the leeks and simmer for 1 hour. Transfer the chicken to a cutting board, discard the bones and skin, and return to the pot. In a bowl, mix the lemon juice with the eggs and black pepper and stir well. Add the 2 cups boiling soup and whisk again. Pour this into soup, season it with salt and black pepper, stir, ladle into bowls, and serve.

Nutrition: Calories - 219, Fat - 3, Fiber - 5, Carbs - 6, Protein - 17

Coconut Chicken Soup

Preparation time: 15 minutes | *Cooking time:* 1 hour and 10 minutes | *Servings:* 6

Ingredients:

- 1 whole chicken
- 1 onion, peeled and cut into quarters
- 1 onion, peeled and chopped
- 3½ quarts water
- 4 carrots, peeled and chopped
- 4 celery stalks, chopped
- 1 garlic clove, peeled and minced
- 1 teaspoon black peppercorns
- 6 parsley sprigs
- A pinch of salt and black pepper
- ¼ cup olive oil
- 2 tomatoes, cored and chopped
- 2 tablespoons fresh ginger, grated
- 2 tablespoons curry powder
- 1 tablespoon tomato paste
- 1 cup coconut milk
- 2 tablespoons fresh parsley, chopped

Directions:

Put the chicken in a pot, add the water, add the quartered onion, and the carrots, stir, and bring to a simmer over medium heat. Add the peppercorns, garlic, and parsley sprigs, stir again, cover, and simmer for 30 minutes. Transfer the chicken to a cutting board, discard bones, shred the meat and return it to the pot. Heat a pan with the oil over medium-high heat, add the chopped onion, tomatoes, ginger, tomato paste, and curry powder, stir, and cook for 7 minutes. Add the coconut milk, stir, bring to a boil, pour everything over the soup, and cook the soup for 30 minutes. Add the cilantro, stir, ladle into soup bowls, and serve.

Nutrition: Calories - 219, Fat - 9, Fiber - 5, Carbs - 10, Protein - 9

Chicken and Collard Green Soup

Preparation time: 10 minutes | Cooking time: 25 minutes | Servings: 4

Ingredients:

- 4 cups chicken stock
- 1 garlic clove, peeled and minced
- ½ onion, peeled and chopped
- 8 ounces chicken breast skinless, boneless and chopped
- 1 cup collard greens, chopped
- ½ cup soft cashew butter
- Salt and ground black pepper, to taste
- 2 tablespoons fresh ginger, grated

Directions:

Put the stock in a pot, add the chicken, onion, garlic, ginger, salt and pepper, toss, bring to a simmer over medium heat and cook for 20 minutes. Add the cashews butter mixed with some of the hot soup and the collard greens, toss, cook for 5 minutes more, ladle into bowls and serve.

Nutrition: Calories - 209, Fat - 5, Fiber - 5, Carbs - 8, Protein - 12

Five Spice and Bok Choy Chicken Soup

Preparation time: 15 minutes | Cooking time: 15 minutes | Servings: 4

Ingredients:

- 1½ tablespoon five spice powder
- 3 chicken thighs boneless, skinless, and cubed
- Salt and black pepper to taste
- 2 tablespoons olive oil
- 1 chili pepper, chopped
- 2 garlic cloves, peeled
- 1 head bok choy, chopped
- 1 carrot, peeled and grated
- 2 tablespoons coconut aminos
- ½ cup fresh cilantro, chopped
- 3 cups chicken stock

Directions:

Heat a pot with the oil over medium heat, add the garlic and chili pepper, stir, and cook for 3 minutes. Add the chicken to the pot, season with salt, pepper and five spice powder, stir, and brown for 5 minutes, Add the carrot, the stock, the aminos and the bok choy, toss, simmer for 5 minutes more, ladle into bowls, sprinkle the cilantro on top and serve.

Nutrition: Calories - 257, Fat - 4, Fiber - 5, Carbs - 10, Protein - 9

Chilli Chicken Soup

Preparation time: 10 *minutes* | *Cooking time:* 22 *minutes* | *Servings:* 4

Ingredients:

- 2 cups chicken breast, skinless, boneless, cooked, and shredded
- 1 tomato, cored and chopped
- 2 avocados, peeled, pitted, and chopped
- 5 cups vegetable stock
- 2 cups scallions, chopped
- 2 garlic cloves, peeled and minced
- ⅓ cup fresh parsley, chopped
- Salt and ground black pepper, to taste
- 2 teaspoons olive oil
- A pinch of chili powder

Directions:

Heat a pot with the oil over medium heat, add the scallions and the garlic, stir, and cook for 2 minutes. Add the tomato, the stock, chili powder, salt and pepper, bring to a boil, reduce heat to low and simmer for 20 minutes. Divide the chicken and the avocado into bowls, pour the soup over them, sprinkle the parsley on top and serve.

Nutrition: Calories - 185, Fat - 5, Fiber - 4, Carbs - 14, Protein - 8

Chicken and Bacon Soup

Preparation time: 10 *minutes* | *Cooking time:* 30 *minutes* | *Servings:* 4

Ingredients:

- 12 ounces chicken thighs, skinless, boneless and cut in small pieces
- 2 smoked bacon slices, chopped
- 1 cup tomato, chopped
- ½ cup onion, chopped
- 1 garlic clove, peeled and minced
- Salt and ground black pepper, to taste
- 4 cups vegetable stock
- 2 tablespoons oregano, chopped
- 2 tablespoons fresh parsley, chopped

Directions:

Heat a pot over medium-high heat, add the bacon, stir, cook for 7 minutes, take off the heat, and set aside. Return the pot to medium heat, add the chicken, stir, cook for 6 minutes, add the garlic and onion, stir, and cook for 4 minutes. Add the tomato, salt, pepper, oregano, bacon, and stock, stir, bring to a boil, and cook for 10 minutes. Add the parsley, stir, ladle into soup bowls, and serve.

Nutrition: Calories - 235, Fat - 4, Fiber - 5, Carbs - 12, Protein - 26

Chicken Sausage and Cabbage Soup

Preparation time: 10 minutes | Cooking time: 30 minutes | Servings: 4

Ingredients:

- ½ teaspoon fennel seeds, toasted and ground
- 1 tablespoon olive oil
- 1½ cups onion, chopped
- ½ cup carrots, chopped
- 3 garlic cloves, minced
- ½ cup celery, chopped
- 5 cups chicken stock
- 4 ounces chicken sausage, sliced
- 8 ounces sweet potato, chopped
- 2 cups chicken breast, cooked and shredded
- 4 cups green cabbage, sliced
- Salt and ground black pepper, to taste
- 1 tablespoon white vinegar

Directions:

Heat a pot with the oil over medium-high heat, add the carrot, onion, celery, and garlic, stir, and cook for 5 minutes. Add the sausage, the fennel, the stock and potato. Stir, bring to a boil, cover, reduce heat to medium-low, and cook for 15 minutes. Add the cabbage, chicken breast, salt, pepper and vinegar, stir, cook for 5 minutes, ladle into bowls, and serve.

Nutrition: Calories - 328, Fat - 9, Fiber - 4, Carbs - 12, Protein - 14

Italian Chicken Wings with Applesauce

Preparation time: 10 minutes | Cooking time: 1 hour | Servings: 6

Ingredients:

- 2 pounds chicken wings
- 1 tablespoon Italian seasoning
- A pinch of salt and black pepper
- 2 tablespoons olive oil
- 2 tablespoons natural apple sauce
- 1¼ cups balsamic vinegar
- 3 garlic cloves, peeled and minced

Directions:

In a baking dish, mix the chicken with salt, pepper, oil and Italian seasoning and toss. Add the apple sauce, vinegar and the garlic, toss, bake in the oven at 400°F for 1 hour, and divide between plates and serve.

Nutrition: Calories - 200, Fat - 4, Fiber - 5, Carbs - 7, Protein - 10

Herbed Chicken Thighs

Preparation time: 10 minutes | Cooking time: 50 minutes | Servings: 6

Ingredients:

- 3 tablespoons olive oil
- 3 garlic cloves, peeled and minced
- 1 tablespoon tomato sauce, unsweetened
- Juice of 1 lemon
- 2 tablespoons dried oregano
- 2 tablespoons dried rosemary
- A pinch of salt and black pepper
- 2 potatoes, chopped
- 6 chicken thighs
- 1 lemon, sliced

Directions:

In a baking dish, mix the chicken with salt, pepper, oil, garlic, tomato sauce, lemon juice, rosemary, oregano, potatoes and top with the lemon slices. Place the dish in the oven and bake at 400°F for 50 minutes. Divide everything between plates and serve.

Nutrition: Calories - 250, Fat - 5, Fiber - 6, Carbs - 7, Protein - 10

Chicken and Tomato Stew

Preparation time: 10 minutes | Cooking time: 1 hour | Servings: 8

Ingredients:

- 3 tablespoons olive oil
- 8 chicken thighs
- A pinch of salt and black pepper
- 3 garlic cloves, peeled and minced
- 8 ounces cherry tomatoes, halved
- ½ teaspoon dried thyme
- 1 cup vegetable stock
- ¼ cup coconut cream
- ½ teaspoon dried basil
- ½ teaspoon dried oregano

Directions:

Heat a pot with the oil over medium-high heat, add the chicken pieces, salt, and pepper, brown for 3 minutes on each side, and transfer to a plate. Heat the same pot over medium heat, add the tomatoes and garlic, stir, and cook for 6 minutes. Add the salt, pepper, stock, oregano, thyme, basil, cream and the chicken, stir, place in the oven at 400°F, and bake for 40 minutes. Divide everything between plates and serve.

Nutrition: Calories - 259, Fat - 5, Fiber - 6, Carbs - 8, Protein - 12

Turkey Casserole

Preparation time: 10 minutes | Cooking time: 30 minutes | Servings: 6

Ingredients:

- 2 tablespoons olive oil
- 1 pound turkey meat, ground
- 2 carrots, peeled and grated
- A pinch of salt and black pepper
- 1 onion, peeled and chopped
- ½ cup orange juice
- 1 cup tomato sauce, unsweetened
- ½ cup fresh parsley, chopped
- 2 tablespoons fresh dill, chopped
- ½ cup coconut milk

Directions:

Heat a pan with the oil over medium heat, add the turkey and brown for 5 minutes. Transfer this to a baking dish, add carrots, onion, salt, pepper, orange juice, tomato sauce, parsley, dill and milk, toss, place in the oven at 375°F. Bake for 25 minutes, divide between plates and serve.

Nutrition: Calories - 300, Fat - 4, Fiber - 6, Carbs - 8, Protein - 12

Creamy Chicken Salad

Preparation time: 10 minutes | Cooking time: 25 minutes | Servings: 4

Ingredients:

- 1 whole chicken, cut into pieces
- 8 black tea bags
- 4 scallions, chopped
- 2 celery stalks, chopped
- 1 cup orange, chopped
- ¼ cup homemade mayonnaise
- ½ cup coconut yogurt
- 1 cup cashews, toasted and chopped
- A pinch of salt and ground black pepper

Directions:

Put the chicken pieces in a pot, add water to cover, add the tea bags, bring to a boil over medium heat, and cook for 25 minutes until chicken is tender. Drain, reserving about 4 ounces of liquid, transfer the chicken to a cutting board, discard the bones. Shred the meat, and put it in a bowl. Add the celery, orange pieces, cashews, scallion, reserved liquid, salt, pepper, mayonnaise, and yogurt. Toss to coat well and serve cold.

Nutrition: Calories - 150, Fat - 3, Fiber - 3, Carbs - 7, Protein - 6

Chicken Stew

Preparation time: 10 minutes | Cooking time: 1 hour and 10 minutes | Servings: 6

Ingredients:

- 1 cup coconut flour
- A pinch of salt and black pepper
- 4 pounds chicken breast, skinless, boneless, and cubed
- 4 ounces olive oil
- 4 ounces celery, chopped
- 3 garlic cloves, peeled and minced
- 2 onions, peeled and chopped
- 2 red bell pepper, seeded and chopped
- 7 ounces poblano pepper, chopped
- 1-quart vegetable stock
- 1 teaspoon chili powder
- ¼ cup fresh cilantro, chopped

Directions:

Heat a pot with the oil over medium-high heat. Coat the chicken in coconut flour, add to the pan, and cook for 5 minutes on each side and transfer to a bowl. Heat the pot again over medium-high heat, add the onion, celery, garlic, bell pepper, poblano pepper, stock, chili powder, salt, pepper and the chicken, stir, bring to a simmer. Reduce heat to medium low, cover, and cook for 1 hour. Add the cilantro, ladle into bowls, and serve.

Nutrition: Calories - 245, Fat - 12, Fiber - 3, Carbs - 9, Protein - 4

Chicken and Mushroom Soup

Preparation time: 10 minutes | Cooking time: 30 minutes | Servings: 6

Ingredients:

- 2 chicken breasts, cooked, skinless, boneless, and shredded
- 2 bacon slices, cooked and crumbled
- A drizzle of olive oil
- A pinch of salt and black pepper
- 1½ cups mushrooms, chopped
- 1 onion, diced
- 2 carrots, peeled and chopped
- 3 garlic cloves, peeled and minced
- 4 cups spinach
- 6 cups vegetable stock
- Zest of ½ lime
- ½ cup cilantro, diced
- 3 green onions, diced

Directions:

Heat a pot with the oil over medium heat, add the mushrooms and onions, stir, and cook for 5 minutes. Add the carrots, garlic, spinach, salt, and pepper, stir, and cook another 3 minutes. Add the stock and chicken, stir, bring to a boil, reduce heat to medium-low, and simmer for 15 minutes. Add the lime zest, stir the soup again, ladle into soup bowls, and serve with the cilantro, bacon and green onions sprinkled on top.

Nutrition: Calories - 245, Fat - 2, Fiber - 3, Carbs - 5, Protein - 6

Chicken and Onion Mix

Preparation time: 10 minutes | Cooking time: 55 minutes | Servings: 4

Ingredients:

- 3½ pounds chicken, cut into medium pieces
- 2 onions, peeled and chopped
- 2 tablespoons olive oil
- 1 garlic clove, peeled and minced
- ¼ pint vegetable stock
- 1 teaspoon dried parsley
- 1 teaspoon dried basil
- A pinch of salt and black pepper
- 14 ounces canned diced tomatoes

Directions:

Heat a pot with the oil over medium heat, add the chicken pieces, brown them for 5 minutes, transfer to a plate, and set aside. Heat the pot again over medium heat, add the onion and garlic, stir, and cook for 4 minutes. Add the tomatoes, parsley, basil, stock, chicken, salt and black pepper, stir, bring to a simmer. Reduce heat to medium, cook for 45 minutes, divide between plates and serve.

Nutrition: Calories - 200, Fat - 4, Fiber - 3, Carbs - 7, Protein - 12

Chicken and Radish Mix
Preparation time: 10 minutes | Cooking time: 30 minutes | Servings: 4

Ingredients:
- 8 chicken thighs
- A pinch of salt and black pepper
- 1 tablespoon olive oil
- 1 cup vegetable stock
- 12 radishes, cut in half
- 1 tablespoon parsley, chopped
- 2 tablespoon fresh chives, minced

Directions:
Heat a pot with the oil over medium-high heat, add the chicken, salt, and pepper, stir, and brown for 5 minutes on each side. Add the stock, radishes and chives, stir, reduce heat to medium, cover, and simmer for 20 minutes. Divide between plates and serve with the parsley sprinkled on top.

Nutrition: Calories - 187, Fat - 10, Fiber - 3, Carbs - 9, Protein - 29

Turkey and Peach Mix
Preparation time: 10 minutes | Cooking time: 12 minutes | Servings: 4

Ingredients:
- 1 pound turkey breast, skinless, boneless, and cut into thin strips
- 3 tablespoon olive oil
- A pinch of salt and black pepper
- 2 tablespoon vinegar
- 3 cups peaches, pitted and sliced
- 1 tablespoon fresh chives, minced
- ¼ cup tomato sauce, unsweetened
- 2 bacon slices, cooked and crumbled

Directions:
In a bowl, mix 1 tablespoon oil with the vinegar, salt, and pepper and whisk. Add the peaches and toss to coat. Heat a pan with the rest of the oil over medium-high heat, add the turkey strips season with salt and black pepper, cook for 10 minutes. Add tomato sauce, toss, cook for 1-2 minutes more, divide between plates and serve with the peaches salad on the side and with crumbled bacon on top.

Nutrition: Calories - 200, Fat - 15, Fiber - 3, Carbs - 10, Protein - 33

Chicken Ramekins

Preparation time: 20 minutes | Cooking time: 20 minutes | Servings: 4

Ingredients:

- 1 onion, peeled and chopped
- 28 ounces canned diced tomatoes
- 2 chipotle chilies, chopped
- 4 garlic cloves, peeled
- A pinch of sweet paprika
- ½ cup fresh cilantro, chopped
- 2 tablespoons olive oil
- A pinch of salt and black pepper
- 2 cups chicken meat, cooked and shredded
- 6 eggs, scrambled
- 2 avocados, pitted, peeled, and sliced
- 1 tablespoon parsley, chopped

Directions:

In a blender, mix the onion with tomatoes, chilies, garlic, paprika, cilantro, oil, salt and pepper, pulse well. Pour into a pan, heat over medium heat, boil for 20 minutes and take off heat. Spoon sauce into 6 ramekins, divide the chicken, scrambled eggs, avocado and top with the parsley and serve.

Nutrition: Calories - 190, Fat - 5, Fiber - 5, Carbs - 8, Protein - 12

Chicken, Radish and Jicama Salad

Preparation time: 10 minutes | Cooking time: 0 minutes | Servings: 4

Ingredients:

- 3 cups rotisserie chicken breast, cooked and shredded
- A pinch of salt and black pepper
- 1 onion, peeled and chopped
- 1 bunch fresh parsley, chopped
- 1 cup coconut cream
- Juice of 1 lime
- 2 jalapeño chilies, chopped
- 12 cups mixed salad greens
- 2 cups Jicama, peeled and chopped
- 1 cup radishes, sliced

Directions:

In a bowl, mix the chicken with salt, pepper, onion, parsley, cream, lime juice, salad greens, jalapenos, Jicama and radishes, toss and serve cold.

Nutrition: Calories - 230, Fat - 4, Fiber - 2, Carbs - 7, Protein - 12

Simple Chicken Soup

Preparation time: 10 minutes | *Cooking time:* 40 minutes | *Servings:* 4

Ingredients:

- 1½ pounds chicken breasts, skinless, boneless and cubed
- 15 ounces canned diced tomatoes
- 1 chili pepper, chopped
- 2 tablespoons olive oil
- 3 garlic cloves, peeled and minced
- 8 cups vegetable stock
- 1 onion, peeled and chopped
- 1 avocado, pitted, peeled, and chopped
- A pinch of salt and black pepper

Directions:

Heat a pot with the oil over medium heat, add the onion and garlic, stir, and cook for 10 minutes. Add tomatoes, chili and the chicken, stir and cook for 6 minutes more. Add the stock, salt and pepper, bring to a simmer, cook for 25 minutes, ladle into bowls, top with avocado and serve.

Nutrition: Calories - 250, Fat - 2, Fiber - 8, Carbs - 10, Protein - 15

Chicken and Potato Stew
Preparation time: 10 minutes | Cooking time: 1 hour | Servings: 6

Ingredients:

- 1½ pounds chicken thighs, boneless and skinless
- ¼ cup olive oil
- 1 onion, peeled and chopped
- A pinch of salt and black pepper
- 1 red bell pepper, seeded and chopped
- 1 carrot, peeled and chopped
- 1 teaspoon cumin
- 1 cup pineapple, peeled and chopped
- 2 canned chipotle peppers, chopped
- 6 garlic cloves, peeled and minced
- 4 cups vegetable stock
- 1 pound potatoes, peeled and cubed,
- 3 cilantro sprigs, chopped
- 14 ounces canned tomatoes in juice, chopped
- Juice of 1 lime

Directions:

Heat a pot with the oil over medium-high heat, add the chicken, salt, and pepper, stir, cook for 15 minutes, transfer to a plate and shred. Heat the same pot over medium heat, add the carrot, bell pepper, and onion, stir, and cook for 8 minutes. Add the cumin, pineapple, chipotle, garlic, return the chicken to the pot. Add the stock, potatoes, tomatoes, and cilantro, bring to a boil, reduce heat to low, and cook for 30 minutes, stirring occasionally. Add the lime juice, stir, ladle into bowls, and serve.

Nutrition: Calories - 250, Fat - 3, Fiber - 4, Carbs - 7, Protein - 10

Chicken and Zucchini Stew

Preparation time: 10 minutes | *Cooking time:* 1 hour | *Servings:* 6

Ingredients:

-
- 1 medium chicken, cut into medium pieces
- 3½ pounds small tomatoes, cored and cut in half
- 3 zucchinis, chopped
- 2 tablespoons olive oil
- 2 onions, peeled and cut into wedges
- 3 garlic cloves, peeled and minced
- 3 red chili peppers, chopped
- 1 tablespoon ground coriander seeds
- 4 tablespoons chipotle chili peppers paste
- Zest of 1 lime
- Juice of 1 lime
- A pinch of salt and black pepper
- ½ cup cilantro leaves, chopped

Directions:

Heat a pot with the oil over medium high heat, add the chicken and brown for 5 minutes. Add the tomatoes, onions, garlic, chili peppers, coriander, chili paste, salt and pepper, toss, cover the pot, reduce heat to medium and simmer the stew for 45 minutes. Add the zucchinis, lime zest, juice, and cilantro, toss, cook for 15 minutes more, divide into bowls and serve.

Nutrition: Calories - 250, Fat - 5, Fiber - 3, Carbs - 7, Protein - 12

Creamy Coconut Chicken

Preparation time: 10 minutes | Cooking time: 30 minutes | Servings: 4

Ingredients:

- 5 chicken thighs
- 1 tablespoon olive oil
- 1 tablespoon fresh thyme, chopped
- 2 garlic cloves, peeled and minced
- 1 teaspoon red pepper flakes
- ½ cup coconut cream
- ¾ cup vegetable stock
- ½ cup sun-dried tomatoes, chopped
- A pinch of salt and black pepper

Directions:

Heat a pan with the oil over medium heat; add the chicken, season with salt and black pepper, brown for 3 minutes on each side and transfer to a plate. Heat the pan over medium heat, add thyme, garlic, chili flakes and the tomatoes, toss and cook for 5 minutes more. Add the stock, the cream and return the chicken, toss, place in the oven and bake at 350°F for 15 minutes. Divide between plates and serve.

Nutrition: Calories - 237, Fat - 5, Fiber - 8, Carbs - 10, Protein - 12

Turkey with Veggies

Preparation time: 10 minutes | Cooking time: 40 minutes | Servings: 4

Ingredients:

- 14 ounces canned diced tomatoes
- 1 pound turkey breast, boneless, skinless and cubed
- 2 tablespoons olive oil
- 1 cup vegetable stock
- A pinch of salt and black pepper
- 2 zucchinis, chopped
- 2 red bell peppers, chopped
- 1 onion, peeled and chopped
- 2 garlic cloves, peeled and minced
- ¼ cup basil leaves, chopped

Directions:

Heat a pan with the oil over medium heat; add the turkey, season with salt and pepper, brown for 6 minutes on each side and transfer to a plate. Heat the same pan over medium heat, add the onion and the garlic, stir and cook for 3 minutes more. Return the turkey, also add the tomatoes, stock, zucchinis and bell peppers, toss, cover the pan and simmer everything for 15 minutes. Add the basil, toss, divide into bowls and serve.

Nutrition: Calories - 250, Fat - 4, Fiber - 6, Carbs - 8, Protein - 10

Fruity Chicken Salad

Preparation time: 10 minutes | Cooking time: 0 minutes | Servings: 6

Ingredients:

- 20 ounces chicken, cooked and chopped
- ½ cup walnuts, chopped
- 1 cup green grapes, cut in half
- 11 ounces canned oranges, drained and chopped
- 1 cup homemade mayonnaise
- 1 cucumber, chopped
- 1 garlic clove, peeled and chopped
- A pinch of salt and white pepper
- 1 teaspoon lemon juice

Directions:

In a bowl, mix the chicken with the walnuts, grapes, oranges, cucumber, garlic, salt, pepper, lemon juice and mayonnaise. Toss and serve.

Nutrition: Calories - 250, Fat - 3, Fiber - 4, Carbs - 10, Protein - 12

Chicken and Chilli Paste

Preparation time: 10 minutes | Cooking time: 15 minutes | Servings: 4

Ingredients:

- 4 chicken breasts, boneless and skinless
- A pinch of salt and black pepper
- 1 tablespoon fresh ginger, grated
- 1 tablespoon garlic, minced
- 2 tablespoons coconut aminos
- 3 tablespoons olive oil
- 1 teaspoon chili paste

Directions:

Heat a pan with the oil over medium high heat, add the chicken and brown for 3 minutes on each side. Add salt, pepper, ginger, garlic, chili paste and aminos, toss well, cook for 10 minutes more, divide between plates and serve with a side salad.

Nutrition: Calories - 240, Fat - 5, Fiber - 8, Carbs - 10, Protein - 10

Moroccan Chicken Soup

Preparation time: 10 minutes | Cooking time: 45 minutes | Servings: 8

Ingredients:

- 6 cups eggplant, diced
- A pinch of salt and black pepper
- ¼ cup olive oil
- 1 cup onion, chopped
- 2 tablespoons garlic, minced
- 1 red bell pepper, seeded and chopped
- 2 tablespoons sweet paprika
- ¼ cup fresh parsley, chopped
- 1 teaspoon turmeric powder
- 1½ tablespoons fresh oregano, chopped
- 7 cups vegetable stock
- 1 pound chicken breast, skinless, boneless, and cubed
- 1 cup coconut cream
- 1 tablespoon lemon juice

Directions:

Heat a pot with the oil over medium high heat, add the chicken, salt and pepper. Stir, brown for 5 minutes and transfer to a bowl. Heat the same pot over medium high heat, add the eggplants, toss, cook for 5 minutes, drain excess grease on paper towels and put in a bowl. Heat the pot again over medium heat, add the onion, garlic, bell pepper, paprika, turmeric, salt and pepper, stir and cook for 5 minutes. Return the chicken and the eggplant, also add the stock and the cream, stir and cook for 25 minutes. Add the oregano and the parsley, toss, divide into bowls and serve.

Nutrition: Calories - 240, Fat - 3, Fiber - 2, Carbs - 7, Protein - 10

Oregano Chicken Stew
Preparation time: 10 minutes | Cooking time: 1 hour | Servings: 4

Ingredients:

- 3½ pounds chicken, cut into medium pieces
- 2 onions, peeled and chopped
- 2 tablespoons olive oil
- 1 garlic clove, peeled and minced
- ¼ pint chicken stock
- 1 tablespoon tapioca flour
- 2 teaspoons oregano, dried
- 14 ounces canned diced tomatoes
- Salt and ground black pepper, to taste

Directions:

Heat a pot with the oil over medium heat; add the chicken, stir, and brown for 5 minutes and transfer to a plate. Heat the pot again over medium heat, add the garlic and the onions, stir and cook for 3 minutes. Add the stock, the tomatoes, the oregano, return the chicken, salt and pepper, stir, bring to a simmer and cook for 45 minutes. Add the tapioca, stir, cook for 10 minutes more, divide into bowls and serve.

Nutrition: Calories - 260, Fat - 5, Fiber - 5, Carbs - 6, Protein - 9

Chicken and Garlic Sauce
Preparation time: 10 minutes | Cooking time: 30 minutes | Servings: 4

Ingredients:

- 10 chicken pieces
- 3 tablespoons olive oil
- Salt and ground black pepper, to taste
- 12 garlic cloves
- 1 bay leaf
- 1 cup red vinegar
- 2 cups chicken stock
- ¼ cup coconut cream

Directions:

Heat a pan with the oil over medium heat, add the chicken and brown it for 5 minutes on each side. Add salt, pepper, garlic, bay leaf, stock and vinegar, toss and bake in the oven at 450ºF for 10 minutes. Discard bay leaf, add the cream, toss, bake for 10 minutes more, divide everything between plates and serve.

Nutrition: Calories - 240, Fat - 4, Fiber - 5, Carbs - 9, Protein - 10

French Chicken Soup

Preparation time: 10 minutes | Cooking time: 3 hours | Servings: 8

Ingredients:

- 1 whole chicken, skinless and cut into medium pieces
- 12 cups chicken stock
- 1 tablespoon Dijon mustard
- ½ teaspoon ground nutmeg
- A pinch of salt and white pepper
- 4 carrots, peeled and sliced
- 6 baby carrots, chopped
- 3 leeks, chopped
- 2 celery stalks, chopped

Directions:

Put the chicken pieces in a big pot, add the stock, stir, bring to a boil over medium-high heat, skim the foam, and reduce heat to medium. Add the mustard, potatoes, celery, carrots, leeks, nutmeg, salt, and pepper, stir well, cover the pot, cook for 3 hours, ladle into bowls and serve.

Nutrition: Calories - 102, Fat - 3, Fiber - 4, Carbs - 10, Protein - 9

Chicken and Asparagus Soup

Preparation time: 15 minutes | Cooking time: 1 hour | Servings: 4

Ingredients:

- 3 carrots, peeled and cut in half
- 1 chicken, cut into medium pieces
- 1 onion, peeled and cut into quarters
- 2 celery stalks, cut in half
- A pinch of salt and black pepper
- 12 ounces asparagus, chopped
- 2 tomatoes, cored and chopped
- 8 cups water

Directions:

Put the chicken in a pot, add the water, also add the onion, celery and carrots, stir, bring to a boil over medium heat, and simmer for 45 minutes skimming foam and discard the veggies. Transfer chicken to a cutting board, discard bones, shred the meat and return it to the soup. Also, add the asparagus, tomatoes, salt and pepper, toss, cook for 10 minutes over medium heat, ladle into bowls and serve.

Nutrition: Calories - 194, Fat - 6, Fiber - 5, Carbs - 13, Protein - 13

Chicken and Mixed Pepper Stew

Preparation time: 10 minutes | Cooking time: 1 hour and 20 minutes | Servings: 6

Ingredients:

-
  - 4 chicken breasts, boneless, skinless and cubed
  - 2 tablespoons olive oil
  - 3 onions, peeled and chopped
  - 2 tablespoons garlic, minced
  - 2 yellow bell peppers, seeded and chopped
  - 2 red bell peppers, seeded and chopped
  - 1 teaspoon chili powder
  - A pinch of red pepper flakes
  - 1 teaspoon cumin, ground
  - A pinch of salt and black pepper
  - 4 cups plum tomatoes, pureed
  - 4 tablespoons fresh basil, chopped

Directions:

Heat a pot with the oil over medium high heat, add the chicken, stir, cook for 5 minutes and transfer to a bowl. Heat the pot over medium heat again, add the onions and the garlic, stir and cook for 5 minutes more. Return the chicken to the pot, also add the yellow bell peppers, the red bell peppers, chili powder, pepper flakes, cumin, salt, pepper and tomatoes, stir, cover the pot, reduce the heat to medium low and cook for 1 hour. Add the basil, stir, cook for 10 minutes more, divide everything between plates and serve.

Nutrition: Calories - 250, Fat - 4, Fiber - 4, Carbs - 7, Protein - 10

Chicken and Pearl Onion Stew

Preparation time: 10 minutes | Cooking time: 1 hour and 10 minutes | Servings: 12

Ingredients:

- 1½ pounds chicken breast, boneless, skinless, and cubed
- 3 cups pearl onions, peeled
- 2 tablespoons olive oil
- 4 garlic cloves, peeled and chopped
- 1 cup green bell peppers, chopped
- 3 tablespoons chili powder
- 2 teaspoons parsley, chopped
- A pinch of salt and black pepper
- 4 cups chicken stock
- 4 cups tomatoes, chopped
- 1½ cups tomato paste

Directions:

Heat a large pot with the oil over medium-high heat, add the onions, garlic, salt and pepper, stir and cook for 5 minutes. Add the chicken, bell pepper, chili powder, stock, tomatoes and tomato paste, toss, cover the pot, reduce heat to medium low and cook for 50 minutes. Divide into bowls and serve with parsley sprinkled on top.

Nutrition: Calories - 265, Fat - 4, Fiber - 4, Carbs - 7, Protein – 10

Chicken, Kale and Purple Potato Mix

Preparation time: 10 minutes | Cooking time: 30 minutes | Servings: 6

Ingredients:

- 1½ pound purple potatoes, peeled and cubed
- A pinch of salt and black pepper
- 1 carrot, peeled and chopped
- ¼ cup olive oil
- 1 pound chicken breasts, boneless, skinless and chopped
- 6 garlic cloves, peeled and minced
- 4 cups kale, chopped
- ¼ cup balsamic vinegar

Directions:

Put the potatoes and carrots in a pot, add the water to cover, add salt, bring to a boil over medium-high heat. Cook for 15 minutes, drain and put in a bowl. Heat a pan with the oil over medium heat, add the chicken, season with salt and pepper, and cook for 4 minutes on each side. Add the garlic, the kale, carrots, potatoes, salt, pepper and vinegar, toss, cook for 5 minutes, divide between plates and serve.

Nutrition: Calories - 160, Fat - 2, Fiber - 3, Carbs - 6, Protein - 10

Baked Chicken

Preparation time: 15 minutes | Cooking time: 30 minutes | Servings: 6

Ingredients:

- 1 and ½ pounds chicken pieces
- Juice of ½ lime
- Zest of ½ lime
- ½ cup celery, chopped
- 1 onion, cut into wedges
- Salt and ground black pepper, to taste
- ½ teaspoon garlic, chopped
- 2 tablespoons olive oil
- 1 cup vegetable stock
- 2 green bell peppers, seeded and chopped
- 4 plum tomatoes, cored and cut into wedges
- 1 cup tomato sauce
- 1 bunch cilantro, chopped

Directions:

Put the chicken pieces in a baking dish. Add lime juice, lime zest, oil, salt and pepper, and rub chicken pieces well. Add the onion, the celery, garlic, tomatoes, bell peppers, stock and tomato sauce, toss a bit, cover the dish, bake in the oven at 380°F for 30 minutes. Add the cilantro, toss, divide between plates and serve.

Nutrition: Calories - 230, Fat - 3, Fiber - 5, Carbs - 6, Protein - 9

Slow Cooked Chicken Stew

Preparation time: 5 minutes | Cooking time: 6 hours | Servings: 6

Ingredients:

- 2 pounds chicken breasts, boneless and skinless
- 28 ounces canned diced tomatoes
- 28 ounces canned artichoke hearts, drained
- 1½ cups chicken stock
- 1 onion, peeled and chopped
- ¼ cup white vinegar
- ½ cup Kalamata olives, pitted and chopped
- 1 tablespoon curry powder
- 2 teaspoons dried thyme
- Salt and ground black pepper, to taste
- ¼ cup fresh cilantro, chopped

Directions:

In a slow cooker, mix the chicken with the tomatoes, artichokes, stock, onion, vinegar, olives, curry powder, thyme, salt and pepper. Toss, cover, cook on Low for 6 hours, add cilantro, stir, divide between plates and serve.

Nutrition: Calories - 260, Fat - 5, Fiber - 4, Carbs - 6, Protein - 10

Herbed Chicken Mix

Preparation time: 10 minutes | Cooking time: 6 hours | Servings: 6

Ingredients:

- 1¾ cups onion, chopped
- 1 teaspoon lemon zest
- 1 tablespoon lemon juice
- 12 Kalamata olives, cut in half
- 2 tablespoons capers, drained
- 15 ounces tomatoes, chopped
- 12 chicken thighs, skinless
- Salt and ground black pepper, to taste
- 1 tablespoon olive oil
- ½ cup fresh rosemary, chopped
- ½ cup fresh parsley, chopped

Directions:

In a slow cooker, mix the chicken with salt, pepper, oil, rosemary, parsley, lemon juice, lemon zest, onion, olives, capers and tomatoes. Toss, cover and cook on Low for 6 hours. Divide into bowls and serve.

Nutrition: Calories - 300, Fat - 3, Fiber - 4, Carbs - 6, Protein – 12

Leftover Chicken Soup

Preparation time: 10 minutes | Cooking time: 25 minutes | Servings: 4

Ingredients:

- Roasted leftover chicken cut into strips
- 6 garlic cloves, peeled and chopped
- 1 onion, peeled and chopped
- 2 zucchinis, chopped
- 2 carrots, peeled and chopped
- 14 ounces canned tomatoes
- 1 bunch fresh parsley, chopped
- 2 pints chicken stock
- 1 tablespoon olive oil
- Salt and ground black pepper, to taste

Directions:

Heat a pot with the oil over medium high heat, add the onion and the garlic, stir and cook for 5 minutes. Add the carrots, the zucchini, the tomatoes, stock, salt and pepper, toss, reduce heat to medium and cook for 15 minutes. Add the chicken and the parsley, stir, cook for 5 minutes, ladle into bowls and serve.

Nutrition: Calories - 278, Fat - 5, Fiber - 7, Carbs - 8, Protein - 12

Chicken Wing Platter

Preparation time: 1 hour | Cooking time: 50 minutes | Servings: 6

Ingredients:

- 12 chicken wings, halved
- 2 garlic cloves, peeled and minced
- Juice of 1 lemon
- Zest of 1 lemon
- 2 tablespoons olive oil
- 1 teaspoon cumin, ground
- Salt and ground black pepper, to taste
- 3 tablespoons black olives, pitted and chopped
- 6 dates, chopped

Directions

In a bowl, mix the lemon zest with the lemon juice, garlic, olive oil, cumin, salt, and pepper. Whisk, add the chicken, toss and keep in the fridge for 1 hour. Transfer the mix to a baking dish, bake for 50 minutes at 350°F, transfer to a platter, and serve with olives and dates on top.

Nutrition: Calories - 265, Fat - 4, Fiber - 4, Carbs - 7, Protein - 10

Coconut Cream Chicken Bites

Preparation time: 10 minutes | Cooking time: 50 minutes | Servings: 4

Ingredients:

- 1 pound chicken breasts, skinless, boneless and cubed
- 2 tablespoons olive oil
- ½ teaspoon paprika
- 1 teaspoon cumin
- 5 ounces chicken stock
- 6 ounces walnuts, chopped
- 1 onion, peeled and chopped
- 2 garlic cloves, peeled and minced
- 1½ tablespoons coconut cream
- ½ cup cilantro, chopped
- Juice of 1 lemon
- Salt and ground black pepper, to taste

Directions:

Put the chicken pieces in a baking dish, add the oil, salt, pepper, paprika, cumin, stock, walnuts, onion, garlic, lemon juice, cilantro and cream. Toss, bake at 350°F for 50 minutes, divide into bowls and serve.

Nutrition: Calories - 340, Fat - 4, Fiber - 7, Carbs - 9, Protein - 12

Lemon Marinated Chicken

Preparation time: 1 hour | Cooking time: 50 minutes | Servings: 4

Ingredients:

- 1 whole chicken without its back bone
- 1 big onion, cut into medium chunks
- 5 lemons, cut in half and juiced
- Salt and ground black pepper, to taste
- 8 garlic cloves, peeled and chopped
- 3 sprigs thyme
- ¼ cup olive oil

Directions:

Put the chicken in a bowl, add the onion, lemons, lemon juice, garlic, bay leaf, thyme, oil, salt, and pepper. Toss well, and keep in the refrigerator for 1 hour. Arrange the chicken in a baking dish, place in the oven at 450°F, and bake for 50 minutes, cut and serve.

Nutrition: Calories - 264, Fat - 4, Fiber - 7, Carbs - 12, Protein - 16

Chicken and Plum Mix

Preparation time: 30 minutes | Cooking time: 15 minutes | Servings: 2

Ingredients:

- ¾ pound plums, pitted and chopped
- ½ onion, peeled and chopped
- 3 tablespoons fresh cilantro, chopped
- 3 jalapeno peppers, chopped
- Salt and ground black pepper, to taste
- ¾ pound chicken breasts, skinless and boneless
- 2 teaspoons fresh parsley, chopped
- 2 teaspoons olive oil

Directions:

In a bowl, mix the plums with the onion, jalapenos, parsley and cilantro, stir, and keep in the refrigerator for 30 minutes. Heat a pan with the oil over medium, add the chicken, season with salt and pepper, cook for 6 minutes on each side, transfer the chicken to plates and serve with the plum salsa on top.

Nutrition: Calories - 232, Fat - 3, Fiber - 2, Carbs - 7, Protein - 9

Basil Chicken Breasts

Preparation time: 1 hour | Cooking time: 2 hours | Servings: 4

Ingredients:

- 5 medium chicken breasts, boneless with the skin on
- 1 bunch fresh basil, chopped
- ½ cup olive oil
- 6 garlic cloves, peeled and minced
- A pinch of salt and black pepper
- ¼ cup balsamic vinegar

Directions:

In a food processor, mix the basil with the salt, pepper, olive oil, and balsamic vinegar and blend well. In a bowl mix chicken breasts with the basil mix, cover, and keep in the refrigerator for 1 hour. Transfer chicken breasts to a slow cooker, add the marinade, cover, cook on high for 2 hours, divide between plates and serve.

Nutrition: Calories - 176, Fat - 3, Fiber - 3, Carbs - 6, Protein - 10

Indian Chicken Stew

Preparation time: 10 minutes | Cooking time: 50 minutes | Servings: 4

Ingredients:

- 2 lime leaves, chopped
- 6 lemongrass stalks, chopped
- 1 red chili pepper, chopped
- 2 teaspoons ginger, grated
- A small bunch of cilantro, chopped
- 2 tablespoons olive oil
- 14 ounces canned coconut milk
- 8 chicken thighs, skinless, boneless, and cut in half
- A pinch of salt and black pepper
- 6 ounces green beans, trimmed
- Zest of 2 limes
- Juice of 2 limes

Directions:

In a blender, mix the lime leaves with the lemongrass, chili pepper, ginger, olive oil and cilantro. Pulse really well, transfer to a pot and heat over medium heat. Add the chicken, toss and cook for 6 minutes. Add the coconut milk, the green beans, salt, pepper, lime zest and juice, toss. Cover the pot, cook for 45 minutes, divide between plates and serve.

Nutrition: Calories - 154, Fat - 4, Fiber - 7, Carbs - 8, Protein - 12

Whole Food Meat Recipes

Beef Stew

Preparation time: 10 minutes | *Cooking time:* 5 hours and 5 minutes | *Servings:* 6

Ingredients:

- 1 green bell pepper, seeded and chopped
- 1 pound beef, cubed
- 1 onion, peeled and chopped
- 4 carrots, peeled and chopped
- Salt and ground black pepper, to taste
- 26 ounces canned diced tomatoes
- 1 teaspoon onion powder
- 1 tablespoon fresh parsley, chopped
- 4 teaspoons chili powder
- 1 teaspoon garlic powder
- 1 teaspoon sweet paprika

Directions:

Heat a pan over medium-high heat, add the beef, brown for 5 minutes, and transfer to a slow cooker. Add the bell pepper, carrots, onions, tomatoes, salt, pepper, onion powder, parsley, chili powder, paprika and garlic powder, stir, cover, and cook on high for 5 hours. Divide into bowls and serve.

Nutrition: Calories - 274, Fat - 6, Fiber - 1, Carbs - 32, Protein - 24

Beef Chilli

Preparation time: 10 minutes | *Cooking time:* 1 hour and 35 minutes | *Servings:* 8

Ingredients:

-
- 2 pounds sweet potatoes, chopped
- 1 onion, peeled and chopped
- A drizzle of olive oil
- 2 pounds ground beef
- 1 tablespoon chili powder
- Salt and ground black pepper, to taste
- ½ teaspoon garlic powder
- ½ teaspoon fresh oregano, chopped
- ½ teaspoon ground cinnamon
- 1 bunch of kale, chopped
- 1 cup water
- 2 avocados, pitted, peeled, and chopped
- ½ cup fresh cilantro, chopped

Directions

Heat a pot with the oil over medium-high heat, add the sweet potatoes and onion stir, cook for 15 minutes, and transfer to a bowl. Heat the pan again over medium-high heat; add the beef, stir, and brown for 5 minutes. Add the salt, pepper, cumin, garlic powder, oregano, cinnamon, water, return the potatoes and onion to the pan, stir, and cook for 1 hour. Add the kale, stir, cook for 15 minutes, divide into bowls and serve with the avocado and cilantro on top.

Nutrition: Calories - 300, Fat - 7, Fiber - 6, Carbs - 32, Protein - 18

Pumpkin Stew

Preparation time: 10 minutes | Cooking time: 6 hours | Servings: 6

Ingredients:

- 1 green bell pepper, seeded and chopped
- 2 cups onion, chopped
- 1 tablespoon olive oil
- 6 garlic cloves, peeled and minced
- 28 ounces canned diced tomatoes
- 1½ pounds ground pork
- 6 ounces tomato paste
- 14 ounces pumpkin puree
- 1 cup chicken stock
- 2½ teaspoons dried oregano
- 1½ teaspoon ground cinnamon
- 1½ tablespoon chili powder
- Salt and ground black pepper, to taste

Directions:

Heat a pot with the oil over medium-high heat, add the bell peppers and onion, stir, and cook for 10 minutes. Add the garlic and the pork, stir, cook for 10 minutes and transfer the whole mixture to a slow cooker. Add the tomatoes, tomato paste, pumpkin puree, stock, oregano, cinnamon, chili powder, salt, and pepper, stir, cover, cook on low for 6 hours, divide into bowls and serve.

Nutrition: Calories - 409, Fat - 12, Fiber - 8, Carbs - 32, Protein - 27

Pork Soup

Preparation time: 10 minutes | Cooking time: 1 hour | Servings: 6

Ingredients:

- 3 carrots, peeled and chopped
- 1 pound pork, boneless and cubed
- 1 tomato, cored and chopped
- 8 mushrooms, chopped
- 4 bay leaves
- 2 tablespoons Sichuan peppercorns
- 1½ tablespoons fennel powder
- 1 teaspoon cilantro, dried
- 1 tablespoon cumin
- ¼ teaspoon five spice powder
- Salt and ground black pepper, to taste
- A bunch of scallions, chopped
- 8 cups vegetable stock
- ⅓ cup coconut aminos

Directions:

Put the stock in a pot and heat over medium heat. Add the carrots, pork, tomato, mushrooms, bay leaves, peppercorns, fennel, cilantro, cumin, five spice, salt, pepper and aminos, stir, bring to a simmer, cover the pot and cook for 50 minutes. Add the scallions, stir, cook for 10 minutes more, ladle into bowls and serve.

Nutrition: Calories - 180, Fat - 2, Fiber - 7, Carbs - 24, Protein - 8

Mexican Beef Soup

Preparation time: 10 minutes | Cooking time: 30 minutes | Servings: 4

Ingredients:

-
- 1 pound ground beef
- 3 carrots, peeled and chopped
- 4 potatoes, chopped
- 1 onion, peeled and chopped
- ½ bunch kale, chopped
- 4 garlic cloves, peeled and minced
- 2 cups squash, cooked and pureed
- 2 quarts beef stock
- Salt and ground black pepper, to taste
- 3 teaspoons Italian seasoning

Directions:

Heat a pot over medium-high heat; add the beef, stir, brown for a few minutes and transfer to a bowl. Heat the pot again over medium heat, add the potatoes, onion, carrots, kale, salt, and pepper, stir, and cook for 10 minutes. Add the garlic, return the beef, add the stock, squash puree and Italian seasoning, stir, and simmer over medium heat for 10 minutes. Divide into bowls and serve.

Nutrition: Calories - 400, Fat - 12, Fiber - 6, Carbs - 27, Protein – 23

Mixed Greens and Beef

Preparation time: 10 minutes | Cooking time: 20 minutes | Servings: 4

Ingredients:

- ¾ pound sirloin steak
- ½ cup mixed greens
- ½ cup fresh cilantro, chopped
- 1 shallot, peeled and chopped
- Salt and ground black pepper, to taste
- 1 teaspoon olive oil
- 3 garlic cloves, peeled and minced
- 2 tablespoons coconut aminos
- 1 red chili pepper, chopped
- 2 teaspoons red pepper sauce
- 3 tablespoons lime juice

Directions:

Heat a pan with the oil over high heat, add the steak, salt, and pepper, cook for 4 minutes on each side, slice, transfer to a bowl, add the cilantro, shallots and greens and toss. In a bowl, mix the garlic with the chili pepper, aminos, and red pepper sauce and stir well. Heat a pan over medium heat, add this mix, lime juice, stir, take off the heat, add over the salad, toss to coat, and serve.

Nutrition: Calories - 307, Fat - 23, Fiber - 12, Carbs - 4, Protein - 33

Steak and Kale Salad

Preparation time: 10 minutes | Cooking time: 10 minutes | Servings: 2

Ingredients:

- 2 peaches, chopped
- 2 cups kale, chopped
- 8 ounces beef filet mignon, sliced in half
- 2 tablespoons olive oil
- A drizzle of balsamic vinegar
- Salt and ground black pepper, to taste

Directions:

Heat a pan with half of the oil over medium-high heat; add the steaks, fry well on both sides, and transfer to a plate. In a bowl, mix the kale with the peaches, the rest of the olive oil, vinegar, salt, and pepper and stir well. Slice the steak thinly, add to the salad, toss to coat, and serve.

Nutrition: Calories - 260, Fat - 5, Fiber - 4, Carbs - 12, Protein - 6

Easy Balsamic Beef

Preparation time: 10 minutes | Cooking time: 8 hours | Servings: 6

Ingredients:

- 4-pound top round beef roast
- 6 garlic cloves, peeled and minced
- 1 onion, peeled and chopped
- ½ cup balsamic vinegar
- 1 cup chicken stock
- 2 tablespoons coconut aminos
- Salt and ground black pepper, to taste
- A pinch of red chili flakes

Directions:

Put the roast in a slow cooker, add garlic, onion, vinegar, stock, aminos, salt, pepper and chili flakes, toss, cover. Cook on Low for 8 hours, slice the roast, divide it and the cooking juices between plates and serve.

Nutrition: Calories - 255, Fat - 7, Fiber - 1, Carbs - 23, Protein - 32

Cocoa and Chilli Beef

Preparation time: 10 minutes | *Cooking time:* 3 hours | *Servings:* 6

Ingredients:

- 2½ pounds beef top round roast
- Salt and ground black pepper, to taste
- 1 teaspoon chili powder
- ½ teaspoon onion powder
- ¼ teaspoon cumin
- 1 teaspoon 100% cocoa powder

Directions:

In a baking dish, mix the roast with salt, pepper, onion powder, cumin, cocoa and chili powder, toss, bake in the oven 325°F for 3 hours. Slice and serve.

Nutrition: Calories - 188, Fat - 5, Fiber - 0, Carbs - 12, Protein - 23

Italian Beef Roast

Preparation time: 10 minutes | *Cooking time:* 11 hours | *Servings:* 6

Ingredients:

- 3 pounds beef round roast
- Salt and ground black pepper, to taste
- 26 ounces canned marinara sauce
- 2 onions, chopped

Directions:

In a slow cooker, mix the roast with the salt, pepper, onions, and marinara sauce, cover, and cook on low for 10 hours. Shred the meat, stir everything, cook on low for 1 hour, divide between plates and serve.

Nutrition: Calories - 300, Fat - 12, Fiber - 6, Carbs - 23, Protein - 18

Coconut Pork Chops

Preparation time: 10 minutes | Cooking time: 15 minutes | Servings: 5

Ingredients:

- 2 tablespoons olive oil
- 5 pork chops
- 1 tablespoon chili powder
- ½ teaspoon cumin
- Salt and ground black pepper, to taste
- ½ teaspoon chili pepper
- 1 teaspoon paprika
- 1 garlic clove, peeled and minced
- 1 cup coconut milk
- ¼ cup fresh cilantro, chopped
- Juice of 1 lemon

Directions:

In a bowl, mix the pork chops with the oil, chili, cumin, salt, pepper, chili pepper, paprika and garlic and toss really well. Heat a pan over medium high heat, add the pork chops, cook them for 5 minutes on each side, mix with the coconut milk, cilantro and lemon juice. Toss, cook for 5 minutes more, divide between plates and serve.

Nutrition: Calories - 200, Fat - 8, Fiber - 1, Carbs - 10, Protein - 12

Pork Tenderloin with Date Sauce

Preparation time: 10 minutes | Cooking time: 40 minutes | Servings: 6

Ingredients:

- 1½ pounds pork tenderloin
- 2 tablespoons water
- ⅓ cup dates, pitted
- ¼ teaspoon onion powder
- ¼ teaspoon smoked paprika
- 2 tablespoons mustard
- ¼ cup coconut aminos
- Salt and ground black pepper, to taste

Directions:

In a food processor, mix the dates with the water, coconut aminos, mustard, paprika, salt, pepper, and onion powder, blend well, pour this into a baking dish. Add the pork, rub well with this mix, bake in the oven at 400°F for 40 minutes. Slice, and serve hot.

Nutrition: Calories - 170, Fat - 8, Fiber - 1, Carbs - 13, Protein - 24

Pork Chop with Baked Apples

Preparation time: 10 minutes | Cooking time: 45 minutes | Servings: 4

Ingredients:

- 1½ cups chicken stock
- Salt and ground black pepper, to taste
- 4 pork chops
- 1 onion, peeled and chopped
- 1 tablespoon olive oil
- 2 garlic cloves, peeled and minced
- 1 apple, sliced
- 2 thyme sprigs

Directions:

Put the pork chops in a baking dish, add the stock, salt, pepper, onion, oil, garlic, apple and thyme. Toss, place in the oven and bake at 400°F for 45 minutes. Divide between plates and serve.

Nutrition: Calories - 370, Fat - 12, Fiber - 9, Carbs - 34, Protein - 27

Smoked Pork Butt

Preparation time: 10 minutes | Cooking time: 10 hours | Servings: 4

Ingredients:

- 5 pounds pork butt, boneless
- 1½ cups unsweetened apple cider
- 1 onion, peeled and chopped
- Salt and ground black pepper, to taste
- 1½ teaspoon smoked paprika
- 1½ teaspoon garlic powder
- ½ teaspoon ground ginger
- ½ teaspoon chili powder

Directions:

In a slow cooker, mix the pork with the apple cider, onion, salt, pepper, paprika, garlic powder, ginger and chili powder. Cover, cook on low for 10 hours, shred the meat, divide it between plates, add cooking juices all over and serve.

Nutrition: Calories - 300, Fat - 7, Fiber - 8, Carbs - 12, Protein - 8

Beef and Mushroom Mix

Preparation time: 10 minutes | *Cooking time:* 8 hours | *Servings:* 6

Ingredients:

- Juice of 1 lime
- 1½ pounds beef skirt steak, sliced into thin strips
- A pinch of cumin
- ½ teaspoon chili powder
- Salt and ground black pepper, to taste
- ½ teaspoon dried oregano
- 2 tablespoons olive oil
- 1 red bell pepper, seeded and chopped
- 1 yellow bell pepper, seeded and chopped
- 1 onion, sliced
- 5 ounces shiitake mushrooms, sliced
- 1 garlic clove, peeled and minced
- 2 green onions, chopped
- 1 jalapeño, chopped
- 1 cup vegetable stock
- ¼ cup fresh cilantro, chopped

Directions:

In a slow cooker, mix the beef with lime juice, cumin, chili powder, salt, pepper, oregano, oil, bell peppers, onion, mushrooms, garlic, stock and jalapeno. Toss, cover, cook on Low for 8 hours, divide between plates and serve with the cilantro and green onions on top.

Nutrition: Calories - 250, Fat - 12, Fiber - 3, Carbs - 7, Protein - 20

Beef with Potatoes

Preparation time: 10 minutes | *Cooking time:* 40 minutes | *Servings:* 4

Ingredients:

For the potatoes:

- 2 tablespoons oil
- Salt and ground black pepper, to taste

For the beef:

- 8 ounces canned pineapple, crushed
- 1 tablespoon olive oil
- 1 pound ground beef
- 1 teaspoon chili powder

- 4 sweet potatoes, chopped

- 1 teaspoon garlic powder
- 1 teaspoon cumin
- Salt and ground black pepper, to taste

Directions:

In a bowl, mix the sweet potatoes with salt, pepper, and 2 tablespoons oil, toss to coat, arrange on a lined baking sheet, place in the oven at 400°F, roast for 15 minutes. Flip, roast for 15 minutes more and divide between plates. Heat a pan with 1 tablespoon oil over medium heat; add the beef, stir, and brown for 3 minutes. Add the garlic, cumin, chili powder, salt, and pepper, stir, and cook for 8 minutes. Add the pineapple, stir, take off the heat, divide next to the potatoes and serve.

Nutrition: Calories - 200, Fat - 6, Fiber - 7, Carbs - 12, Protein - 22

Steak and Pesto

Preparation time: 10 minutes | Cooking time: 15 minutes | Servings: 4

Ingredients:

- ¼ cup balsamic vinegar
- 1 pounds sirloin steak
- ¼ cup fresh basil, chopped
- 1 tablespoons garlic, minced
- 2 tablespoons avocado oil

For the pesto:

- ½ cup bell peppers, roasted
- ½ cup fresh basil, chopped
- ¼ cup olive oil
- ¼ cup pine nuts

- Salt and ground black pepper, to taste
- 1 teaspoon onion powder

- 1 garlic clove, peeled
- Salt and ground black pepper, to taste

Directions:

In a bowl, mix the steak with the vinegar, avocado oil, basil, garlic, onion, salt, and pepper, toss to coat and keep in the fridge for 10 minutes. Heat a grill over medium-high heat, add the steak, cook for 4 minutes on each side and divide between plates. In a food processor, mix the basil with the roasted peppers, pine nuts, olive oil, garlic, salt, and pepper, pulse well, and top the steak with this mix and serve.

Nutrition: Calories - 350, Fat - 12, Fiber - 5, Carbs - 20, Protein - 12

Hungarian Beef

Preparation time: 10 minutes | Cooking time: 15 minutes | Servings: 4

Ingredients:

- 2 shallots, peeled and chopped
- 2 tablespoons olive oil
- 4 garlic cloves, peeled and minced
- 1 pound ground beef
- 1 eggplant, cubed
- 14 ounces canned diced tomatoes
- Salt and ground black pepper, to taste
- ⅓ cup fresh basil, chopped
- ¾ cup coconut cream

Directions:

Heat a pan with the oil over medium heat, add the garlic and shallots, stir, and cook for 4 minutes. Add the beef, stir, and brown for 5 minutes. Add the eggplant, tomatoes, salt, pepper, basil and cream, stir, cook for 10 minutes more, divide into bowls and serve.

Nutrition: Calories - 261, Fat - 11, Fiber - 1, Carbs - 8, Protein - 32

Marsala Lamb

Preparation time: 10 minutes | Cooking time: 20 minutes | Servings: 4

Ingredients:

- ½ cup marsala
- 1 cup fresh raspberries
- 1 garlic clove
- 8 lamb chops
- Salt and ground black pepper, to taste
- 1 shallot, peeled and chopped
- 1 tablespoon olive oil
- 1 tablespoon mint, chopped

Directions:

In a food processor, mix the raspberries with the garlic and Marsala and blend well. Heat a pan with the oil over medium-high heat, add the lamb chops, season with salt and pepper, cook for 5 minutes on each side, add the shallot, stir, and cook for 2 minutes. Add the raspberry sauce, stir, and cook for 5 minutes, divide everything between plates, sprinkle the mint on top and serve.

Nutrition: Calories - 250, Fat - 12, Fiber - 2, Carbs - 5, Protein - 32

Minty Lamb Chops

Preparation time: 30 minutes | Cooking time: 10 minutes | Servings: 4

Ingredients:

- 8 lamb chops
- ¼ cup mint leaves
- ¼ cup fresh basil leaves, chopped
- ¼ cup fresh parsley, chopped
- ¼ cup white vinegar
- ½ cup olive oil
- 2 garlic cloves, peeled and minced
- Salt and ground black pepper, to taste
- ¼ teaspoon red pepper flakes

Directions:

In a blender, mix the mint with the basil, parsley, vinegar, oil, garlic, salt, pepper, and pepper flakes, blend well. Combine the lamb chops with this mix and keep in the fridge for 30 minutes. Place the lamb chops on preheated grill over medium-high heat, cook for 5 minutes on each side, divide between plates and serve with the mint sauce drizzle all over.

Nutrition: Calories - 160, Fat - 6 Fiber 1, Carbs - 3, Protein - 23

Thyme and Apple Pork Chops

Preparation time: 10 minutes | Cooking time: 15 minutes | Servings: 4

Ingredients:

- 1 tablespoon olive oil
- 2 cups apple, cut into wedges
- Salt and ground black pepper, to taste
- 1 tablespoon fresh thyme, chopped
- 4 medium pork loin chops, bone-in
- 1 teaspoon white vinegar
- ½ teaspoon tapioca flour
- ½ cup chicken stock

Directions:

Put the stock in a pot, add the tapioca, stir well, heat, bring to a boil, and cook for 2 minutes. Add the vinegar, stir, cook for 1 minute more and take off the heat. Heat a pan with the oil over medium high heat, add pork chops, salt, pepper, thyme and the apple, toss and cook for 5 minutes on each side. Arrange the pork chops and apples on plates and serve with the sauce drizzled on top

Nutrition: Calories - 240, Fat - 10, Fiber - 2, Carbs - 10, Protein - 24

Ground Beef Stir Fry

Preparation time: 10 minutes | Cooking time: 20 minutes | Servings: 4

Ingredients:

- 1 onion, peeled and chopped
- 1½ pounds ground beef
- 1 red bell pepper, seeded and chopped
- 28 ounces canned diced tomatoes
- Salt and ground black pepper, to taste
- 1 teaspoon smoked paprika
- 1 tablespoon chili powder

Directions:

Heat a pan over medium heat; add the beef, stir, and brown for 5 minutes. Add the onion, bell pepper, paprika, chili powder, salt and pepper, stir and cook for 2-3 minutes more, Add the tomatoes, toss, cook for 10 more minutes, divide into bowls and serve.

Nutrition: Calories - 210, Fat - 3, Fiber - 2, Carbs - 7, Protein - 10

Pork Tenderloin and Zucchini Mix

Preparation time: 10 minutes | Cooking time: 25 minutes | Servings: 3

Ingredients:

- 8 ounces pork tenderloin, sliced
- 2 tablespoons balsamic vinegar
- Salt and ground black pepper, to taste
- 1 teaspoon fresh ginger, grated
- 2 tablespoons olive oil
- 3 garlic cloves, peeled and minced
- 2 dried chili peppers, chopped
- 2 teaspoons coconut aminos
- 2 zucchinis, sliced

Directions:

In a bowl, mix the pork with the vinegar, salt, pepper, and ginger, toss to coat, and set aside for 10 minutes. Heat a pan with half of the oil over medium-high heat, add the pork, stir, cook for 2 minutes on each side, and transfer to a plate. Heat the pan with the rest of the oil over medium heat, add the chili peppers, garlic, and zucchini, stir, cook for 5 minutes. Return the pork to the pan, add the aminos, some salt and pepper, stir, cook for 6 minutes, divide between plates and serve.

Nutrition: Calories - 234, Fat - 3, Fiber - 7, Carbs - 8, Protein - 10

Simple Pork Stew
Preparation time: 10 minutes | Cooking time: 50 minutes | Servings: 6

Ingredients:
- 2 pounds pork butt, boneless, trimmed, and cubed
- 2 onions, peeled and chopped
- 1 tablespoon olive oil
- 1 garlic clove, peeled and minced
- 3 cups vegetable stock
- 2 tablespoons paprika
- 1 teaspoon caraway seeds
- Salt and ground black pepper, to taste
- 28 ounces sauerkraut, drained
- 1½ cups coconut cream
- 2 tablespoons fresh parsley, chopped

Directions:

Heat a pot with the oil over medium heat, add the pork, and brown for 5 minutes. Add the onions, and the garlic, stir, and cook 5 minutes. Add the stock, caraway seeds, paprika, salt, and pepper, bring to a boil, cover, and cook for 30 minutes. Add the sauerkraut, stir, cook for 2 minutes, take off the heat, add the parsley and cream, stir, and return the stew to heat for 5 minutes, divide into bowls and serve.

Nutrition: Calories - 234, Fat - 3, Fiber - 2, Carbs - 6, Protein – 10

Beef and Tomato Stew
Preparation time: 10 minutes | **Cooking time**: 2 hours | **Servings**: 4

Ingredients:
- 1 pound round steak, cubed
- Salt and ground black pepper, to taste
- ¼ teaspoon sweet paprika
- 1 tablespoon avocado oil
- 1 onion, peeled and chopped
- ½ cup tomato sauce unsweetened
- ½ teaspoon caraway seeds
- 2 turnips, peeled and cubed
- 2 potatoes, cubed
- 2 carrots, peeled and sliced

Directions

Heat a pot with the oil over medium-high heat, add the beef, salt, pepper, and paprika, stir, and cook for 2 minutes. Add the onion, tomato sauce and caraway seeds, stir and simmer for 1 hour. Add the carrots, potatoes, and turnips, cover again, and cook for 45 minutes. Take the stew off the heat, divide into bowls, and serve.

Nutrition: Calories - 245, Fat - 3, Fiber - 5, Carbs - 7, Protein - 10

Pork and Cabbage Mix

Preparation time: 10 minutes | Cooking time: 6 hours | Servings: 6

Ingredients:

- 1 tablespoon olive oil
- 1 pound pork butt, cubed
- 20 ounces coconut cream
- 3 cups cabbage, chopped
- 3 carrots, peeled and chopped
- 2 red potatoes, chopped
- Salt and ground black pepper, to taste
- ¼ teaspoon caraway seeds

Directions

Heat a pan with the oil over medium-high heat, add the meat, brown it on all sides, drain, and transfer the meat to a slow cooker. Add the cream, the cabbage, carrots, potatoes, salt, pepper and caraway seeds, cover, cook on Low for 6 hours, stir, divide into bowls and serve.

Nutrition: Calories - 243, Fat - 3, Fiber - 6, Carbs - 10, Protein - 9

Pork Chops with Juniper Berries

Preparation time: 1 day | Cooking time: 20 minutes | Servings: 6

Ingredients:

- 2 pork chops
- ¼ cup olive oil
- 2 yellow onions, peeled and cut into wedges
- 2 garlic cloves, peeled and minced
- 2 teaspoons Dijon mustard
- 4 juniper berries
- 1 teaspoon paprika
- Salt and ground black pepper, to taste
- ½ teaspoon dried oregano
- ½ teaspoon dried thyme
- A pinch of cayenne pepper

Directions

In a small bowl, mix the oil with the garlic, mustard, berries, paprika, black pepper, oregano, thyme, and cayenne pepper and whisk. Add the meat and the onions, toss to coat, cover, and keep in the refrigerator for 1 day. Place meat and the onions on preheated grill over medium-high heat and cook for 10 minutes on each side. Divide everything between plates and serve.

Nutrition: Calories - 265, Fat - 3, Fiber - 2, Carbs - 7, Protein - 12

Pork Stir Fry

Preparation time: 10 minutes | Cooking time: 20 minutes | Servings: 4

Ingredients:

- 9 ounces bacon, cooked and chopped
- 2 tablespoons olive oil
- 1 pound pork loin, cut into thin strips
- 2 cups mushrooms, sliced
- ¾ cup balsamic vinegar
- ½ cup onion, chopped
- 3 tablespoons coconut cream
- Salt and white pepper, to taste

Directions

Heat a pan with half of the oil over medium heat, add the pork strips, salt, and pepper, stir, cook for 5 minutes on each side and transfer to a bowl. Return the pan to medium heat, add the rest of the oil, onions, mushrooms and the vinegar, stir, and cook for 10 minutes. Add the cream, pork, salt, and pepper, stir, heat up, divide between plates, top with the crispy bacon and serve.

Nutrition: Calories - 241, Fat - 4, Fiber - 3, Carbs - 7, Protein - 9

Cucumber and Pork Soup

Preparation time: 15 minutes | Cooking time: 1 hour and 20 minutes | Servings: 4

Ingredients:

- 2 cucumbers, sliced
- 8 ounces pork, cubed
- 3 garlic cloves, peeled and minced
- ½ cup carrots, sliced
- 1 tablespoon coconut aminos
- Ground black pepper, to taste
- 32 ounces chicken stock
- 1 tablespoon cilantro, chopped

Directions

Put the stock in a pot, heat over medium heat, add the pork, the garlic, carrots, aminos and black pepper, stir and cook for 1 hour. Add the cucumber and the cilantro, stir, cook for 20 minutes more, ladle into bowls and serve.

Nutrition: Calories - 253, Fat - 4, Fiber - 7, Carbs - 8, Protein - 10

Pork and Eggplant Soup

Preparation time: 10 minutes | *Cooking time: 25 minutes* | *Servings: 3*

Ingredients:

- ½ pounds pork loin, sliced
- 1 onion, peeled and chopped
- 3 teaspoons coconut aminos
- 1 big eggplant, chopped
- 4 tomatoes, cored and chopped
- 4 cups water
- 1 bunch mint leaves, chopped

Directions

Heat a pot over medium-high heat, add the onions, stir, and cook for 5 minutes. Add the pork, stir, and cook for 5 minutes. Add the water, tomatoes, and eggplants. Stir, bring to a boil, reduce heat to medium, and simmer for 15 minutes. Add the aminos and the mint, stir well, ladle into soup bowls and serve.

Nutrition: Calories - 324, Fat - 2, Fiber - 4, Carbs - 7, Protein - 12

Beef and Nutmeg Soup

Preparation time: 10 minutes | *Cooking time: 30 minutes* | *Servings: 6*

Ingredients:

- 1 onion, peeled and chopped
- 1 tablespoon olive oil
- 1 garlic clove, peeled and minced
- 1 pound ground beef
- 1 pound eggplant, chopped
- ¾ cup celery, chopped
- ¾ cup carrots, chopped
- Salt and ground black pepper, to taste
- 29 ounces canned diced tomatoes, drained
- 28 ounces vegetable stock
- ½ teaspoon ground nutmeg
- 2 teaspoons fresh parsley, minced

Directions

Heat a pot with the oil over medium heat, add the onion, garlic, and meat, stir, and cook for 5 minutes. Add the celery, carrots, eggplant, tomatoes, stock, salt, pepper, and nutmeg, stir, and cook for 20 minutes. Add the parsley, stir, ladle into bowls, and serve.

Nutrition: Calories - 320, Fat - 4, Fiber - 4, Carbs - 7, Protein - 10

Braised Pork with Grapes

Preparation time: 10 minutes | Cooking time: 1 hour and 30 minutes | Servings: 4

Ingredients:

- 2 pounds pork loin roast, boneless
- 3 tablespoons olive oil
- Salt and ground black pepper, to taste
- 2 cups chicken stock
- 2 garlic cloves, peeled and minced
- 1 teaspoon fresh thyme, chopped
- 1 tablespoon rosemary, chopped
- ½ onion, peeled and chopped
- ½ pound grapes, halved

Directions

Put the pork in a baking dish. Add the oil, salt, pepper, stock, garlic, thyme, rosemary, onion and grapes, cover, and bake in the oven at 380°F for 1 hour and 30 minutes. Slice the roast, divide it and the grapes mix between plates and serve.

Nutrition: Calories - 321, Fat - 3, Fiber - 3, Carbs - 6, Protein - 10

Lamb Chops with Apples

Preparation time: 10 minutes | Cooking time: 20 minutes | Servings: 4

Ingredients:

- 1½ cups pearl onions
- 2 cups apple, cut in wedges
- 1 tablespoon olive oil
- Salt and ground black pepper, to taste
- 2 teaspoons fresh rosemary, chopped
- 4 medium lamb chops
- ½-cup vegetable stock

Directions

Heat a pan with oil over medium high heat, add the lamb chops, salt, pepper and the rosemary, cook for 4 minutes on each side, take off heat, add the stock, the apple and the onions. Place the pan in the oven and bake at 400°F for 10 minutes more. Divide everything between plates and serve.

Nutrition: Calories - 240, Fat - 10, Fiber - 3, Carbs - 10, Protein - 18

Pork Roll

Preparation time: 10 minutes | Cooking time: 35 minutes | Servings: 4

Ingredients:

- 1 pound pork tenderloin
- Salt and ground black pepper, to taste
- 1 teaspoon olive oil
- ¾ cup apple, peeled and chopped
- ¾ cup onion, chopped
- 2 teaspoons garlic, minced
- 1 teaspoon fresh rosemary, chopped
- 1 tablespoon white vinegar
- 1 teaspoon Dijon mustard
- ⅓ cup chicken stock

Directions

Heat a pan with the oil over medium-high heat, add the apple, onion, and garlic, stir, and cook for 5 minutes. Add the vinegar and rosemary, stir, and transfer to a bowl. Butterfly the pork lengthwise, butterfly each half lengthwise, cover with the plastic, and flatten a bit using a meat tenderizer. Season the pork with salt and pepper, arrange with the apple mixture, and roll up. Heat the same pan over medium heat; add the pork roulade, brown for 4 minutes, place in the oven at 425°F, and bake for 15 minutes. Slice the pork and arrange on a platter. Heat the pan again over medium-high heat, add the stock and the mustard, stir, bring to a boil, cook for 2 minutes, drizzle over pork roll, and serve.

Nutrition: Calories - 181, Fat - 4, Fiber - 2, Carbs - 9, Protein - 24

Lamb Stew

Preparation time: 10 minutes | Cooking time: 7 hours | Servings: 4

Ingredients:

- 2 pounds lamb meat, cubed
- Salt and ground black pepper, to taste
- 2 cups vegetable stock
- 2 tablespoons olive oil
- 2 bay leaves
- ¼ cup tapioca flour
- 1 onion, peeled and chopped
- 2 tablespoons fresh thyme, chopped
- 4 garlic cloves, peeled and minced
- 16 ounces mushrooms, chopped
- 3 carrots, peeled and chopped
- 3 celery stalks, chopped
- 28 ounces canned crushed tomatoes
- ½ cup fresh parsley, chopped

Directions

In a bowl, mix the beef with the salt, pepper and coat in tapioca flour. Heat a pan with the oil over medium-high heat, add the meat, brown it for a few minutes, and transfer to a slow cooker. Add the stock, bay leaves, onion, thyme, garlic, mushrooms, carrots, celery and tomatoes. Cover, cook on Low for 7 hours, add the parsley, stir, divide into bowls and serve.

Nutrition: Calories - 240, Fat - 7, Fiber - 4, Carbs - 15, Protein - 13

Beef, Watercress and Radish Salad

Preparation time: 10 minutes | Cooking time: 0 minutes | Servings: 4

Ingredients:

- ½ cup olive oil
- Salt and ground black pepper, to taste
- 2 tablespoon balsamic vinegar
- 2 teaspoons mustard
- 4 ounces cherry tomatoes, cut in half
- 4 ounces baby plum tomatoes, cut in quarters
- 2 tablespoons sun-dried tomatoes in oil, drained and chopped
- 4 ounces radishes, chopped
- 4 ounces watercress
- 8 slices roast beef, cut into thin strips
- 4 green onions, sliced

Directions

In a salad bowl, mix the beef with green onions, watercress, radishes, sun-dried tomatoes, plum tomatoes, cherry tomatoes, mustard, vinegar, salt, pepper and the oil, toss and serve.

Nutrition: Calories - 154, Fat - 4, Fiber - 3, Carbs - 8, Protein - 10

Beef Brisket with Tomato Sauce

Preparation time: 10 minutes | Cooking time: 7 hours and 20 minutes | Servings: 6

Ingredients:

- 1 pound onions, peeled and chopped
- 4 pounds beef brisket
- 1 pound carrots, peeled and chopped
- 8 Earl Grey tea bags

For the sauce:

- 16 ounces canned diced tomatoes
- ½ pound celery, chopped
- 1 ounce garlic, minced

- ½ pound celery, chopped
- Salt and ground black pepper, to taste
- 4 cups water

- 4 ounces olive oil
- 1 pound onions, peeled and chopped
- 1 cup white vinegar

Directions

Put the water in a pot, add 1 pound onion, carrot, ½-pound celery, salt, and pepper, stir, and bring to a simmer over medium-high heat. Add the beef brisket and the tea bags, stir, cover, reduce heat to low, and cook for 7 hours. Heat a pan with the olive oil over medium-high heat; add 1 pound onion, stir, and sauté for 10 minutes. Add the garlic, ½ pound celery, tomatoes, vinegar, salt and pepper, stir, bring to a simmer and cook for 20 minutes Transfer the beef brisket to a cutting board, set aside to cool down, slice, divide between plates. Drizzle the tomato sauce all over and serve.

Nutrition: Calories - 400, Fat - 12, Fiber - 4, Carbs - 18, Protein - 3

Pork Chops and Tomato Sauce

Preparation time: 10 minutes | Cooking time: 1 hour and 20 minutes | Servings: 4

Ingredients:

- 4 pork chops
- ½ teaspoon ground cinnamon

For the sauce:

- 30 ounces canned tomato sauce
- 2 tablespoons cumin. ground
- 10 garlic cloves, peeled and minced
- Ground black pepper, to taste
- ¼ teaspoons ground black pepper
- 2 tablespoons dry mustard
- ¼ teaspoons red pepper flakes
- ½ teaspoon ground cinnamon
- ½ cup red vinegar

Directions

Rub the ribs with a mixture of cloves, pepper, and ½-teaspoon cinnamon, rub with the oil. Place on preheated grill and cook over medium high heat for 7 minutes on each side. In a pan, mix the tomato sauce with the cumin, garlic, black pepper, mustard, pepper flakes, ½-teaspoon cinnamon, and vinegar. Stir, bring to a boil over medium heat, and simmer for 1 hour covered. Divide the ribs between plates, drizzle the sauce all over and serve.

Nutrition: Calories - 242, Fat - 4, Fiber - 2, Carbs - 5, Protein - 10

Beef and Beets Salad

Preparation time: 10 minutes | Cooking time: 5 minutes | Servings: 4

Ingredients:

- 3 red beetroot, peeled and sliced
- Juice of 1 lemon
- 2 sirloin steaks
- 2 tablespoons olive oil
- 1 small bunch fresh dill, chopped
- 4 ounces coconut cream
- 2 tablespoon olive oil
- Salt and ground black pepper, to taste

Directions

In a salad bowl, mix the beetroot with half of the lemon juice and toss to coat, then set aside. Heat a kitchen grill over medium-high heat, add the steaks, season with salt and pepper, rub them with half of the olive oil, cook for 2 minutes on each side. Slice, and put in a bowl. In another bowl, mix the dill with the coconut cream, the rest of the lemon juice, and remaining olive oil then whisk. Mix the beetroot and apple slices with the beef slices, divide between plates, drizzle with the dressing, and serve.

Nutrition: Calories - 234, Fat - 2, Fiber - 4, Carbs - 5, Protein - 10

Pork Rib Stew

Preparation time: 10 minutes | Cooking time: 2 hours and 20 minutes | Servings: 6

Ingredients:

- 8 cups water
- 4 ounces tomatillos, husked
- 2 cups cilantro leaves
- 2 jalapeños
- 4 garlic cloves, peeled
- 6 garlic cloves, peeled and minced
- 1 teaspoon dried oregano
- 2 pounds baby back pork ribs, ribs divided
- Salt and ground black pepper, to taste
- 1 onion, peeled and cut in wedges

Directions

Put the tomatillos and jalapeños in a pan, add water to cover, heat up over high heat, bring to a boil, cook for 5 minutes, drain. Transfer to a blender, add the cilantro and whole garlic cloves and pulse very well. Put the pork ribs in a pot, add 4 cups water, bring to a boil, and cook for 1 hour and 15 minutes. Add the onion, cilantro, oregano and the tomatillo sauce, stir, and cook for another 15 minutes. Add the remaining water, stir, bring to a boil, and reduce the heat to low, and cook pork for 30 minutes. Season with salt and pepper, stir, divide between bowls, and serve.

Nutrition: Calories - 231, Fat - 2, Fiber - 3, Carbs - 7, Protein - 10

Pork Chops and Green Chillies
Preparation time: 10 minutes | Cooking time: 30 minutes | Servings: 4

Ingredients:

- 4 pork chops, boneless
- 1 teaspoon ancho chili powder
- 1 teaspoon cumin
- Salt and ground black pepper, to taste
- ¾ cup chicken stock
- 3 tablespoons jarred jalapeños, chopped
- 4 ounces canned green chilies, chopped
- 1 tablespoon white vinegar
- 1 yellow onion, peeled and sliced
- 3 tablespoons olive oil

Directions

In a bowl, mix the chili powder with the salt, pepper, and cumin and stir. Sprinkle this over the pork chops, place them in a preheated pan with 2 tablespoons oil over medium heat, and cook for 4 minutes on each side and transfer to a bowl. In a food processor, mix the stock with the jalapeños, green chilies, and vinegar and pulse well. Heat a pan over medium-high heat, add the rest of the oil and the onions, stir, and cook for 4 minutes. Add the green chili mixture, salt and pepper, stir, bring to a boil, and simmer for 8 minutes. Divide the pork chops on plates, drizzle the sauce over them, and serve.

Nutrition: Calories - 312, Fat - 4, Fiber - 4, Carbs - 6, Protein - 10

Sautéed Pork

Preparation time: 4 hours | Cooking time: 1 hour and 20 minutes | Servings: 4

Ingredients:

- 2 pounds pork shoulder, boneless and cubed
- 1 teaspoon ginger, grated
- ⅓ cup white vinegar
- 1 teaspoon cumin seeds
- 10 black peppercorns
- 4 garlic cloves, peeled and minced
- ½ teaspoon turmeric
- 3 red chili peppers
- 2 green chili peppers
- 1 teaspoon black mustard seeds
- ⅓ cup olive oil
- 1¼ cup water
- 1 teaspoon cinnamon powder
- 1 yellow onion, peeled and sliced
- A pinch of salt and black pepper

Directions

Heat a pot with the oil over medium high heat, add the pork, salt, pepper, cumin, mustard seeds and peppercorns, stir and cook for 5-6 minutes. Add the ginger, the vinegar, garlic and all the chili peppers, stir and cook for 6 minutes. Add the onion, cinnamon and the water, stir, cover the pot, reduce heat to low and simmer for 1 hour. Divide into bowls and serve.

Nutrition: Calories - 321, Fat - 4, Fiber - 4, Carbs - 7, Protein – 10

Beef and Apple Soup

Preparation time: 10 minutes | Cooking time: 1 hour and 35 minutes | Servings: 6

Ingredients:

- 2 carrots, peeled and chopped
- 1 onion, peeled and chopped
- 1 tablespoon olive oil
- 1 apple, peeled, cored, and chopped
- 4 teaspoons curry powder
- 5 cups vegetable stock
- 1 cup cooked beef meat, minced
- A pinch of salt and black pepper
- 14 ounces canned diced tomatoes

Directions

Heat a pot with the oil over medium heat, add the onion, carrots, and apple, stir, and cook them for a few minutes. Add the curry powder, the stock, tomatoes, salt, and pepper. Bring to a boil, reduce heat to low, cover, and simmer for 1 hour and 30 minutes, stirring from time to time. Strain the liquid, return it to the pot, add the beef, stir, heat up over medium heat. Bring to a boil, cook for 5 minutes, ladle into bowls, and serve.

Nutrition: Calories - 214, Fat - 3, Fiber - 3, Carbs - 6, Protein - 10

Thai Grilled Beef

Preparation time: 15 minutes | Cooking time: 15 minutes | Servings: 4

Ingredients:

- 1 cup green onion, sliced
- 2 tablespoons coconut aminos
- ½ cup water
- ½ cup balsamic vinegar
- ¼ cup sesame seeds
- 5 garlic cloves, peeled and minced
- 1 teaspoon ground black pepper
- 1 pound lean beef steaks

Directions

In a bowl, mix the onion with the aminos, water, vinegar, garlic, sesame seeds, and pepper and stir well. Place meat in a large dish, pour the marinade over, cover, and leave aside for 10 minutes. Place on a preheated kitchen grill, and cook for 15 minutes, flipping once. Divide the meat on plates and serve.

Nutrition: Calories - 214, Fat - 4, Fiber - 4, Carbs - 7, Protein - 10

Pork and Papaya Stir-fry

Preparation time: 15 minutes | Cooking time: 10 minutes | Servings: 4

Ingredients:

- 1 teaspoon avocado oil
- 2 teaspoons coconut aminos
- ½ teaspoon fresh ginger, grated
- 1 pound papaya, peeled and cubed
- 3 garlic cloves, peeled and minced
- ½ pound pork tenderloin, cut into strips
- Juice of 1 lime
- ¼ cup fresh parsley, chopped

Directions

Heat a large pan with the oil over medium-high heat, add the pork, and cook for 2-3 minutes. Add the aminos, garlic, ginger, lime juice and parsley, stir, cook for 5 minutes, take of the heat, add the papaya, toss, divide into bowls and serve.

Nutrition: Calories - 306, Fat - 4, Fiber - 7, Carbs - 12, Protein - 20

Chinese Beef Mix

Preparation time: 4 hours | Cooking time: 20 minutes | Servings: 6

Ingredients:

-
  - 3 tablespoons olive oil
  - ¼ cup tamari sauce
  - 1½ teaspoons sesame oil
  - 1 teaspoon ginger, grated

- 2 garlic cloves, peeled and chopped
- 2 pounds beef meat, cubed
- 2 scallions, chopped

Directions

In a bowl, mix the olive oil with the tamari, ginger, garlic, and the oil, whisk well, add the beef, toss to coat, and keep in the refrigerator for 4 hours. Heat a kitchen grill over medium heat, add the beef, cook for 8 minutes, turning from time to time. Divide between plates, sprinkle the scallions on top and serve.

Nutrition: Calories - 150, Fat - 4, Fiber - 3, Carbs - 7, Protein - 12

Spiced Beef Stew

Preparation time: 30 minutes | **Cooking time:** 1 hour | *Servings:* 8

Ingredients:

For the spice mix:
- ¼ teaspoon ground nutmeg
- ½ teaspoon cumin seeds, toasted
- 1 teaspoon fenugreek seeds, toasted
- ¼ teaspoon turmeric powder
- ½ teaspoon black pepper
- 4 tablespoons red chili flakes
- 1 teaspoon ground ginger

- 2 tablespoons sweet paprika
- 2 teaspoons dried onion flakes
- ¼ teaspoon allspice
- ½ teaspoon garlic powder
- 1 teaspoon coriander
- ½ teaspoon ground cloves
- ½ teaspoon ground cinnamon

For the stew:
- 3 tablespoons olive oil
- 3 pounds beef, cubed
- 2 garlic cloves, peeled and minced
- 1 onion, peeled and chopped

- 2 tablespoons tomato paste
- Salt and ground black pepper, to taste
- 2 cups vegetable stock

Directions

In a bowl, mix the nutmeg with the cumin seeds, fenugreek, turmeric, black pepper, chili flakes, ginger, paprika, onion flakes, allspice, coriander, garlic powder, cloves and cinnamon stir well. Transfer 3 teaspoons of this mix to another bowl, add the meat, toss and keep in the fridge for 30 minutes. Heat a pot with the oil over medium-high heat, add the onion, stir well, cook for 3-4 minutes. Add the meat, the garlic, tomato paste, the stock, salt and pepper, toss, cover the pot, and simmer over medium heat for about 1 hour. Divide between plates and serve.

Nutrition: calories-214, fat-7, fiber-5, carbs-14, protein-11

Cardamom Beef

Preparation time: 10 minutes | Cooking time: 10 minutes | Servings: 6

Ingredients:

- 1 and ½ pounds beef tenderloin, trimmed and cubed
- 1 teaspoon cardamom powder
- 6 teaspoons cayenne pepper
- 4 tablespoons coconut oil, melted
- Salt and ground black pepper, to taste
- ¼ teaspoon onion powder
- ¼ teaspoon garlic powder

Directions

Heat a pan with the oil over medium high heat, add the beef and brown it for 2-3 minutes. Add salt, pepper, cayenne, cardamom, onion powder and garlic powder, toss. Cook for 8 minutes more, divide between plates and serve with a side salad.

Nutrition: Calories - 120, Fat - 3, Fiber - 3, Carbs - 4, Protein – 6

Beef Chuck and Celery Soup

Preparation time: 10 minutes | Cooking time: 1 hour and 20 minutes | Servings: 8

Ingredients:

-
- 1 pound beef chuck, cubed
- 2 tablespoons olive oil
- 3 celery stalks, chopped
- 1 onion, peeled and chopped
- Salt and ground black pepper, to taste
- 6 garlic cloves, peeled and chopped
- 32 ounces canned beef stock
- 1½ teaspoons parsley, dried
- 1 teaspoon dried oregano
- 28 ounces canned diced tomatoes
- ¼ cup fresh cilantro, minced

Directions

Heat a pot with the oil over medium-high heat; add the beef, stir, and brown for 8 minutes. Add the celery, garlic, onion, oregano, and dried parsley, stir, and cook for 10 minutes more. Add the stock, salt, pepper and tomatoes, bring to a boil, reduce heat to medium, and cook for 1 hour. Add parsley, stir, ladle into soup bowls, and serve.

Nutrition: Calories - 241, Fat - 4, Fiber - 4, Carbs - 5, Protein - 9

Pork and Basil Soup

Preparation time: 10 minutes | *Cooking time: 1 hour and 10 minutes* | *Servings: 6*

Ingredients:

- 1 onion, peeled and chopped
- 1 tablespoon olive oil
- 3 teaspoons fresh basil, chopped
- 3 garlic cloves, diced
- Salt and ground black pepper, to taste
- 1 carrot, peeled and chopped
- 1 pound pork chops, bone-in
- 3 cups chicken stock
- 2 tablespoons tomato paste
- 2 tablespoons lime juice
- 1 teaspoon red chili flakes

Directions

Heat a pot with the oil over medium-high heat, add the garlic, onion, basil, salt and pepper, stir well, and cook for 6 minutes. Add the carrots and the pork chops, stir and brown for 5 minutes. Add the tomato paste, salt, pepper and stock, stir well, bring to a boil, reduce heat to medium, and simmer for 50 minutes. Transfer the pork to a plate, discard the bones, shred it, return to soup, add the chili flakes, and lime juice, stir, ladle into bowls, and serve.

Nutrition: Calories - 321, Fat - 4, Fiber - 4, Carbs - 7, Protein - 17

Meatballs and Hoisin Sauce

Preparation time: 10 minutes | *Cooking time: 10 minutes* | *Servings: 4*

Ingredients:

For the meatballs:

- 1 pound ground beef
- ⅓ cup fresh cilantro, chopped
- 1 cup onion, chopped
- 4 garlic cloves, peeled and chopped

For the sauce:

- 2 tablespoons coconut aminos
- ¼ cup hoisin sauce
- 1 tablespoon fish sauce
- 1 tablespoon fresh ginger, grated
- 1½ tablespoon coconut aminos
- 1 Serrano chili pepper, chopped
- 2 tablespoons olive oil

- 2 tablespoons water
- 1 Serrano chili pepper, chopped

Directions

In a bowl, mix the beef with the onion, garlic, cilantro, ginger, aminos and chili, stir well and shape medium meatballs out of this mix. Heat up a pan with the oil over a medium-high heat, add the meatballs, cover, cook for 5 minutes on each side and transfer them to a platter. In a bowl, mix the hoisin sauce with the fish sauce, aminos, water and Serrano chili, whisk well and drizzle over the meatballs.

Nutrition: Calories - 245, Fat - 4, Fiber - 4, Carbs - 7, Protein - 9

Beef and Walnut Mix

Preparation time: 10 minutes | *Cooking time*: 20 minutes | *Servings*: 4

Ingredients:

- 2 tablespoons lime juice
- 2 tablespoons coconut aminos
- 5 garlic cloves, peeled and minced
- 3 tablespoons olive oil
- 1 onion, peeled and cut into wedges
- 1½ pound beef tenderloin, cubed
- 3 tablespoons walnuts, toasted and chopped
- 2 scallions, sliced

Directions

Heat a pan with the oil over medium high heat, add the beef and brown it for 3 minutes on each side. Add the garlic and the onion, stir and cook for 2 minutes more. Add the lime juice, the aminos and the walnuts, toss, cook for 10 minutes over medium low heat. Divide into bowls, sprinkle the scallions on top and serve.

Nutrition: Calories - 300, Fat - 3, Fiber - 4, Carbs - 6, Protein - 12

Lemongrass Beef Bowls

Preparation time: 30 minutes | *Cooking time*: 2 hours | *Servings*: 4

Ingredients:

-
- 2 pounds beef, boneless and cubed
- 3 tablespoons coconut aminos
- 1 stalk lemongrass, chopped
- 1½ teaspoons five spice powder
- 2½ tablespoons fresh ginger, grated
- 3 tablespoons olive oil
- 1 onion, peeled and chopped
- 2 cups tomatoes, chopped
- 1 pound carrots, peeled and chopped
- Salt and ground black pepper, to taste
- 3 cups water
- 2 tablespoons cilantro, chopped

Directions

In a bowl, mix the coconut aminos with the lemongrass, 5 spice powder, ginger, and beef, cover, and set aside for 30 minutes. Heat a pot with the oil over medium-high heat, add the beef, stir, cook for 3-4 minutes and transfer to a plate. Heat the pot again over medium heat, add the onions, and cook for 5 minutes, stirring often. Add the tomato, salt, pepper, the water, the carrots, return the beef and the lemongrass mix. Stir, cover, and cook for 15 minutes. Reduce the heat to low and simmer the stew for 1 hour and 30 minutes. Add the cilantro, stir, divide into bowls and serve.

Nutrition: Calories - 320, Fat - 4, Fiber - 4, Carbs - 7, Protein - 12

Garlic Rib Eye Steaks

Preparation time: 30 minutes | Cooking time: 10 minutes | Servings: 4

Ingredients:

- 11 ounces rib eye steak, sliced
- 4 garlic cloves, peeled and chopped
- 2 tablespoons olive oil
- 1 red bell pepper, seeded and cut into strips
- A pinch of salt and black pepper
- 2 tablespoons fish sauce
- ½ cup vegetable stock
- 4 green onions, sliced

Directions

In a bowl, mix the beef with the oil, garlic, black pepper, and bell pepper. Stir, cover, and keep in the refrigerator for 30 minutes. Heat a pan over medium-high heat, add the beef, the marinade, fish sauce and the stock, stir, and cook for 8 minutes. Add the green onions, cook for 1-2 minutes, divide between plates, and serve.

Nutrition: Calories - 321, Fat - 4, Fiber - 5, Carbs - 7, Protein - 15

Pork and Spinach Soup

Preparation time: 10 minutes | Cooking time: 20 minutes | Servings: 4

Ingredients:

- 2 inches ginger piece, grated
- ½ pound pork loin, cubed
- 1 onion, peeled and cut in half
- 2 tablespoons fish sauce
- 1 cup baby spinach
- 6 cups vegetable soup

Directions

Put the stock in a pot and bring to a simmer over medium heat. Add the pork, fish sauce and ginger, stir and simmer for 20 minutes. Add the spinach, stir, take off the heat, cover, set aside for 2-3 minutes, ladle into bowls and serve.

Nutrition: Calories - 254, Fat - 3, Fiber - 3, Carbs - 6, Protein - 10

Pork, Shrimp and Pickled Veggie Salad
Preparation time: 10 minutes | Cooking time: 2 hours | Servings: 4

Ingredients:

- 2 jars pickled root vegetables, drained and chopped
- 3 cups pickled carrots, drained
- 1 bunch mint leaves, chopped
- 1 bunch cilantro, chopped
- ½ pound pork shoulder
- ½ pound shrimp, cooked, peeled and deveined
- 2 teaspoons walnuts, roasted and ground
- 2 tablespoons shallots
- ½ cup fish sauce

Directions

Put the pork shoulder in a pot, add the water to cover and a pinch of salt, bring to a boil over medium heat, cook for 2 hours, drain, shred, and set aside. Put the pickled vegetables and carrots in a salad bowl, add the sliced pork, shrimp, cilantro, mint, shallots, walnuts, and fish sauce. Toss everything to coat, and serve.

Nutrition: Calories - 230, Fat - 4, Fiber - 4, Carbs - 6, Protein - 10

Bacon and Sausage Stew
Preparation time: 30 minutes | Cooking time: 3 hours | Servings: 12

Ingredients:

- 4 sausages, sliced
- 1 pound bacon, sliced
- 4 heads green cabbage, chopped
- 2 yellow onions, peeled and sliced
- 5 pounds sweet potatoes, chopped
- 4 ounces garlic, minced
- Ground black pepper, to taste
- 4 cups water
- 3 tablespoons coconut oil, melted

Directions

Heat a pot with the oil over medium-high heat, add the onions and garlic, stir, and cook for 5 minutes. Add the black pepper, ⅓ of the cabbage and half of the potatoes. Add the 2 cups water and half of the sausages and stir. Add ⅓ of cabbage, the other half of the potatoes, the rest of the cabbage, sausages, garlic, and 2 cups water. Stir again, cover, cook for 3 hours, divide into bowls and serve.

Nutrition: Calories - 232, Fat - 4, Fiber - 3, Carbs - 6, Protein - 12

Apple and Ginger Pork Chops

Preparation time: 20 minutes | Cooking time: 20 minutes | Servings: 6

Ingredients:
- ½ cup natural apple juice
- 1 tablespoon coconut aminos
- 4 tablespoons olive oil
- Salt and ground black pepper, to taste
- ½ teaspoon fresh ginger, grated
- ½ cup water
- 6 boneless pork chops

Directions

Heat a pan with the oil over medium heat, add the aminos, apple juice, ginger, salt, and pepper, stir, bring to a simmer, cook for 10 minutes and take off the heat. Brush the pork chops with this half of mixture, place them on a preheated grill over medium heat, and cook for 10 minutes, turning them once. Divide the pork chops on plates serve with the rest of the sauce on top.

Nutrition: Calories - 231, Fat - 4, Fiber - 3, Carbs - 5, Protein – 9

Pork and Kimchi Soup

Preparation time: 10 minutes | Cooking time: 10 minutes | Servings: 2

Ingredients:
-
- ⅛ pound pork loin, sliced
- Ground black pepper, to taste
- 1 cup Kimchi, chopped
- 1 green onion, sliced
- ¼ cup mushrooms, chopped
- 3 tablespoons green chili peppers, sliced
- 1½ cup vegetable soup
- 1 tablespoon olive oil
- 4 teaspoons red chili flakes
- 2 teaspoons chili paste
- 4 teaspoons coconut aminos
- ½ teaspoon garlic, minced

Directions

Heat pot with the oil over medium-high heat, add the Kimchi, cook for 5 minutes, and transfer to a bowl. In another bowl, mix the chili flakes with the chili paste, aminos, garlic, and black pepper. Add the Kimchi, green onion, green chili peppers, and mushrooms. Transfer everything to the pot, add the stock and the meat. Stir, bring to a boil over medium-high heat, simmer everything for 5 minutes, ladle into bowls, and serve.

Nutrition: Calories - 130, Fat - 1, Fiber - 5, Carbs - 7, Protein - 10

Baked Pork with Blueberry Sauce

Preparation time: 10 minutes | Cooking time: 30 minutes | Servings: 4

Ingredients:

- 1 cup blueberries
- ½ teaspoon dried thyme
- 2 pounds pork loin
- 1 tablespoon balsamic vinegar
- ½ teaspoon red chili flakes
- 1 teaspoon ground ginger
- Ground black pepper, to taste
- 2 tablespoon water

Directions

Heat a pan over medium heat, add the blueberries, vinegar, water, thyme, black pepper, chili flakes, and ginger, stir, cook for 5 minutes, and take off the heat. Put the pork in a baking dish, pour the sauce all over, place in the oven at 375°F, bake for 25 minutes. Slice the meat, divide it between plates, drizzle the sauce all over and serve.

Nutrition: Calories - 335, Fat - 5, Carbs - 6, Fiber - 1, Protein - 14

Whole Food Vegetable Recipes

Herbed Tomato Salad
Preparation time: 10 minutes | Cooking time: 0 minutes | Servings: 4

Ingredients:
- 1 pound cherry tomatoes, cut in half
- 1 onion, peeled and chopped
- 2 tablespoons balsamic vinegar
- 1 tablespoon olive oil
- A pinch of salt and ground black pepper
- ¼ cup basil

Directions:
In a salad bowl, mix the tomatoes with the onions, salt, pepper, vinegar, oil, and basil, toss well and serve.

Nutrition: Calories - 70, Fat - 2, Fiber - 2, Carbs - 6 Protein 4

Avocado and Asparagus Salad
Preparation time: 10 minutes | Cooking time: 2 minutes | Servings: 4

Ingredients:
- 1 pound asparagus, steamed and cut in half
- 6 cups cherry tomatoes, cut in half
- ¼ cup avocado oil
- A pinch of salt and ground black pepper
- 1 avocado, peeled, pitted, and cubed
- 1 cup fresh basil, chopped
- 2 teaspoons Dijon mustard
- 2 teaspoons lemon juice

Directions:
In a salad bowl, mix the avocado with the asparagus, tomatoes, salt, pepper, oil, mustard, lemon juice and basil, toss and serve cold.

Nutrition: Calories - 140, Fat - 4, Fiber - 2, Carbs - 7, Protein - 10

Zucchini Stir-fry

Preparation time: 10 minutes | Cooking time: 15 minutes | Servings: 4

Ingredients:

-
  - 2 tablespoons olive oil
  - 4 zucchinis, sliced
  - 2 garlic cloves, peeled and minced
  - 1 onion, peeled and chopped
  - 1 carrot, peeled and sliced
  - Zest of 1 lemon
  - 1 teaspoon red chili flakes
- 2 tablespoons pine nuts, chopped
- 4 tablespoons mint leaves, chopped
- 2 tablespoons cilantro, chopped
- Salt and ground black pepper, to taste
- 2 cups mixed salad greens

Directions:

Heat a pan with the oil over medium-high heat, add the onion and cook for 3 minutes. Add the garlic, the chili flakes, salt and pepper, stir and cook for 1 more minute. Add the zucchinis, the carrot and lemon zest, stir, cook for 8 minutes and transfer to a bowl. Add pine nuts, mint, and cilantro and salad greens, toss well and serve.

Nutrition: Calories - 140, Fat - 7, Fiber - 1, Carbs - 7, Protein - 7

Minty Watermelon Salad

Preparation time: 10 minutes | Cooking time: 0 minutes | Servings: 4

Ingredients:

- 2 cucumbers, chopped
- 2 tablespoons olive oil
- 1 onion, sliced
- 1 small watermelon, cubed
- 2 tablespoons lime juice
- ½ cup mint leaves, chopped
- Salt and ground black pepper, to taste

Directions:

In a bowl, mix the cucumbers with the onion, watermelon, mint, salt and pepper. Add the oil and the lime juice, toss and serve.

Nutrition: Calories - 160, Fat - 14, Fiber - 3.2, Carbs - 13.4, Protein - 4.6

Tomato Salad with Basil Dressing

Preparation time: 10 minutes | Cooking time: 10 minutes | Servings: 4

Ingredients:

- 2 pounds plum tomatoes, cored and sliced
- A pinch of salt and black pepper
- *For the basil dressing:*
- ⅓ cup olive oil
- 1 teaspoon lemon zest
- ¼ cup fresh lemon juice
- 1 tablespoon Dijon mustard
- 1 bunch fresh basil, chopped

Directions:

Mix the oil with the mustard, basil, lemon zest, salt, black pepper, and lemon juice, and whisk well. In a salad bowl, mix the tomatoes with a pinch of salt and black pepper, add the basil dressing, toss well, and serve.

Nutrition: Calories - 86, Fat - 3.8, Fiber - 2.1, Carbs - 9.2, Protein - 5.3

Okra Mix

Preparation time: 10 minutes | Cooking time: 20 minutes | Servings: 4

Ingredients:

-
- ⅓ cup extra virgin olive oil
- 1 tablespoon mustard seeds, toasted
- 1 onion, peeled and chopped
- 2 teaspoons fresh ginger, grated
- 2 garlic cloves, peeled and minced
- ½ pound small potatoes, cubed
- 1 pound okra, trimmed and sliced
- 2 teaspoons cilantro, dried
- 2 teaspoons cumin
- 1 teaspoon turmeric
- 1½ tablespoons sesame seeds, toasted
- ½ teaspoon red pepper flakes
- Salt and ground black pepper, to taste

Directions:

Heat a pan with the olive oil at a medium-high heat, cook mustard seeds and the onion, and cook for 2 minutes. Add the garlic, ginger, stir, potatoes, salt, and red pepper, stir, cover, and cook for 8 minutes, stirring often. Add the okra, cumin, turmeric, and cilantro, stir, and cook for 10 minutes. Add the sesame seeds, transfer to plates, and serve.

Nutrition: Calories - 120, Fat - 6.4, Fiber - 3, Carbs - 10, Protein - 4

Lime Okra Mix
Preparation time: 60 minutes | Cooking time: 10 minutes | Servings: 4

Ingredients:

- 2 tablespoons olive oil
- 2 pounds okra, trimmed
- Zest of 2 limes
- Juice of 2 limes
- 2 garlic cloves, peeled and chopped
- 1 tablespoon garam masala
- ¼ cup fresh cilantro, chopped
- Salt and ground black pepper, to taste

Directions:

In a bowl, mix the okra with the lime zest, lime juice, olive oil, garam masala, garlic, salt, pepper, stir well, and set aside in the refrigerator for 1 hour. Heat a kitchen grill at a high heat, cook marinated okra for 10 minutes, transfer the okra to plates, and serve with the chopped cilantro on top.

Nutrition: Calories - 78, Fat - 2, Fiber - 3, Carbs - 8.5, Protein - 4

Basil Summer Squash
Preparation time: 10 minutes | Cooking time: 10 minutes | Servings: 4

Ingredients:

- 1½ pounds summer squash, sliced
- A pinch of salt and black pepper
- 2 tablespoons olive oil
- ½ cup basil, torn
- 1 teaspoon balsamic vinegar

Directions:

Arrange the summer squash on a lined baking sheet, season with salt and black pepper, drizzle with the oil, toss well, bake in the oven at 400°F for 10 minutes. Arrange the squash slices on plates, drizzle with vinegar, sprinkle with basil, and serve.

Nutrition: Calories - 80, Fat - 2.6, Fiber - 0 Carbs 0.2, Protein - 1

Dijon Fennel Salad
Preparation time: 10 minutesc | Cooking time: 0 minutes | Servings: 4

Ingredients:

- 1 tablespoon olive oil
- 1 teaspoon Dijon mustard
- 1 tablespoon lime juice
- 1 fennel bulb, trimmed and shaved

- A pinch of salt and ground black pepper
- 1 cup fresh parsley, chopped

Directions:

In a salad bowl, mix the fennel with the parsley and stir. Add salt, pepper, lime juice, mustard and oil, toss and serve cold.

Nutrition: Calories - 90, Fat - 0.5, Fiber - 1, Carbs - 1, Protein - 4

Endive and Almond Salad
Preparation time: 10 minutes | Cooking time: 0 minutes | Servings: 4

Ingredients:

- 2 tablespoons lemon juice
- ¼ cup olive oil
- A pinch of salt and ground black pepper
- 1 teaspoon mustard

- 4 endives, cut into small pieces
- ½ cup almonds, chopped
- 2 tablespoons fresh parsley, chopped

Directions:

In a salad bowl, mix the endives with almonds, parsley, salt, pepper, lemon juice, oil, and mustard, whisk well, and serve.

Nutrition: Calories - 70, Fat - 0, Fiber - 1, Carbs - 0, Protein - 6

Lettuce and Radicchio Salad
Preparation time: 6 minutes | Cooking time: 0 minutes | Servings: 4

Ingredients:

- ½ cup olive oil
- A pinch of salt and ground black pepper
- 2 tablespoons shallots, chopped
- ¼ cup Dijon mustard

- Juice of 2 lemons
- ½ cup fresh cilantro, chopped
- 5 baby romaine lettuce heads, chopped
- 3 radicchios, sliced

Directions:

In a salad bowl, mix the romaine lettuce with the radicchios, shallots, salt, pepper, oil, mustard, lemon juice and cilantro, toss and serve.

Nutrition: Calories - 87, Fat - 2, Fiber - 1, Carbs - 1, Protein - 2

Tomato and Radish Salad

Preparation time: 10 minutes | Cooking time: 0 minutes | Servings: 4

Ingredients:

- 12 ounces tomatoes, chopped
- 1 cucumber, chopped
- 3 onions, chopped
- 7 ounces red radishes, cut into wedges
- 3 tablespoons olive oil
- 1 teaspoon mustard
- 1 teaspoon mustard seeds
- Juice of 2 limes
- 3 tablespoons basil, chopped
- 1 red chili pepper, chopped

Directions:

In a salad bowl, mix the tomatoes with the cucumber, onion, radishes, chili, oil, mustard, mustard seeds, lime juice and basil, toss and serve cold.

Nutrition: Calories - 98, Fat - 3, Fiber - 2, Carbs - 8, Protein - 2

Cabbage and Blueberry Salad

Preparation time: 8 minutes | Cooking time: 0 minutes | Servings: 4

Ingredients:

- 1 napa cabbage, shredded
- 1 cup almonds, chopped
- 1 bunch green onions, chopped
- ¼ cup dried blueberries
- ¼ cup balsamic vinegar
- 2 tablespoons coconut aminos
- ½ cup olive oil
- ¼ teaspoon fresh ginger, grated
- A pinch of ground black pepper

Directions:

In a salad bowl, mix the cabbage with the green onions, almonds, and blueberries, ginger, black pepper, oil, aminos and vinegar, toss and serve.

Nutrition: Calories - 140, Fat - 3, Fiber - 3, Carbs - 8, Protein - 6

Minty Cabbage Salad

Preparation time: 10 minutes | Cooking time: 0 minutes | Servings: 4

Ingredients:

- 1 small green cabbage head, shredded
- 1 cup red cabbage, shredded
- 1 cup mint leaves, chopped
- 1 large avocado, pitted, peeled, and cubed
- 1 orange bell pepper, sliced
- 1 tablespoon coconut aminos
- ¼ cup walnuts, roasted and crushed
- Juice of 2 limes

Directions:

In a bowl, mix the green cabbage with the red cabbage, bell pepper, avocado, walnuts, mint, lime juice and aminos, toss and serve.

Nutrition: Calories - 111, Fat - 9, Fiber - 5, Carbs - 8.5, Protein - 1.8

Pumpkin Chilli

Preparation time: 10 minutes | Cooking time: 6 hours | Servings: 4

Ingredients:

- 1 squash, chopped
- 1 potato, chopped
- 2 carrots, sliced
- 1 cup cherry tomatoes, cut in half
- 1 yellow bell pepper, seeded and sliced
- 2 red chilies, chopped
- 10 ounces coconut milk
- 2 tablespoons orange rind, grated
- 4 garlic cloves, peeled and minced
- 2½ tablespoons coconut aminos
- Juice of ½ lime
- Juice from 1 orange
- ⅓ onion, peeled and chopped
- ½ teaspoon turmeric
- 1 tablespoon coriander seeds
- 1 tablespoon cider vinegar
- 1 teaspoon fennel seeds
- 1 teaspoon pumpkin seeds
- ½ small bunch fresh cilantro, chopped

Directions:

In a slow cooker, mix the squash with the potato, carrots, tomatoes, bell pepper, chilies, coconut milk, orange rind, garlic, aminos, lime juice and orange juice, onion, turmeric, vinegar, coriander and fennel. Toss, cover, cook on Low for 6 hours, add pumpkin seeds and cilantro, toss again, divide into bowls and serve.

Nutrition: Calories - 250, Fat - 8, Fiber - 3, Carbs - 20, Protein - 16

Squash and Zucchini Salad

Preparation time: 10 minutes | Cooking time: 0 minutes | Servings: 4

Ingredients:

- ½ pound summer squash, shaved
- ½ pound zucchini, shaved
- 3 tablespoons almonds, roasted and crushed
- 2½ tablespoons olive oil
- 2 tablespoons lemon juice
- A pinch of salt and ground black pepper
- 1 garlic clove, peeled and minced
- 1 cup salad greens

Directions:

In a bowl, mix the squash with the zucchini, almonds, garlic, salad greens, oil, lemon juice, salt and pepper, toss and serve.

Nutrition: Calories - 110, Fat - 2, Fiber - 2, Carbs - 4, Protein - 5

Cold Summer Soup

Preparation time: 10 minutes | Cooking time: 0 minutes | Servings: 4

Ingredients:

- 1 pound tomatoes, cored and chopped
- 1 yellow bell pepper, seeded and chopped
- 1 small summer squash, chopped
- 2 green onions, peeled and chopped
- 1 cup fresh carrot juice
- 2 tablespoons sherry wine vinegar
- Salt and ground black pepper, to taste
- ½ cup fresh mint leaves, chopped

Directions:

In a food processor, mix the tomatoes with the bell pepper, squash, onions, carrot, juice, vinegar, salt and pepper, pulse well, divide into bowls, sprinkle the mint all over and serve cold.

Nutrition: Calories - 60, Fat - 1, Fiber - 2, Carbs - 14, Protein - 2.4

Fennel and Cabbage Salad

Preparation time: 10 minutes | Cooking time: 0 minutes | Servings: 4

Ingredients:

- 4 cups red cabbage, shredded
- 2 apples, cored and sliced
- 1½ cup fennel, shredded
- ½ cup mayonnaise
- 3 tablespoons balsamic vinegar
- ½ teaspoon caraway seeds
- Ground black pepper, to taste

Directions:

In a bowl, mix the fennel with the cabbage, apple, black pepper, vinegar, mayo and caraway seeds, toss and serve cold.

Nutrition: Calories - 160, Fat - 4, Fiber - 6, Carbs - 10, Protein - 3

Balsamic Roasted Carrots

Preparation time: 10 minutes | Cooking time: 30 minutes | Servings: 4

Ingredients:

- 2 tablespoons clarified butter, melted
- 1½ pounds carrots, peeled
- 2 garlic cloves, peeled and minced
- 2 tablespoons balsamic vinegar
- ½ cup fresh parsley, chopped
- A pinch of salt and ground black pepper

Directions:

Arrange the carrots on a lined baking sheet, season with salt and black pepper, add the garlic, clarified butter, and vinegar, toss well, place in the oven at 400°F and roast for 30 minutes. Arrange the carrots on plates sprinkle the parsley on top and serve.

Nutrition: Calories - 130, Fat - 5, Fiber - 1, Carbs - 3, Protein - 6

Balsamic Roasted Onions

Preparation time: 10 minutes | Cooking time: 40 minutes | Servings: 4

Ingredients:

- 2 pounds onions, peeled and cut in half
- ¼ cup avocado oil
- 1 tablespoon balsamic vinegar
- 2 teaspoons smoked paprika
- A pinch of salt and black pepper

Directions:

Put the onions on a baking dish, add the salt, pepper, vinegar, oil, and paprika, toss well, cover, place in the oven at 450ºF, and bake for 40 minutes. Divide between plates and serve.

Nutrition: Calories - 110, Fat - 2, Fiber - 3, Carbs - 7, Protein - 2

Glazed Veggies

Preparation time: 10 minutes | Cooking time: 35 minutes | Servings: 4

Ingredients:

- ¾ pound tomatoes, cored and chopped
- ¾ pound carrots, peeled and chopped
- ¾ pound, radishes, cut in half
- ¼ cup red wine
- ¼ cup balsamic vinegar
- Salt and ground black pepper, to taste
- 2 tablespoons extra virgin olive oil
- 1 tablespoon parsley, chopped

Directions:

In a small pot, mix the red wine with the balsamic vinegar, bring to a boil at a medium heat, reduce heat, and simmer for 25 minutes. Rub the vegetables with olive oil, season them with salt and pepper, place on a heated grill, cook the carrots and radishes for 10 minutes and the tomatoes for 2 minutes on each side. Transfer the vegetables to a platter, sprinkle parsley all over, drizzle glaze on top and serve.

Nutrition: Calories - 120, Fat - 1, Fiber - 3, Carbs - 9, Protein - 2

Dill and Cucumber Salad

Preparation time: 10 minutes | Cooking time: 0 minutes | Servings: 4

Ingredients:

- 7 small cucumbers, sliced
- 5 tomatoes, cored and chopped
- 3 tablespoons onion, chopped
- ¼ cup balsamic vinegar
- 1 tablespoon fresh dill, chopped
- A pinch of salt and ground black pepper
- 3 tablespoons olive oil

Directions:

In a salad bowl, mix the cucumbers with onion, tomatoes, salt, pepper, oil and vinegar and toss. Add the dill, toss and serve.

Nutrition: Calories - 120, Fat - 3, Fiber - 2, Carbs - 5, Protein - 10

Potato Cakes

Preparation time: 10 minutes | Cooking time: 10 minutes | Servings: 4

Ingredients:

- 1 onion, peeled and chopped
- 1 pound russet potatoes, grated
- Salt and ground black pepper, to taste
- 2½ teaspoons, ground nutmeg
- 2 tablespoons coconut flour
- 1 egg
- 1½ tablespoons coconut oil, melted

Directions:

In a bowl, mix the potatoes with the salt, onion, nutmeg, pepper, flour, and egg and stir well. Heat up ¾ tablespoon oil in a pan at a medium-high temperature, put 3 tablespoons of the potato mixture in the pan, flatten the mixture with a spatula, reduce heat, cook for 5 minutes on each side, and transfer to a plate. Repeat this with the rest of the ingredients and serve the cakes warm.

Nutrition: Calories - 70, Fat - 2, Fiber - 3, Carbs - 10, Protein - 4

Artichoke Mix and Vinaigrette

Preparation time: 10 minutes | Cooking time: 0 minutes | Servings: 4

Ingredients:

- 12 ounces jarred artichokes hearts, drained and chopped
- 3 tablespoons lime juice
- ⅓ cup extra virgin olive oil
- 10 ounces mixed greens
- Salt and ground black pepper, to taste

Directions:

In a bowl, mix the lime juice with the artichokes, greens, salt, pepper, and oil, toss and serve.

Nutrition: Calories - 112, Fat - 9, Fiber - 2, Carbs - 6, Protein - 2

Mushroom and Parsley Salad

Preparation time: 4 hours | Cooking time: 0 minutes | Servings: 3

Ingredients:

- 5 pounds mushrooms, sliced
- 2 cups olive oil
- 2 bunches fresh parsley, chopped
- 1 cup lemon juice
- 8 garlic cloves, peeled and minced
- Salt and ground black pepper, to taste

Directions:

In a bowl, mix the mushrooms with the parsley, garlic, salt, pepper, lemon juice and oil, toss well and serve after keeping the salad in the fridge for 4 hours.

Nutrition: Calories - 76, Fat - 1, Fiber - 2, Carbs - 3, Protein - 3

Baked Vegetable Mix
Preparation time: 10 minutes | Cooking time: 1 hour | Servings: 4

Ingredients:
- 2 cups cauliflower florets
- 8 medium potatoes, well-scrubbed
- 2 cups white mushrooms, cut in quarters
- 6 tomatoes, cubed
- 1 small garlic clove, peeled and minced
- 1 onion, peeled and chopped
- 3 tablespoons fresh basil, chopped
- 3 tablespoons fresh parsley, chopped

Directions:
Place the potatoes in the oven at 350°F, bake for 45 minutes, peel them, arrange them on a lined baking sheet. Add the cauliflower, mushrooms, tomatoes, onion, garlic, salt, pepper, basil and parsley, toss and bake at 350°F for 15 minutes. Divide between plates and serve.

Nutrition: Calories - 215, Fat - 2, Fiber - 5, Carbs - 10, Protein - 9

Carrot Pancakes
Preparation time: 10 minutes | Cooking time: 10 minutes | Servings: 4

Ingredients:
- 1 carrot, grated
- 10 medium potatoes, grated
- 1 onion, peeled and chopped
- 5 garlic cloves, peeled and minced
- 1 tablespoon fresh dill, chopped
- 1 tablespoon fresh parsley, chopped
- 2 tablespoons lemon juice
- 2 tablespoons almond flour
- ¼ cup extra virgin olive oil
- Salt and ground black pepper, to taste
- ¼ cup olive oil, for frying

Directions:
In a bowl, mix the carrot with the onion, potatoes, parsley, dill, garlic, lemon juice, flour, ¼-cup olive oil, salt, and pepper and stir well. Heat a pan with the rest of the oil over medium heat, drop spoonfuls of potato pancake batter into circular shapes, cook for 4 minutes, flip, cook for another 4 minutes, transfer to plates, and serve warm.

Nutrition: Calories - 60, Fat - 3, Fiber - 1, Carbs - 6, Protein - 1.3

Kale Hummus

Preparation time: 10 minutes | Cooking time: 7 minutes | Servings: 2

Ingredients:

- 2 cups kale, chopped
- 1 teaspoon olive oil
- 1 garlic clove, peeled and minced
- Salt and ground black pepper, to taste

Directions:

Heat a pan with the olive oil over medium-high heat, add the kale, garlic, salt and pepper, stir, and cook for 7 minutes. Transfer to a blender, pulse well and serve as a spread.

Nutrition: Calories - 93, Fat - 5, Fiber - 3, Carbs - 9, Protein - 4

Balsamic Green Salad

Preparation time: 10 minutes | Cooking time: 0 minutes | Servings: 4

Ingredients:

-
- 4 cups salad greens
- 1 scallion, chopped

For the salad dressing:

- 2 tablespoons Dijon mustard
- 2 tablespoons balsamic vinegar
- 2 figs, sliced
- ½ teaspoon garlic powder
- Salt and ground black pepper, to taste

Directions:

In a salad bowl, mix the salad greens with scallions and figs. Add the mustard, the vinegar, salt, pepper and garlic powder, toss well and serve.

Nutrition: Calories - 130, Fat - 3, Fiber - 1, Carbs - 5, Protein - 7

Grilled Asparagus

Preparation time: 10 minutes | Cooking time: 8 minutes | Servings: 4

Ingredients:

- 4 tablespoons tapioca flour
- A pinch of salt and black pepper
- ½ teaspoon garlic powder
- 10 asparagus spears, trimmed
- 1 tablespoon water

Directions:

In a bowl, mix the flour with the salt, black pepper, garlic powder, and water and stir well. Dredge the asparagus in this mixture, place on preheated grill over medium-high heat, cook for 4 minutes on each side, divide between plates, and serve.

Nutrition: Calories - 140, Fat - 2, Fiber - 1, Carbs - 3, Protein - 5

Arugula Dressing

Preparation time: 10 minutes | Cooking time: 0 minutes | Servings: 3

Ingredients:

- ¼ cup nutritional yeast
- 1½ cups cashews, roasted
- 1 garlic clove, peeled
- 3 cups arugula
- 2 tablespoons lemon juice
- ¼ cup olive oil
- Salt and ground black pepper

Directions:

In a blender, mix the yeast with the cashews and garlic, olive oil, lemon juice, salt, pepper and arugula, pulse well, divide into bowls and serve.

Nutrition: Calories - 75, Fat - 0, Fiber - 3, Carbs - 4, Protein - 6

Spiced Cauliflower Soup

Preparation time: 10 minutes | Cooking time: 25 minutes | Servings: 4

Ingredients:

- 2 white onions, peeled and sliced
- 2 tablespoons olive oil
- 1 cauliflower head, florets separated
- 4 garlic cloves, peeled and chopped
- Salt and ground black pepper
- 4½ cups vegetable stock

- ½ teaspoon coriander
- ½ teaspoon turmeric
- 1¼ teaspoon cumin
- 1 cup coconut milk
- ¼ cup toasted cashews, cut in half
- ¼ cup fresh parsley, chopped

Directions:

Heat a pot with the oil over medium heat, add the onions, stir, and cook for 8 minutes. Add the garlic, cauliflower, stock, turmeric, coriander, and cumin, bring to a boil, and simmer for 15 minutes. Transfer to a food processor, pulse, return to the pot, heat again over medium heat, add the coconut milk, salt, and pepper, stir, and ladle into soup bowls. Sprinkle parsley and cashews on top and serve.

Nutrition: Calories - 174, Fat - 3, Fiber - 3, Carbs - 7, Protein - 6

Vegetable Soup

Preparation time: 10 minutes | Cooking time: 20 minutes | Servings: 6

Ingredients:

- 1 onion, peeled and chopped
- 2 teaspoons olive oil
- 3 celery stalks, chopped
- 1 teaspoon fresh thyme, chopped
- 3 garlic cloves, peeled and minced
- 6 cups vegetable stock
- 5 small red potatoes, cubed
- ½ pound green beans, chopped
- 6 ounces spinach, torn
- A pinch of salt and ground black pepper

Directions:

Heat a pot with the oil over medium heat, add the celery and onion, stir, and cook for 8 minutes. Add the thyme, garlic, stock and potatoes, bring to a boil, and simmer for 5 minutes. Add the green beans, salt and black pepper and simmer for 10 minutes. Add the spinach, stir, cook for 3 minutes, ladle into soup bowls, and serve.

Nutrition: Calories - 154, Fat - 3, Fiber - 4, Carbs - 6, Protein – 5

Minty Bell Pepper Salad

Preparation time: 10 minutes | Cooking time: 0 minutes | Servings: 4

Ingredients:

- 1 onion, peeled and chopped
- ½ cup sun-dried tomatoes, chopped
- 1 yellow bell pepper, seeded and cut into strips
- 1 red bell pepper, seeded and cut into strips
- 1 orange bell pepper, seeded and cut into strips
- 2 tablespoons olive oil
- 1 cup fresh parsley, chopped
- 1 cup toasted walnuts, chopped
- 1 cup mint leaves, chopped
- Juice and zest of 1 lemon
- Salt and ground black pepper, to taste

Directions:

Put the sun-dried tomatoes in a bowl, cover with some boiling water, set aside for a few minutes, drain and put in a salad bowl. Add onion, yellow bell pepper, red bell pepper, orange bell pepper, parsley, mint, walnuts, lemon zest and juice, salt, pepper, the oil, toss well and serve cold.

Nutrition: Calories - 121, Fat - 3, Fiber - 4, Carbs - 6, Protein - 8

Potato Cream Soup
Preparation time: 10 minutes | Cooking time: 25 minutes | Servings: 4

Ingredients:

- 3 tablespoons olive oil
- 1 garlic clove, peeled and minced
- 2 sweet potatoes, chopped
- 1 onion, peeled and chopped
- 3 cups tomato juice
- 4 ounces green chilies, chopped
- 15 ounces vegetable stock
- 1 teaspoon allspice
- A pinch of salt and ground black pepper
- 2 teaspoons fresh ginger, grated
- 1 tablespoon parsley, chopped

Directions:

Arrange the potatoes on a lined baking sheet, place in the oven at 350°F, bake for 10 minutes, and set aside to cool down. Heat a Dutch oven with 1 tablespoon oil over a medium heat, add the onion, and brown for 4 minutes. Add the garlic, tomato juice, green chilies, allspice, and ginger, stir, and cook for 10 minutes. Add half of the potatoes, stir, and cook for a few minutes. Put the other half of the potatoes in a food processor, add the stock, salt, pepper and the rest of the oil, pulse well. Add this to the pot, stir well, ladle into soup bowls, sprinkle with the parsley on top and serve.

Nutrition: Calories - 153, Fat - 3, Fiber - 3, Carbs - 5, Protein - 8

Eggplant and Lettuce Salad

Preparation time: 10 minutes | Cooking time: 20 minutes | Servings: 4

Ingredients:

- 4 tablespoons olive oil
- 2½ teaspoons curry powder
- 2½ teaspoons chili powder
- 2 eggplants, cubed
- ¼ cup Whole Food salsa
- ⅓ cup lime juice
- Salt and ground black pepper, to taste
- 4 cups romaine lettuce leaves, torn
- 3 green onions, chopped
- 2 mangos, peeled and chopped
- ¼ cup fresh cilantro, chopped

Directions:

In a bowl, mix 1 tablespoon oil with 2 teaspoons chili powder, 2 teaspoons curry powder and eggplant pieces, toss to coat. Spread them on a lined baking sheet, place in the oven at 400°F, and bake for 15 minutes. In another bowl, mix the rest of the oil with the rest of the chili and curry powder, lime juice, salsa, salt and pepper and whisk well. Add the eggplant pieces, green onions, mango, lettuce and cilantro, toss and serve.

Nutrition: Calories - 232, Fat - 3, Fiber - 4, Carbs - 6, Protein - 9

Lime Cantaloupe Soup

Preparation time: 10 minutes | Cooking time: 0 minutes | Servings: 2

Ingredients:

- ⅓ cup orange juice
- 1 chilled cantaloupe, peeled and cut into medium-sized chunks
- 1 teaspoon lime juice
- 1-teaspoon lime zest

Directions:

In a food processor, mix the cantaloupe with the orange juice, pulse well, and divide into bowls, drizzle lime juice, lime zest all over, and serve cold.

Nutrition: Calories - 81, Fat - 0, Fiber - 2, Carbs - 6, Protein - 2

Mushroom Soup
Preparation time: 10 minutes | Cooking time: 27 minutes | Servings: 4

Ingredients:

- 2 onions, peeled and chopped
- 1½ tablespoons olive oil
- Salt and ground black pepper, to taste
- 1 carrot, peeled and chopped
- 20 ounces button mushrooms, sliced
- 2 celery stalks, chopped
- 5 cups vegetable stock
- 2 teaspoons fresh thyme, chopped

Directions:

Heat a pot over medium heat with the oil, add the onions, salt, and pepper, stir, and cook for 7 minutes. Add the celery, carrot and mushrooms stir, cover, and cook for 10 minutes. Add the stock and thyme, cook for 10 minutes, ladle into bowls, and serve.

Nutrition: Calories - 143, Fat - 4, Fiber - 3, Carbs - 6, Protein - 5

Green Bean Soup
Preparation time: 10 minutes | Cooking time: 6 minutes | Servings: 3

Ingredients:

- 1 teaspoon fresh ginger, grated
- 1 tablespoon red curry paste
- 2 cups vegetable stock
- Salt and ground black pepper
- 14 ounces coconut milk
- ½ pound white mushrooms, sliced
- 2 carrots, sliced
- 4 ounces green beans, halved
- 2 tablespoons lime juice
- ¼ cup fresh cilantro, chopped

Directions:

Put the ginger and curry paste in a pot, stir, heat over medium heat, add the stock, salt, pepper, and coconut milk, stir, and bring to a boil. Add the green beans, mushrooms, lime juice and carrots, stir, and simmer for 5 minutes. Ladle into soup bowls, sprinkle the cilantro on top and serve.

Nutrition: Calories - 121, Fat - 2, Fiber - 3, Carbs - 4, Protein - 10

Spiced Vegetables

*Preparation time: 10 minutes | **Cooking time:** 45 minutes | **Servings:** 4*

Ingredients:

- 1 onion, peeled and chopped
- 1 tablespoon olive oil
- 3 garlic cloves, peeled and minced
- 1 teaspoon smoked paprika
- 3 carrots, peeled and sliced
- 1 tablespoon dried thyme
- 2 celery stalks, chopped
- 1 red bell pepper, seeded and chopped
- 1 yellow bell pepper, seeded and chopped
- 28 ounces canned diced tomatoes
- 8 ounces vegetable stock
- 2 zucchinis, sliced
- Salt and ground black pepper, to taste

Directions:

Heat a pot with the olive oil over medium-high heat, add the onions, stir, and cook for 10 minutes. Add the garlic, paprika, thyme, carrots, bell peppers, and celery, stir, and cook for 5 minutes. Add the stock, tomatoes, salt, pepper and zucchini, stir, cook for 25 minutes, divide between plates, and serve.

Nutrition: Calories - 200, Fat - 2, Fiber - 1, Carbs - 5, Protein - 10

Mediterranean Salad

*Preparation time: 10 minutes | **Cooking time:** 0 minutes | **Servings:** 4*

Ingredients:

-
- 2 heads romaine lettuce, torn
- 1 cucumber, chopped
- 2 cups cherry tomatoes chopped

For the salad dressing:

- ¼ cup olive oil
- 3 garlic cloves, peeled and chopped
- 3 tablespoons lemon juice
- 1 shallot, sliced
- ¼ cup Kalamata olives, pitted and chopped
- Salt and ground black pepper, to taste
- 2 tablespoons mustard
- ¼ cup fresh basil, chopped

Directions:

In a bowl, mix the lettuce with the cucumber, tomatoes, shallot and olives. In another bowl, mix the garlic with the oil, lemon juice, salt, pepper, basil and mustard, whisk well, and add to the salad, toss and serve.

Nutrition: Calories - 132, Fat - 3, Fiber - 3, Carbs - 4, Protein – 8

Watercress Soup

Preparation time: 10 minutesn | Cooking time: 40 minutes | Servings: 4

Ingredients:

- 2 potatoes, chopped
- 2 onions, chopped
- 2 garlic cloves, peeled and minced
- 1 teaspoon olive oil
- 14 ounces vegetable stock
- 3 bunches watercress, chopped
- Salt and ground black pepper, to taste

Directions:

Heat a pot with the olive oil over medium heat. Add the potato, garlic, and onion, stir, and cook for 6 minutes. Add the stock, bring to a boil, and simmer for 25 minutes. Add the watercress, salt and pepper, cook for 5 minutes, transfer to a food processor. Pulse well until you obtain a creamy soup, divide into bowls and serve.

Nutrition: Calories - 200, Fat - 2, Fiber - 2, Carbs - 4, Protein - 8

Mixed Vegetable Salad

Preparation time: 10 minutes | Cooking time: 40 minutes | Servings: 4

Ingredients:

- 6 tomatoes, cored and cut in half
- 2 onions, peeled and cut into quarters
- 4 red bell peppers
- 2 yellow bell peppers
- 6 garlic cloves, peeled
- 1 tablespoon capers, drained
- 1 teaspoon hot paprika
- 4 tablespoons
- Juice of ½ lime
- Salt and ground black pepper, to taste

Directions:

Arrange the tomatoes, bell peppers, garlic cloves, and onions on a lined baking sheet, season with salt and pepper, drizzle half of the oil, toss and bake in the oven at 375°F for 40 minutes. Take the peppers out of the oven, peel them, cut into thin strips, and put them, the tomatoes, onions and garlic in a salad bowl. Add the capers, paprika, and the rest of the oil, lemon juice, salt, and pepper, toss to coat, and serve.

Nutrition: Calories - 159, Fat - 3, Fiber - 4, Carbs - 7, Protein - 4

Jambalaya

Preparation time: 10 minutes | Cooking time: 40 minutes | Servings: 4

Ingredients:

- ½ cup onions, chopped
- 1 butternut squash, peeled and cubed
- 1 tablespoon olive oil
- ½ cup green bell pepper, seeded and chopped
- ¼ cup red bell pepper, seeded and chopped
- 1 garlic clove, peeled and minced
- ¼ cup celery, chopped
- ½ cup tomatoes, chopped
- 2 cups vegetable stock
- 1 teaspoon garlic powder
- 1 teaspoon sweet paprika
- 1 cup tomato sauce, unsweetened
- ½ teaspoon dried oregano
- ½ teaspoon dried thyme
- ½ teaspoon onion powder
- Salt and ground black pepper, to taste

Directions:

Heat a pan with the oil over medium-high heat, add the bell peppers, onions, and celery, stir, and cook for 3-4 minutes. Add the squash, garlic, and tomatoes, stir, and cook for 3 minutes more. Add the tomato sauce, stock, garlic powder, paprika, thyme, oregano, onion powder, salt, pepper and stir. Bring to a boil, reduce heat to medium, simmer for 30 minutes, divide between plates and serve.

Nutrition: Calories - 200, Fat - 2, Fiber - 2, Carbs - 5, Protein - 8

Almond Bell Pepper Cream

Preparation time: 10 minutes | Cooking time: 50 minutes | Servings: 4

Ingredients:

- 2 tablespoons olive oil
- 5 red bell peppers
- 1 onion, peeled and chopped
- 2 garlic cloves, peeled and minced
- 2 tablespoons tapioca flour
- 2 tablespoons balsamic vinegar
- Salt and ground black pepper, to taste
- 2 cups vegetable stock
- 1½ cups almond milk
- ¼ cup fresh cilantro, chopped

Directions:

Arrange the bell peppers on a lined baking sheet, place in the oven at 400°F, bake for 40 minutes. Peel, chop, and put them in a bowl. Heat a pan with the oil over medium heat, add the onion and garlic, stir, and cook for 5 minutes. Add the salt, pepper, tapioca, vinegar, stock, and bell peppers, stir, bring to a boil, reduce to a simmer, and cook for 5 minutes. Take the soup off the heat, add the almond milk, stir, transfer to a blender, pulse well, ladle into serving bowls, top with the cilantro and serve.

Nutrition: Calories - 200, Fat - 3, Fiber - 4, Carbs - 6, Protein - 9

Cold Avocado Gazpacho

Preparation time: 10 minutes | Cooking time: 0 minutes | Servings: 4

Ingredients:

- 6 scallions, chopped
- 2 garlic cloves, peeled and minced
- 2 avocados, peeled, pitted, and chopped
- ¼ teaspoon cumin
- 1 tablespoon lime juice
- 2¾ cups vegetable stock
- 1 cup coconut milk
- Salt and ground black pepper, to taste
- ½ cup fresh cilantro, chopped
- 6 cherry tomatoes, chopped

Directions:

In a blender, mix the scallions with the garlic, avocado, cumin, lime juice, stock, milk, salt and pepper, pulse well, divide into bowls, sprinkle the tomato pieces and the cilantro on top and serve cold.

Nutrition: Calories - 100, Fat - 4, Fiber - 4, Carbs - 6, Protein - 9

Cream of Cabbage Soup

Preparation time: 10 minutes | *Cooking time:* 20 minutes | *Servings:* 4

Ingredients:

- 2 onions, peeled and chopped
- 1 pound cabbage, shredded
- 2 cups chicken stock
- 2 garlic cloves, peeled and minced
- Salt and ground black pepper, to taste
- ½ cup parsley, chopped

Directions:

Put the cabbage in a pot, add the garlic, onions, stock, salt, and pepper. Stir, bring to a boil over medium heat, cover, simmer for 20 minutes. Transfer to a food processor, pulse well, add the parsley, ladle into soup bowls, and serve.

Nutrition: Calories - 100, Fat - 3, Fiber - 2, carb 4, Protein - 8

Creamy Mushroom Mix

Preparation time: 10 minutes | *Cooking time:* 20 minutes | *Servings:* 4

Ingredients:

- 1 tablespoon coconut oil, melted
- 1 onion, peeled and chopped
- 2 cups vegetable stock
- 3 tablespoons coconut flour
- 1 teaspoon lemon juice
- 1 tablespoon coconut aminos
- 1 teaspoon tomato paste
- ½ teaspoon dried thyme
- 1½ pounds button mushrooms, cut in half
- Salt and ground black pepper, to taste
- 1 tablespoon white vinegar
- ¼ cup fresh parsley, chopped

Directions:

Heat a pan with the olive oil over medium heat, add the onions, stir, and cook for 3 minutes. Add the flour, stock, lemon juice, aminos, tomato paste, stir well, and cook for 1 minute. Add the salt, pepper, mushrooms, thyme, and vinegar, stir, and cook for 10 minutes. Add the parsley, stir, cook for 5 extra minutes, transfer to plates, and serve.

Nutrition: Calories - 200, Fat - 4, Fiber - 1, Carbs - 7, Protein - 9

Chinese Mushroom Soup

Preparation time: 10 minutes | Cooking time: 21 minutes | Servings: 4

Ingredients:

- 6 green onions, sliced
- 64 ounces vegetable stock
- Salt and black pepper to taste
- 1 tablespoon fresh ginger, grated
- 6 ounces shiitake mushrooms
- 2 teaspoons olive oil
- 8 ounces Brussels sprouts, chopped
- 2 jalapeño peppers, sliced
- 1½ tablespoon olive oil
- 1 tablespoon fresh cilantro, chopped
- 1 tablespoon fresh basil, chopped
- 1 lime, cut in wedges, for serving

Directions:

Put the stock in a pot, heat over medium-high heat, add the ginger, salt, and green onions, stir, bring to a boil, reduce heat, and simmer for 15 minutes. Heat a pan with the oil over medium heat, add the mushrooms, stir, and cook for 6 minutes. Ladle the stock into a bowl; add the mushrooms, sprouts, jalapeños, basil and cilantro, and serve with lime wedges.

Nutrition: Calories - 200, Fat - 4, Fiber - 1, Carbs - 5, Protein – 9

Jicama and Cabbage Salad

Preparation time: 10 minutes | Cooking time: 0 minutes | Servings: 4

Ingredients:

-
- 2 tablespoons lime juice
- 1 garlic clove, peeled and minced
- 1 red chili pepper, sliced
- 2 teaspoons coconut aminos
- 1 grapefruit, peeled, and cut into segments
- 1 Jicama bulb, cut into sticks
- 2 cups napa cabbage, shredded
- ½ cup fresh cilantro, chopped
- ¼ cup cashews, roasted and crushed
- 2 tablespoons shallots, chopped

Directions:

In a bowl, mix the Jicama with the cabbage, shallots, grapefruit, chili pepper and garlic. Add lime juice, aminos, cashews and cilantro, toss and serve.

Nutrition: Calories - 124, Fat - 1, Fiber - 1, Carbs - 2, Protein - 4

Green and Fruit Salad

Preparation time: 10 minutes | Cooking time: 0 minutes | Servings: 4

Ingredients:

- 1 tablespoon avocado oil
- A pinch of black pepper
- 3 plums, pitted and sliced
- 1 tablespoon balsamic vinegar
- 8 cups mixed greens
- 2 nectarines, peeled and sliced
- 2 apricots, pitted and sliced
- 2 peaches, pitted and sliced
- ¾ cup cherries, pitted and cut in half

Directions:

In a bowl, mix the greens with the plums, nectarines, apricots, peaches, cherries, and almonds. Add vinegar, black pepper and oil, toss to coat, and serve.

Nutrition: Calories - 110, Fat - 2, Fiber - 1, Carbs - 1, Protein - 4

Baked Rosemary Zucchini

Preparation time: 10 minutes | Cooking time: 20 minutes | Servings: 4

Ingredients:

- 1 onion, sliced
- 4 zucchinis, chopped
- 1 tablespoon lemon rind, grated
- 1 tablespoon olive oil
- ¼ cup lemon juice
- 2 tablespoon rosemary, chopped
- Salt and ground black pepper, to taste

Directions:

Put the zucchini in a baking dish, add salt, pepper, onion, lemon juice, oil, and lemon rind, toss, place in the oven at 400°F, and bake for 18 minutes. Divide between plates, sprinkle rosemary on top, and serve.

Nutrition: Calories - 100, Fat - 2, Fiber - 3, Carbs - 4, Protein - 4

Parsnip and Pear Mix
Preparation time: 10 minutes | Cooking time: 1 hour | Servings: 4

Ingredients:

- 4 parsnips, peeled and cut into medium wedges
- 1 onion, cut into wedges
- 1 red pear, cored and cut into wedges
- ⅓ cup sage leaves
- ¼ teaspoon red chili flakes
- 2 tablespoons olive oil
- A pinch of salt and ground black pepper

Directions:

In a bowl, mix the pear with the parsnips, onion, sage, chili flakes, oil salt and black pepper. Toss to coat, arrange on a lined baking sheet, place in the oven at 300°F, and bake for 1 hour. Divide between plates and serve hot.

Nutrition: Calories - 200, Fat - 2, Fiber - 3, Carbs - 6, Protein - 8

Celeriac and Olive Salad
Preparation time: 10 minutes | Cooking time: 0 minutes | Servings: 4

Ingredients:

- 1 celeriac, peeled and cut into sticks
- 2 tablespoons lemon juice
- 4 oranges, peeled and sliced
- 10 green olives, pitted and sliced
- 1 onion, peeled and sliced
- 2 ounces baby spinach
- ⅓ cup orange juice
- 1 tablespoon balsamic vinegar
- Salt and ground black pepper, to taste
- 2 teaspoons olive oil

Directions:

In a bowl, mix the orange slices, baby spinach, onion, olives and celeriac. In a smaller bowl, mix the orange juice with the olive oil, lemon juice, salt, pepper, and vinegar, whisk well. Drizzle this dressing over salad, toss to coat, and serve.

Nutrition: Calories - 121, Fat - 2, Fiber - 2, Carbs - 5, Protein - 8

Peach Salsa

Preparation time: 10 minutes | Cooking time: 0 minutes | Servings: 3

Ingredients:

- 2 jalapeños, chopped
- 1-inch lemongrass, minced
- 3 peaches, pitted and chopped
- 1 tablespoon fresh basil, chopped
- Salt and ground black pepper, to taste
- 1 tablespoon balsamic vinegar
- 2 tablespoons olive oil

Directions:

In a bowl, mix the lemongrass with the jalapeños and stir. In a bowl, mix the peaches with the basil, lemongrass mixture, salt, pepper, vinegar, and oil, toss well, and serve.

Nutrition: Calories - 100, Fat - 2, Fiber - 1, Carbs - 1, Protein - 2

Cold Garlic Mushroom Mix

Preparation time: 4 hours and 10 minutes | Cooking time: 0 minutes | Servings: 6

Ingredients:

-
- 5 pounds mushrooms, sliced
- 2 cups olive oil
- 2 bunches fresh parsley, chopped
- 1 cup lemon juice
- 8 garlic cloves, peeled and minced
- Salt and ground black pepper, to taste

Directions:

In a bowl, mix the oil with the parsley, lemon juice, salt, black pepper, garlic and mushrooms. Toss well and keep in the refrigerator for 4 hours before serving.

Nutrition: Calories - 90, Fat - 1, Fiber - 2, Carbs - 3, Protein - 3

Balsamic Beet Mix

Preparation time: 10 minutes | *Cooking time:* 50 minutes | *Servings:* 4

Ingredients:

- 4 red beets
- 1 avocado, pitted and cubed
- 1 tablespoon + 1 teaspoon olive oil
- 1 teaspoon balsamic vinegar
- 2 teaspoon lemon juice
- Sea Salt and black pepper
- ½ bunch fresh parsley, chopped

Directions:

Rub the beets with 1 tablespoon olive oil. Arrange in a pan, cover with the aluminum foil, place in the oven at 400°F, and bake for 50 minutes. Peel, cool down, cut into small pieces and put in a bowl. In a smaller bowl, mix the lemon juice with the salt, pepper, and 1 teaspoon olive oil and stir well. Add the avocado, the beets and the parsley, toss and serve

Nutrition: Calories - 127, Fat - 2, Fiber - 1, Carbs - 4, Protein – 6

Mustard and Gold Potato Salad

Preparation time: 10 minutes | *Cooking time:* 25 minutes | *Servings:* 4

Ingredients:

-
- 2 pounds gold potatoes, cut into quarters
- 3 tablespoons vegetable stock
- ¼ cup balsamic vinegar
- 1 teaspoon Dijon mustard
- A pinch of salt and black pepper
- ⅓ cup green onions, chopped

Directions:

Put the potatoes in a pot, add the water to cover, bring to a boil over medium heat. Cook for 25 minutes, drain, peel them, cut into medium-sized pieces and put them in a bowl. Add mustard, stock, vinegar, salt, and pepper, and green onions, toss and serve cold.

Nutrition: Calories - 110, Fat - 3, Fiber - 2, Carbs - 5, Protein - 9

Avocado and Asparagus Soup

Preparation time: 5 minutes | Cooking time: 0 minutes | Servings: 2

Ingredients:

- 8 ounces mushrooms, chopped
- 12 asparagus spears, trimmed
- 1 avocado, pitted and peeled
- A pinch of salt and white pepper
- 1 yellow onion, peeled and chopped
- 3 cups vegetable stock

Directions:

In a blender, mix the mushrooms with the asparagus, avocado, onion, stock, salt, and pepper and puree well. Ladle into soup bowls and serve.

Nutrition: Calories - 124, Fat - 2, Fiber - 2, Carbs - 4, Protein - 5

Carrot Cream

Preparation time: 10 minutes | Cooking time: 5 minutes | Servings: 2

Ingredients:

- 1 garlic clove, peeled and minced
- 2 celery stalks, chopped
- 1 avocado, pitted, peeled, and chopped
- 4 carrots, peeled and chopped
- A pinch of salt and black pepper
- 4 tablespoons + ½ teaspoon olive oil
- 1 green onion, chopped
- 1½ cups water
- 1 tomato, cored and chopped

Directions:

In a blender, mix the celery with the avocado, carrots, garlic, salt, 4 tablespoons oil, onion, and water, pulse well, transfer this to a pot. Stir, heat for a few minutes over medium heat, ladle into soup bowls, garnish with the tomato and drizzle the rest of the oil all over and serve.

Tomato Gazpacho

Preparation time: 5 minutes | Cooking time: 0 minutes | Servings: 2

Ingredients:

- 1 red bell pepper, seeded and chopped
- 3 tomatoes, cored and chopped
- 4 tablespoons sesame paste
- 2 carrots, peeled and chopped
- Juice of 1 lime
- 1 teaspoon chili pepper
- A pinch of sea salt and black pepper
- 1 garlic clove, peeled and minced
- 1 tablespoon olive oil
- 4 tablespoons celery, chopped

Directions:

In a blender, mix the bell pepper with the tomatoes, sesame paste, carrots, lime juice, chili pepper, salt, pepper, garlic, oil and celery, pulse well, divide into bowls and serve cold.

Nutrition: Calories - 110, Fat - 1, Fiber - 2, Carbs - 4, Protein - 1

Mango and Squash Soup

Preparation time: 10 minutes | Cooking time: 0 minutes | Servings: 2

Ingredients:

- 3 cups orange juice
- 2 cups butternut squash, peeled, seeded and chopped
- 1 mango, chopped
- A pinch of ground nutmeg
- A pinch of ground cinnamon

Directions:

In a blender, mix the squash with orange juice, mango, nutmeg and cinnamon, pulse well, divide into bowls and serve.

Nutrition: Calories - 121, Fat - 1, Fiber - 2, Carbs - 4, Protein - 6

Tomato and Olive Salad

Preparation time: 10 minutes | Cooking time: 0 minutes | Servings: 4

Ingredients:

- 2 tomatoes, cored and cut into small wedges
- 2 bell peppers, seeded and chopped
- 1 cucumber, chopped
- 1 small onion, sliced thin
- ½ cup Kalamata olives, pitted and sliced
- ¼ cup lemon juice
- ½ cup olive oil
- 1 tablespoon fresh oregano, chopped
- Salt and ground black pepper, to taste
- 2 garlic cloves, peeled and minced

Directions:

In a bowl, mix the tomatoes with the bell peppers, cucumber, onion, olives, lemon juice, oil, oregano, salt, pepper and garlic, toss well and serve.

Nutrition: Calories - 165, Fat - 3, Fiber - 1, Carbs - 2, Protein - 4

Spinach and Bacon Salad

Preparation time: 10 minutes | Cooking time: 0 minutes | Servings: 4

Ingredients:

- Salt and ground black pepper, to taste
- 6 bacon slices, cooked and crumbled
- 2 tablespoons red vinegar
- 2 tablespoons extra virgin olive oil
- 2 scallions, chopped
- 6 cups baby spinach

Directions:

In a salad bowl, mix the spinach with the scallions, vinegar, oil, salt, pepper and the bacon, toss and serve.

Nutrition: Calories - 156, Fat - 4, Fiber - 2, Carbs - 2, Protein - 1

Rosemary Potato Wedges

Preparation time: 10 minutes | Cooking time: 45 minutes | Servings: 8

Ingredients:

- 3 pounds assorted potatoes, cut into medium wedges
- Salt and ground black pepper, to taste
- 1 garlic head
- 1 tablespoon fresh rosemary, chopped
- 3 tablespoons olive oil

Directions:

Place the potatoes in a baking pan, add the garlic, sprinkle the rosemary, season with salt and pepper, drizzle with the oil, toss well, and bake in the oven at 400°F for 45 minutes. Transfer the potatoes to a platter, squeeze garlic on top, and serve.

Nutrition: Calories - 142, Fat - 1, Fiber - 2, Carbs - 3, Protein - 4

Japanese Seaweed Salad

Preparation time: 10 minutes | Cooking time: 5 minutes | Servings: 4

Ingredients:

-
- 2 tablespoons dried wakame seaweed
- 3 tablespoons coconut aminos
- 2 tablespoons balsamic vinegar
- 1 tablespoon olive oil
- 2 garlic cloves, peeled and minced
- 1 tablespoon arrowroot powder
- 1 teaspoon fresh ginger, grated
- 2 teaspoons sesame seeds

Directions:

Put the seaweed in a bowl, add the hot water to cover, set aside for a few seconds. Drain, rinse and put it in a pot. In a blender, mix the vinegar with the coconut aminos, ginger, and garlic and blend well. Add the dressing over the seaweed, bring to a boil over medium-high heat, simmer for 1 minute, add the arrowroot powder, simmer for 4 minutes more. Transfer to a bowl, sprinkle sesame seeds and oil and serve cold.

Nutrition: Calories - 140, Fat - 1, Fiber - 1, Carbs - 1, Protein - 5

Coconut Zucchini Soup

Preparation time: 10 minutes | Cooking time: 12 minutes | Servings: 4

Ingredients:

- 2 tablespoons olive oil
- 2 tablespoons green curry paste
- 1 cup shallots, chopped
- 6 zucchinis, chopped
- 1 cup coconut milk
- 1 cup water
- Juice of 1 lime
- Salt and ground black pepper, to taste
- Roasted cherry tomatoes, for serving
- 1 tablespoon fresh cilantro, chopped, for serving

Directions:

Heat a pan with the olive oil over medium-high heat, add the shallots, salt, and pepper, stir, and cook for 2 minutes. Add the curry paste, and the zucchini, stir, and cook for 10 minutes. Add the coconut milk, lime juice, water, stir, bring to a simmer, and ladle into soup bowls. Serve with roasted tomatoes and chopped cilantro on top.

Nutrition: Calories - 140, Fat - 1, Fiber - 1, Carbs - 2, Protein – 6

Tomato Soup

Preparation time: 10 minutes | Cooking time: 35 minutes | Servings: 6

Ingredients:

- 2 cups yellow onion, sliced
- 2 cups tomatoes, diced
- 4 teaspoons olive oil
- A pinch of salt and ground black pepper
- 2 and ⅔ cups tomato juice
- 2 cups vegetable stock
- 2 tablespoons fresh basil, chopped
- 2 teaspoons fresh oregano, chopped

Directions:

Heat a pot with the oil over medium-high heat, add the onion, stir, and cook for 6 minutes. Add the water, tomato juice, salt and black pepper, basil, and oregano, stir, bring to a boil, reduce the heat to medium-low, and simmer for 20 minutes. Add the tomatoes, stir, cook for 10 minutes, ladle into soup bowls and serve.

Nutrition: Calories - 140, Fat - 1, Fiber - 1, Carbs - 0, Protein - 5

Tomato and Citrus Soup

Preparation time: 10 minutes | Cooking time: 1 hour and 10 minutes | Servings: 4

Ingredients:

- 1½ pounds small tomatoes, cut in halves
- 4 tablespoons extra virgin olive oil
- 2 garlic cloves, diced
- 2 yellow onions, diced
- Salt and ground black pepper, to taste
- 2 carrots, diced
- 1 celery stalk, chopped
- 3 ounces orange juice
- 20 ounces vegetable stock
- Zest of 1 orange

Directions:

Arrange the tomatoes on a lined baking sheet, spread garlic, drizzle half of the oil, add the salt and pepper, place in the oven at 350°F and bake for 45 minutes. Heat a pot with the rest of the oil over medium heat, add the onions, celery, and carrots, stir, reduce heat to low, and cook for 20 minutes. Add the roasted tomatoes and garlic, the stock and orange juice, stir well, bring to a boil, cook for 2 minutes. Take off the heat, transfer to a blender, pulse well, return it to the pot, heat up the soup again for a few minutes, ladle into bowls, and serve with the orange zest on top.

Nutrition: Calories - 140, Fat - 2, Fiber - 1, Carbs - 4, Protein - 6

Baked Eggplant Soup

Preparation time: 10 minutes | Cooking time: 35 minutes | Servings: 4

Ingredients:

- 2 pounds eggplants, pricked
- 2 cups yellow onion, sliced
- 5 tablespoons olive oil
- 6 garlic cloves, peeled and minced
- Salt and ground black pepper, to taste
- 4 tablespoons lemon juice
- ½ teaspoon lemon zest
- 6 cups vegetable stock
- 2 tablespoons fresh parsley, minced

Directions:

Arrange the eggplants on a baking sheet, place in a broiler, and cook them for 4 minutes on each side. Peel, chop, and transfer them to a bowl. Heat a pot with the 3 tablespoons oil over medium-high heat, add the onion, salt, and pepper, stir, and cook for 7 minutes. Add the garlic, eggplant, and the stock, bring to a boil, reduce heat to medium, and simmer for 10 minutes. Transfer the soup to a blender, pulse well, return to pot, add the lemon juice, stir again and ladle into bowls. In a bowl, mix the lemon zest with the rest of the olive oil, and whisk. Drizzle this over the soup, sprinkle parsley on top, and serve.

Nutrition: Calories - 180, Fat - 3, Fiber - 3, Carbs - 5, Protein - 9

Creamy Mushroom Stew

Preparation time: 10 minutes | Cooking time: 20 minutes | Servings: 3

Ingredients:

- 1 teaspoon olive oil
- 1 garlic clove, peeled and chopped
- 1 onion, sliced
- 1-inch fresh ginger, peeled and grated
- 1 green chili pepper, chopped
- ½ teaspoon garam masala
- ¼ teaspoon ground cinnamon
- 5 ounces coconut milk
- 1 teaspoon almonds, flaked
- 6 ounces mushrooms, sliced
- Salt and ground black pepper, to taste

Directions:

Heat a pan with the oil over a low heat, add the onion, chili, ginger, garlic, salt, pepper, garam masala and cinnamon, stir, and cook for 3 minutes. Add the milk, cook for 7 minutes, transfer to a blender, pulse well, and set aside. Heat the same pan at a medium temperature, add the mushrooms, and cook for 2-3 minutes. Add the coconut sauce, stir, cook for 8 minutes, divide into bowls and serve with almond flakes on top.

Nutrition: Calories - 173, Fat - 4, Fiber - 5, Carbs - 10, Protein - 12

Simple Veggie Stir-fry

Preparation time: 10 minutes | Cooking time: 35 minutes | Servings: 2

Ingredients:

- 9 ounces beet, chopped
- 12 ounces butternut squash, chopped
- 1 onion, peeled and chopped
- 1 garlic clove, peeled and chopped
- ¼ teaspoon cumin seeds
- ½ teaspoon ground cinnamon
- 1 tablespoon olive oil
- 3 ounces green beans, cut in half
- 1.5 ounces spinach, chopped
- A small bunch fresh parsley, chopped
- Salt and ground black pepper, to taste
- 1-cup veggie stock

Directions:

Heat a large pan with the oil over medium-high heat, add the onion and the garlic, stir and cook for 5 minutes. Add the cumin seeds, the cinnamon, salt and pepper, stir and cook for 5 minutes more. Add the beets, the squash, green beans, and the stock, toss, cover the pan, reduce heat to low and cook for 20 minutes. Add the spinach and the parsley, toss, cook for 5 minutes more, divide between plates and serve.

Nutrition: Calories - 220, Fat - 3, Fiber - 3, Carbs - 10, Protein - 12

Baked Potato Salad

Preparation time: 10 minutes | Cooking time: 25 minutes | Servings: 4

Ingredients:

- 4 gold potatoes, chopped
- 2 rosemary sprigs, chopped
- 1 tablespoon balsamic vinegar
- 2 teaspoons mustard
- 1 teaspoon shallot, sliced
- 1 teaspoon fresh parsley, chopped
- 2 tablespoons olive oil
- Salt and ground black pepper, to taste
- 1 onion, peeled and chopped
- 2 leaf lettuce heads, leaves separated
- 2 tomatoes, cored and cut into wedges

Directions:

Arrange the potatoes on a baking sheet, add half of the oil and rosemary sprigs, toss, and place in the oven at 375 ° F, bake for 25 minutes and transfer to a salad bowl. Add the tomatoes and the lettuce and toss. Add the vinegar, the mustard, shallot, onion, salt, pepper, parsley and the rest of the oil, toss and serve.

Nutrition: Calories - 241, Fat - 7, Fiber - 4, Carbs - 10, Protein - 14

Coconut Pumpkin Soup

Preparation time: 10 minutes | Cooking time: 15 minutes | Servings: 4

Ingredients:

- 2 tablespoons coconut oil, melted
- 1 cup onion, chopped
- 2 garlic cloves, peeled and minced
- 1½ cups vegetable stock
- 2 cups pumpkin puree
- ½ cup coconut cream
- Salt and ground black pepper, to taste
- ¼ cup parsley, chopped

Directions:

Heat a pot with the oil over medium heat, add the garlic, stir, and cook for 4 minutes. Add the stock, pumpkin puree, coconut cream, salt, and black pepper. Bring to a boil, and simmer for 10 minutes. Ladle into bowls, sprinkle parsley on top, and serve.

Nutrition: Calories - 100, Fat - 3, Fiber - 4, Carbs - 11, Protein - 4

Broccoli and Mayonnaise Salad

Preparation time: 10 minutes | Cooking time: 0 minutes | Servings: 6

Ingredients:

- ¼ cup homemade avocado mayonnaise
- 1 garlic clove, peeled and minced
- 6 cups broccoli florets, chopped
- 3 slices bacon, cooked and crumbled
- 2 teaspoons white vinegar
- ¼ cup coconut cream
- 3 tablespoons dried cranberries
- Salt and ground black pepper, to taste

Directions:

In a bowl, mix the mayonnaise with the garlic, vinegar, and coconut cream and whisk well. In a salad bowl, mix the broccoli with cranberries, bacon, salt, and pepper and toss. Add the mayonnaise mix, toss to coat, and serve cold.

Nutrition: Calories - 92, Fat - 5, Fiber - 2, Carbs - 11, Protein - 3

4 Week Meal Plan
Week one meal plan

DAY	BREAKFAST	LUNCH	DINNER	SNACK
Monday	Sweet Potato and Avocado Breakfast	Spiced Potato Cream	Shrimp, Avocado and Tomato Mix	Peach, Chive and Turkey Wraps
Tuesday	Mango Chicken Breakfast Balls	Tomato and Sweet Potato Bake	Chicken and Cilantro Marinade	Beef Nachos
Wednesday	Pineapple, Mango and Coconut Smoothie	Smoked Salmon Lunch Mix	Fruity Salmon Mix	Eggplant Appetizer
Thursday	Banana Pudding	Chicken and Lemongrass Soup	Mexican Beef Soup	Cucumber Bites
Friday	Strawberry and Chia Smoothie	Carrot and Coconut Cream	Salmon and Tomato Mix	Sweet Potato Bites
Saturday	Turkey and Apple Breakfast Cakes	Shrimp, Carrots and Cabbage Salad	Pork Chop with Baked Apples	Pineapple and Chicken Bites
Sunday	Grapes Smoothie	Citrus Lettuce Salad	Eggplant and Lettuce Salad	Tuna Cucumber Rounds

Week two meal plan

DAY	BREAKFAST	LUNCH	DINNER	SNACK
Monday	Blueberry Pudding	Lemony Salmon	Tuna and Lettuce Salad	Mango and Tomato Salad
Tuesday	Avocado Boats	Turkey Patties	Italian Chicken Mix	Basil Mushroom Salad
Wednesday	Chicken, Apple and Grape Salad	Kale and Chicken Soup	Cod and Cucumber Salad	Beef and Caper Tartar
Thursday	Almond Milk and Berries Smoothie Bowls	Sweet Potato and Apple Noodle Salad	Marsala Lamb	Smoked Salmon Platter
Friday	Cucumber and Ginger Smoothie	Tuna Lunch Mix	Shrimp and Bacon Cold Mix	Endive Appetizer Salad
Saturday	Apple and Spinach Smoothie	Sausage and Kale Lunch Mix	Pork Tenderloin with Date Sauce	Fresh Tomato Salad
Sunday	Pork and Chard Bowls	Carrot and Coconut Cream	Mushroom and Parsley Salad	Tuna Cube Salad

Week three meal plan

DAY	BREAKFAST	LUNCH	DINNER	SNACK
Monday	Banana Pudding	Beef Burgers	Shrimp and Veggie Salad	Roasted Beet Spread
Tuesday	Pumpkin and Almond Bowls	Spiced Potato Cream	Chicken and Collard Green Soup	Cucumber, Fennel and Chive Slaw
Wednesday	Beet and Cherry Smoothie Bowl	Flavoured Chicken Mix	Shrimp and Crab Salad	Zucchini and Green Onion Salad
Thursday	Strawberry and Chia Smoothie	Egg and Sausage Muffins	Pork Chops with Juniper Berries	Mango and Tomato Salad
Friday	Mango Chicken Breakfast Balls	Tomato and Sweet Potato Bake	Salmon Stew	Mushroom Bites
Saturday	Pumpkin and Coconut Shake	Purple Potato and Cauliflower Cream	Beef, Watercress and Radish Salad	Roasted Nut and Fruit Bowls
Sunday	Bacon Sandwich with Avocado Spread	Lemony Salmon	Dijon Fennel Salad	Nori Chips

Week four meal plan

DAY	BREAKFAST	LUNCH	DINNER	SNACK
Monday	Coconut, Almond and Cashew Porridge	Carrot and Coconut Cream	Rosemary Shrimp Mix	Coffee Balls
Tuesday	Coconut Banana Pudding	Greek Veggie Salad	Herbed Chicken Thighs	Stuffed Dates
Wednesday	Date and Walnut Granola	Cod and Fennel	Herbed Shrimp Mix	Beef Nachos
Thursday	Pear and Plum Smoothie	Leek and Broccoli Cream	Meatballs and Hoisin Sauce	Green Bean Snack
Friday	Herbed Eggs	Shrimp, Carrots and Cabbage Salad	Asian Shrimp Salad	Plantain Chips and Salsa Dip
Saturday	Blueberry Salad	Sweet Potato and Apple Noodle Salad	Apple and Ginger Pork Chops	Eggplant Appetizer
Sunday	Egg and Meatball Breakfast Salad	Lemony Salmon	Squash and Zucchini Salad	Sweet Potato Bites

Conclusion

The Whole food diet has become one of the most appreciated lifestyles ever. It has gained so much popularity over the last years due to its multiple health benefits. This amazing diet is easy to follow as long as you respect its main principles.

You might think that the Whole food diet is a complex and restrictive one but once you discover it you will understand that it is actually very easy to follow. You are allowed to eat many great products. You can make so many Whole food recipes that will definitely impress you with their tastes and flavors.

Do not hesitate and start a Whole food diet right away, if you want to look great and feel incredible! Trust us! We know!